ACADEMIC WRITING

Exploring Processes and Strategies

SECOND EDITION

Ilona Leki
University of Tennessee, Knoxville

CAMBRIDGE
UNIVERSITY PRESS

PUBLISHED BY THE PRESS SYNDICATE OF THE UNIVERSITY OF CAMBRIDGE
The Pitt Building, Trumpington Street, Cambridge, United Kingdom

CAMBRIDGE UNIVERSITY PRESS
The Edinburgh Building, Cambridge CB2 2RU, UK
40 West 20th Street, New York, NY 10011–4211, USA
10 Stamford Road, Oakleigh, Melbourne 3166, Australia
Ruiz de Alarcón 13, 28014 Madrid, Spain
Dock House, The Waterfront, Cape Town 8001, South Africa

http://www.cambridge.org

First published by St. Martin's Press, Inc. 1995
Reprinted 1998
Third printing 2000

Printed in the United States of America

Library of Congress Cataloging-in-Publication Data Available

ISBN 0 521 65768 7 Student's Book
ISBN 0 521 65767 9 Instructor's Manual

Acknowledgments are given on pages 427-8.

Preface

Academic Writing: Exploring Processes and Strategies is aimed at students who are learning to write for academic contexts. Its goal is to help students develop two types of strategies: strategies for producing texts and strategies for preparing and polishing texts for readers in academic settings. The novice writer needs instruction on the process that writers go through in order to produce texts: a process of exploration and generation of ideas on paper; of seeking out appropriate feedback; and of reworking and revising the presentation of those ideas. The novice writer also needs to learn how to meet the demands of the academy by attention to form, format, accuracy, and correctness. *Academic Writing: Exploring Processes and Strategies* helps writers develop competence in all these areas.

The text is divided into three parts and is followed by appendixes. Part One orients students to the writing processes they will explore and develop as they work their way through the book. Here they will initially engage in actual writing tasks with minimal guidance in order, first, to become more aware of their current writing strategies and, second, to familiarize themselves with the types of demands and support they can expect to encounter in writing assignments throughout the term. In Part Two, students are taken through the writing process and given the opportunity to discover for themselves which kinds of approaches to writing are most useful to them. Students explore their ideas through journal writing, practice a variety of techniques for generating text, and learn how to elicit feedback on their writing from their classmates and how to respond to such feedback. Students are introduced to the rhetorical expectations of English-speaking readers on organization and development of written ideas, and they learn how to accommodate these expectations. Finally, students turn their attention to form, learning how to focus on technical and grammatical accuracy for writing situations that require such attention.

Part Three provides students with the opportunity to practice doing a variety of academic assignments. Assignments emphasize developing an objective tone, responding to already published material, and incorporating the ideas of other writers into academic assignments. Because students are likely to be asked to write essay exams, the last section provides strategies for and practice in writing essay exams based on selected readings.

The appendixes contain a collection of readings, a series of editing exercises, and answers to exercises in the text. The readings were chosen because they are intellectually stimulating and challenging; they are loosely linked thematically to the Writing Assignments in the text. Each reading is accompanied by pre-reading and postreading questions, headnotes, and journal suggestions.

Academic Writing: Exploring Processes and Strategies embodies the notion that beginning writers develop confidence in their ability by having many opportunities to express ideas to which they themselves are committed. The text assumes that developing conviction in writing is closely tied to receiving thoughtful feedback in a nonthreatening environment and that it is extremely important for beginning writers to experience success. Consequently, the book encourages group work, provides many examples of writing done by students in writing courses, and, through the explanations and especially the Writing Assignments, strives to create the proper context in which students can explore and share written ideas that are meaningful to them. This book takes student writing seriously and trusts students to be intellectually alive, to appear in the classroom with a store of experience and information that they are willing to share and that is worth sharing. In many years of teaching, I have not found this trust to be misplaced.

CHANGES IN THE SECOND EDITION

The second edition of *Academic Writing* retains the features of the first edition that teachers and students have found helpful:

- Many examples of actual student writing
- Suggestions throughout the text for journal entries related to Writing Assignments
- A wide variety of Writing Assignments from which to select, drawing both on students' own personal experience and on new information and knowledge developed from reading
- Clear and carefully sequenced instructional material
- Many exercises to help students grasp concepts being discussed
- Suggestions for appropriate readings for the Writing

Assignments throughout the book—for teachers who believe in the usefulness of readings in helping students learn to write. The readings relate generally to the subject matter of the writing assignment; occasionally, students may be referred to a reading selection as an example of one approach to take in dealing with a topic.

NEW AND EXPANDED FEATURES

In response to comments and suggestions by teachers who have used the first edition of this book, the second edition now also includes new and expanded features that make the book easier to use, more academically oriented, and better grounded in current theories of academic reading and writing.

Readings

In keeping with the belief that academic writing in particular draws heavily on reading, the second edition more than doubles the number of readings in the first edition. As in the first edition, the readings are accompanied by *prereading information* (in the case of particularly challenging readings, a great deal) and *postreading activities*.

The readings were selected to appeal to a wide variety of student and teacher interests, but their subject matter is also intended to be compelling, ranging from serious issues that plague the consciences of people in this culture and around the world to more amusing subjects that reveal insights into the qualities and activities of human beings. The readings also vary in difficulty so that increased teacher intervention may be called for in some of the more challenging sections. However, the gains in knowledge, information, and experience with real texts aimed at educated, thoughtful, and reflective readers repay the extra effort that may be required to grasp the ideas presented in the text.

Sequenced Writing Project

A new feature of the second edition is the inclusion of a Sequenced Writing Project, which students can carry out throughout the course of an entire term. Directions for completing the five assignments in the Project are included with each chapter as an alternative to the regular Writing Assignments. The idea of a series of assignments forming a Sequenced Writing Project grows from the belief that students develop their writing skills best when each writing assignment they do can build quite directly on the experience and knowledge gained from completing the previous writing assignments. In fact, in the Sequenced Writing Project, students are encouraged to cite and reference their own previously completed assignments. Again, this Sequenced Writing Project is offered as an option.

Changes to Make This Book Easier for Teachers and Students to Use

New Part One: "Overview of the Writing Process." In order to give students a sense of what their work will entail and what they will learn to do in using this book, the introductory material in the second edition has been restructured and revised. Part One now includes an explanation of how the book is organized and how each of the chapters contributes to developing a specific aspect of writing expertise; hints for writing to communicate effectively; and two Writing Assignments based on the premise that "the best way to learn to write is by writing": The first is designed to allow students to demonstrate the writing skills and habits they now have and to then engage in analyzing that writing to identify their own particular strengths and weaknesses; the second—a full Writing Assignment modeled after one they might encounter in one of their college courses—provides an overview of the kinds of expertise the students will develop as they explore their own writing processes.

Schematic Diagram of the Writing Process. A schematic diagram now appears at the beginning of each major section of the book. This schematic graphically illustrates where the users of this book are in terms of what they have already covered and what they have to cover still.

Improved Interior Design. First, the layout of all Writing Assignments, Journal Suggestions, Reading Suggestions, Exercises, and Examples has been redesigned to distinguish them from one another and from the narrative instructional sections of the text. This makes it easier for users of this book to locate these features quickly and easily within chapters.

Second, important instructional points are now signaled in

the margin by a star (☆). These points constitute the essential information or key issues to be grasped or remembered. Also, the corners of pages that detail information about how to cite sources have been marked to allow easy and quick reference to these sections.

Third, references to other sections of the text that might be helpful in understanding or completing assignments are signaled in marginal notes.

Finally, while the conversational tone of the first edition has been retained, the narrative instructional material has been streamlined.

The revised, added, and expanded features of this new edition are intended to meet the needs of new users of this text effectively and to respond to the suggestions of the professors and students who have used the first edition successfully.

ACKNOWLEDGMENTS

I would again like to express my gratitude to all the international students who not only inspired and then sampled the material in the many earlier versions of this text but who also created the best of it. I am most grateful as well to my editor, Naomi Silverman, whose creativity and artistry have contributed so greatly to the improvements in this second edition. A special thanks to Iris Esau Moye, University of Oregon, who generously shared with me numerous and particularly useful insights on the first edition of *Academic Writing* that helped me to see new directions for this edition. Thank you to Sara Picchi, Carl Whithaus, and Linda Henigin for all their help and kind friendliness, and to my colleagues across the country who patiently reacted to the first edition of the book and those who read the manuscript of the second edition: Marcia Cooley, California State University-Fullerton; Katya Fairbanks, Pitzer College, The Claremont Colleges, California; Pamela Goins, University of the Pacific; Suzanne Leibman, College of Lake County (Illinois); Tamas G. K. Marius, University of Central Florida; Judith Rehm, Writing Center, Embry-Riddle Aeronautical University; Guinn Roberts, Educational Testing Service; and Jessica Williams, University of Illinois at Chicago. Their thoughtful comments and suggestions were illuminating.

Thank you to my colleagues at the University of Tennessee: John Zomchick, Julia Williamson, Jill Vincent, Gema Klein,

Marilyn Hardwig, and Leslie LaChance. And to my wonderful family, the best part of my life, especially Debbie and Pete for thinking so long and carefully with me about writing and other important matters, and Ken, for always being there for me with boundless patience, love, and tenderness.

Ilona Leki

Brief Contents

Contents

Suggested Readings for Chapter Writing Assignments

To Ken with love,
great joy, and gratitude

PART ONE

Overview of Writing Processes

> 1 <

Getting Started

Do you remember the first time you tried to ride a bike? One thing that makes a skill like bike riding hard to learn is that you have to do many things at the same time that you do not yet know how to do well: pedal, keep your balance, steer, watch the road ahead of you, and so on. Learning how to write seems to present similar kinds of problems. Even in the first paragraph, you must have an idea of what you want to say, how to explain it, and how to sound convincing to your reader, and you have to do all of this in English.

But in some important ways, learning the skill of writing well is different from and *easier* than learning the skill of bike riding because when you write, it is possible to concentrate on the different parts of the writing activity one at a time. This possibility makes writing much more like making a clay pot than like riding a bike. When you make a piece of pottery, first you must gather and prepare your materials: select the kind of clay you want, soften the clay by kneading it, perhaps find a pottery wheel, and so on. Next you need some idea of what you want to make, how the piece of pottery is going to be used, and who is going to use it. Only then can you start working on your piece. As you are working, you may change your mind about what you want it to become; instead of becoming a cup, your piece may start to look as though it would be a better flowerpot. If this happens, you revise your image of the final product and who you are making it for. As you work, you show your piece to others, who give you opinions and advice on how to improve it. Sometimes you may decide that you are no longer interested in this particular project or that the project is not coming out the way you had originally hoped. You may then decide to abandon the project and begin something entirely different. If you finally manage to produce a pot you like, the good qualities of that pot will be the result of good materials, good planning, good advice from critics, and good execution on your part.

The same is true of good writing. Before you have a finished product, you must gather ideas on the subject you want to write about. You also have to consider who you are writing this essay

3

for and why. As you write, you will consult with others about their ideas and about their opinion of what you have done so far. You may decide to abandon your project and begin something else entirely. Or you may change your ideas about what you are saying, who you are saying it for, or why you want to say it. This book is meant to help you discover, develop, and arrange your ideas in a shape you can be satisfied with.

HOW THIS BOOK IS ORGANIZED

Part One of this book will introduce you to a number of ways to approach a writing task. You will learn how to:

Gather ideas by keeping a working journal and using invention techniques (Chapter 2)

Consider your audience, purpose, and focus (Chapter 3)

Write the first draft of a paper and get and give feedback on that draft (Chapter 4)

Express the main ideas of your paper explicitly (Chapter 5)

Develop and shape those ideas (Chapter 6)

Write effective introductions, conclusions, and titles (Chapter 7)

Revise a draft (Chapter 8)

Edit a revised draft (Chapter 9)

In Part Two, you will apply all the strategies you developed in Part I to writing academic papers. You will learn how to:

Summarize, paraphrase, and quote from published sources (Chapter 10)

Document any material you take from other sources (Chapter 11)

Write a paper analyzing an issue (Chapter 12)

Read and respond in writing to written arguments (Chapter 13)

Use written material to develop your own argument (Chapter 14)

Prepare for essay exams, including those in your other academic courses (Chapter 15)

Practice writing some essay exams under time limits (Chapter 16).

By the time you finish this book you will have experience with many types of writing required in academic settings. This experience should make you feel confident about your ability to gather ideas, express them, get feedback on your writing, prepare final drafts, and take essay exams in many of the other academic courses you will take.

HINTS

Writing is *communicating*. Good writing helps your reader understand your ideas as clearly as possible. The following are suggestions for making the task of writing easier in English assignments—or any other writing you may need to do.

1. Whenever possible, write on subjects that actually interest you.
2. Write on subjects that you know about or want to know about.
3. Before you begin to write a draft, explore your ideas freely with the help of invention techniques.
4. Have an idea of the audience you are writing for, and keep that person or group of people in your mind as you write.
5. Decide what your purpose is and what you want your writing to accomplish. Will it inform? Persuade? Entertain? Will it help you discover your own ideas?
6. Don't worry about details in your first draft. Try just to get your ideas down on paper. You can shape your ideas later.
7. Reread your own writing frequently. Try to read objectively, as though you were not the author and you were seeing it for the first time.
8. Let others read what you have written and give you feedback.
9. Don't be afraid to add, delete, or move your ideas around.
10. Once your ideas are on paper, check the grammar, vocabulary, spelling, and punctuation to make the writing as correct as you can.

THE BEST WAY TO LEARN TO WRITE IS BY WRITING

➤ *Writing Assignment 1.1: Writing Samples*

Writing
Assignment 1.1

Choose one of the following suggestions and write an essay as you normally would. This assignment is meant to show your teacher the writing skills and habits you have now.

1. Think of a place from your childhood that you remember well. Describe the place in as much detail as possible and explain its significance to you either then or now.

2. Do people from your country have a reputation for being friendly? Easygoing? Hard working? Serious? Independent? What stereotypes do outsiders have of your country or of the people in your country? Do any of these stereotypes seem at all true to you? How would people in your country describe or characterize themselves? Choose two or three stereotypes of people in your country and explain or illustrate how they are true or untrue.

3. Think of the last time you were forced to do something you did not want to do. What did you have to do? Why? Who forced you to do it? What would have happened if you hadn't done it? Now are you glad or not glad that you did it? Tell the story of this incident. Then explain your own reaction to it then and now.

4. What has surprised you about the United States? Did you have expectations about the community where you now live? Were these expectations met? What is striking to you about the place you live now and the people who now surround you? Choose two or three surprises you have had since your arrival here and explain what you had expected and what you found instead.

Self-Analysis

Now answer these questions.

1. To whom were you "speaking" as you wrote your essay? Who did you assume would read what you were writing? Your English teacher? Your classmates in your English class? The general public?

2. Reread what you wrote. Are there any sections, ideas,

phrases, even words that you are particularly proud of having written? Put brackets around them.

3. Reread the parts you bracketed. Why are you especially happy with these sections?   ◄

Now discuss with your class how you wrote your essay. Use these questions as guidelines, and include anything else that comes to mind.

How did you decide which subject to write about?

Did you sit and think or write notes for a while before you began to write the essay itself?

How did you begin? With the first sentence?

How did you decide what to include or exclude?

Who did you assume you were communicating with as you wrote?

What did you think your audience wanted to find out by reading your piece?

What did you enjoy about your first writing assignment for this class?

TRYING OUT THE PROCESS

Your answers to these questions tell you something about the processes you now use when you write. As you work through this book, you will have a chance to try out many techniques other writers use to help themselves write well. To give you an idea of some of these writing processes, you will now work through one full writing assignment. This will give you a brief overview of the work you will be doing this term.

➤ *Writing Assignment 1.2: Historical Change*

Writing
Assignment 1.2

Imagine that you are taking a class in U.S. history or culture. In this class you are studying the invasion of the western hemisphere by Europeans, beginning with the voyages of Christopher Columbus in 1492. Discuss with your class everything you already know about the effects of this invasion on the people who originally lived in what is now called North and South America. What has happened to those original inhabitants since the Europeans first landed on this continent?

(Or see the end of Appendix A for an alternative subject to explore.)

Now read the text on page 290.

Reading

Excerpt from *Bury My Heart at Wounded Knee*, page 290.

Here is the writing assignment for your imaginary history class:

Based on the reading from *Bury My Heart at Wounded Knee*, write a short paper on the following topic:

> Change is the essence of history. Some changes are slow and peaceful; others, like the changes the Europeans forced on the native peoples of North and South America, are violent. Often these changes come about as foreign ideas, inventions, technologies, and sometimes armies come into a country from abroad. Think of the history of your own country. Has your country ever been forced to change its ways as the result of foreign influence? Has your country ever introduced changes into another country? Take any point of view that interests you, and compare this aspect of the history of your own country with the information from the passage you just read from *Bury My Heart at Wounded Knee*. Discuss how the two situations are similar and/or different.

This paper is due in one week. ◄

Writing First Drafts

Chapter 2 will help you gather and generate ideas.

Before actually writing, many people find that they write more easily if they prepare themselves to write. In Chapter 2 you will learn about several invention techniques to help you to prepare to write. For now, begin the first draft of this simulated history assignment by writing down a list of everything you can think of about the two situations you will compare.

Now you have a base from which to begin your assignment.

Who Is Your Audience, and What Is Your Purpose?

Before you begin writing, however, think about these things:

Who will read this text you will write?

Why will this audience be reading what you write?

What will this person expect to read?

What qualities in your paper would make this audience consider this an excellent piece of writing?

Chapter 3 will help you focus on your audience and purpose for writing.

In Chapter 3 you will analyze in much greater detail your audience and your readers' purposes and expectations in reading your writing, but for now, discuss the questions above with your classmates.

Chapter 4 will help you write first drafts.

Do you feel that you are ready to write now? In Chapter 4 you will get detailed instructions on writing a first draft, but for now, if you feel ready to write, put your list of ideas in front of you and write a first draft of your assignment. This is a *first* draft. That means it does not have to be perfect—so don't worry about grammar, spelling, punctuation, or other details yet. (Chapters 5, 6, and 7 will help you with writing an introduction, developing and organizing your ideas, and writing a conclusion.)

Chapter 5 will help you determine or develop your main idea.

Chapter 6 will help you decide how best to support and analyze your ideas.

Chapter 7 will help you write introductions, conclusions, and titles.

Gathering and Generating Ideas. If you don't quite feel you are ready yet, perhaps it would help you to consider your topic from different but related angles. One way to do this is to discuss your topic with others—your classmates, your roommates, or your friends from your own country or from others.

Chapter 2 will get you started keeping a writing journal.

Keeping a Writing Journal. Another way to try to look at the topic from another perspective is to write informally on a related topic, as though you were writing a journal of your own thoughts. In Chapter 2 you will get instructions for beginning a writing journal. For now, think about the history of your country and read the following journal suggestions.

Journal Suggestions

- Is your country racially or culturally mixed, with some people from different backgrounds and traditions? Or do all the people in your country share the very same ethnic or racial or cultural background? If your country is mixed, how do the different groups of people get along? What do they think of one another as a group? How did these different groupings come together in the same country?

- If all the people in your country share exactly the same background and traditions, how has this similarity affected your country's history? How are outsiders, like foreigners, considered?

- The popular culture, the economy, and sometimes the political ideas of the United States have had an effect on many other parts of the world. Have you seen this influence in your own country? How has this influence affected the tastes or the opinions of people in your country?

Now choose one or more of these groups of questions and respond to them in writing—but informally. Spend ten to fifteen minutes writing your answers. No one will read what you have written except you, so don't worry about correct grammar or spelling. Just write freely.

Now that you have finished writing the answers to these questions, you may be ready to write your first draft of Writing Assignment 1.2. First reread everything you have already written; then write your first draft. In this draft, you can use anything, or nothing, from what you have already written.

When you finish your first draft, reread it. If you are not yet satisfied, try writing a new list of ideas that you didn't think of before and see if you can include these new ideas in your text.

Getting Feedback

Chapter 4 will help you get feedback on your writing.

Many writers find it helpful when they write a draft to ask a friend or colleague to read the draft before they give it to its real intended audience to read. If you are fairly satisfied, it is time to give your paper to a classmate to read. In Chapter 4 you will practice responding to your classmates' writing, but for now, you will just ask your classmates for feedback on your paper. Before you do this, write down any questions you would like your classmates to answer that might help you improve your ideas in this paper. Don't ask questions about grammar. You can worry about that later.

If you can, give your draft to several people to read and ask them all for their written or oral comments. These comments will help you see your paper as others see it and may help you locate sections that need improvement.

Revising Your First Draft

After you have collected feedback from as many readers as possible, you can reconsider what you have written. You should have several important items in front of you:

the text from *Bury My Heart at Wounded Knee*

the directions for the assignment

your invention lists

your responses to the Journal Suggestions, if you wrote them

your first draft

your ideas about who will read this paper and why

your classmates' reactions to your writing.

Reread everything you have. Ask yourself if this paper can be improved in any way by adding ideas, deleting sections, or reorganizing what you have written. You may want to make another list of changes to make for your second draft and show this list to a few classmates for their opinions.

Now, write a second version of this paper, taking into account everything you have learned from writing your first draft. In Chapter 8 you will learn more about revising and see examples of how other students have revised their work.

Chapter 8 will help you revise your writing.

Editing

If you are now satisfied that this draft is ready for its intended audience to read, reread the draft once more, carefully, looking for any mistakes you can find in grammar, spelling, or punctuation. Chapter 9 will help you see what kinds of errors you make and will give you ideas on how to correct those mistakes. If you are not satisfied, return to any of the parts of the process you have just gone through and try again. Different people approach their problems with a piece of writing in different ways. You may want to do one or more of the following:

Chapter 9 will help you edit your writing.

reread the text from *Bury My Heart at Wounded Knee*

read something related to this subject, for example, the following articles in Appendix A that discuss changes forced on traditional societies by the majority culture:

Readings

"Discovering the Truth about Columbus," page 295

"Do Not Disturb," page 297

"Sacred Places," page 299

"Auto-cracy Is Being Exported to the Third World," page 303

discuss the text with someone

create a new list of ideas

get more feedback from another classmate

perhaps even put everything aside and write an entirely new first draft.

Do these activities in any order that you think will help you write the best paper you can.

CONCLUSION

You have now completed a writing assignment using processes that you may use in any writing you ever do. As you went through this process you may have had trouble with parts of it. Perhaps you weren't sure what kinds of questions to ask your classmates about your paper. Or perhaps when you tried to list ideas, none came to you. Or perhaps you were not sure how to write the first draft of this assignment. The rest of this book will take you through each of these activities in much greater detail with many examples of what other students like you have done. Looking more carefully at the activities and suggestions in this book will give you the opportunity to try many things that have worked for other students to help them write efficiently and well. Knowing about a variety of options will help you understand and develop your own writing processes as you realize what works well for you.

➤ PART TWO

Writing from Observation and Experience

➤ *UNIT ONE*

Getting to Draft One

➤ *2* ⤙

Getting Ideas
and Starting to Write

JOURNALS: WHERE WILL YOUR IDEAS COME FROM?

The purpose of keeping a writing journal is to help you explore subjects to write about. A journal entry is like a letter to yourself. You are your own audience. You have to please no one but yourself. Writing in your journal will help you learn to think on paper instead of in your head. Keeping a journal also will help you preserve your precious ideas, insights, and memories.

The journal you will write for this class is to be a storehouse for your ideas. It is also a place to practice and experiment with English without worrying about making errors. Throughout this book you will find suggestions to help you get started, but if you do not feel like following them, write about whatever is on your mind at the moment. Feel free to add comments to your regular entries whenever an idea comes to you that you may someday want to write about. Most of your entries will probably never turn into formal essays, but they may contain seeds that will eventually grow into writing projects.

Suggestions for Keeping a Writing Journal

1. Write your journal on looseleaf paper. By using this type of paper, you can add entries to your journal even when you do not have your notebook with you. Get a looseleaf binder in which to store all your entries.
2. Begin each entry on a new sheet of paper.
3. Date each entry. Also, write down at the top of the entry where you are as you are writing. Try to write in a place where you are not likely to be interrupted.

Hint 1: Whenever possible, write on subjects that actually interest you.

4. Before you begin to write anything, relax and let your mind empty itself. Sometimes it helps to concentrate only on your own breathing for one minute.

5. Once you begin to write, keep writing continuously for fifteen minutes.

6. Write legibly and leave plenty of space in case you want to add comments later.

7. Use the suggestions for journal entries given throughout this book to stimulate your thoughts. However, allow your thoughts to take whatever direction they will. If you run out of things to say on the topic suggested, just keep writing on whatever topic is in your mind. If you can think of nothing to say, either repeat what you have been saying or describe what it feels like to find nothing to write about. You will most likely discover that the very act of writing itself stimulates your thinking.

8. After fifteen minutes, go back and reread what you wrote. Add comments if you feel like doing so.

9. Do this three times each week, and keep all your journal entries—dated, numbered, and located—in your journal binder. The binder should contain nothing except your journal entries.

10. Notice that this writing journal is not the same as a diary. Your journal is meant to be a source of raw material from which you can draw ideas for your formal writing. It should include observations about life around you, about yourself, about other people. It should include descriptions of significant events, insights, memories, thoughts, and opinions. It will probably *not* include information such as what time you got up and what you had for breakfast. Include in your journal any ideas you think might eventually be useful to you in an essay.

Determine with your teacher whether these journals are to be private (no one reads what you write except you), semiprivate (you occasionally read from your journal to your classmates), or public (your teacher or your classmates will read your entries).

The following are some sample journal entries written by students in a course like yours.

■ STUDENT EXAMPLES

There is a big puzzle which I could never solve. It is "Freedom." All the Americans I have met believe strongly in the right to be free, free to travel, to think, or to do whatever one wants to. I also heard on TV and read so many articles in newspapers about how eager the Americans are to defend freedom in the U.S. and everywhere in the world, so that I expect to read the word Freedom in each line of any American publication. It is not strange that they believe that free is the adjective of the American people. At the same time they have strange ideas about the peoples of the other countries like mine. They believe that the other peoples are used to oppression, they accept their rulers without questioning them, they have different cultures that suppress the freedom of the individual, and they are different, oriental, poor, ignorant, etc. Therefore, the other peoples are not like the free American people because first, the word freedom describes American not human, and second, because the other peoples are not as eager as the Americans in defending their freedom: they don't write to their representative in Congress, and they don't walk down the street holding signs; they merely fight and die for freedom.

Hazem Najar (Syria) ▪

I am curious about something which is taboo to me. I was taught to act like a lady; that meant to be modest, gentle, and follow all our community's moral principles. Something the Americans take for granted and do naturally may be taboo for me.

I have noticed an ad for Mouse's Ear in the *Daily Beacon* for a long time. The girl in the ad is just taking off her shirt. The words of the ad, like "fantasy show," "exotic dancer," entice you to think more. What's fantasy in it? My husband told me it is a nude show and women are forbidden to enter. What a pity it is! I am not a naive girl anymore. Couldn't I know something that was unknown before?

The weather is getting hotter day by day. You can see some girls wearing sexy bikinis lying down on the ground to have a sun tan. You might be used to seeing this, never am I used to it. I can't pass by without having a good look. It is incredible that girls reveal their bodies to get sun tans. They look very easy and enjoy it very much. Sometimes I feel really embarrassed when she watches me looking at her. To my surprise they always give me a smile. Shame on me! Don't you know it is their requirement in summer? It's not easy to learn to get a tan ten. They need to practice every day.

These are things that I am curious about, but I would not get involved in them.

Ying-Ru Lai (Taiwan) ▪

I remember last year when I got back to my country after 10 months of staying in the U.S. Everytime I heard something I kept asking "Why?" One of my friends told me: "What is the matter with you? Didn't you know?" Know what? I wasn't there! How could I know? After a while I felt that I was almost a stranger in my home town because I went away 10 months. I didn't expect that things would change that way. Even in my family they changed the place where they usually sit in the afternoons drinking tea. I knew the old place and I always loved it. What I did was take my tea and go sit in my lovely old place. After a while, the whole family came and sat with me underneath the peach tree in our beautiful garden. I hope they didn't go back to the new place again. I'm going back home this summer, and I'm going to drink my tea underneath the peach tree again whether they drink it with me or without me. I can't change my habit of drinking my tea in my old place because I'm so used to it.

Nizar Ben Ali (Tunisia)   ▨

Journal Suggestions

These journal suggestions are meant to stimulate your thinking. You may want to answer some or all of the questions, but you do not have to. Write for more than fifteen minutes if you feel inspired.

Hint 2: Write on subjects that you know about or want to know about.

- Begin your journal with a time line of your life. Write down the date of your birth and then record as many events as you can remember of your life up to the present in approximate chronological order. These may include strong childhood memories, births of siblings, changes of residence, travels, political events that affected you, and so on. Try to remember what events you associate with each year. Include trivial events as well as major events. When you have finished, look over your time line. Did you remember anything you hadn't thought of for years?

- Begin your journal by spending at least ten minutes listing the subjects you are most interested in and/or most knowledgeable about. After ten minutes, choose one or two of the subjects and spend ten more minutes or so writing about it or them.

- Think about what your parents were like before they had children. Do you know any stories about them from that time? Have you seen any pictures of them from that time? What do you know about their childhood years? How do you think they have changed?

- Think of something or someone that is popular right now that you dislike: a hairstyle or way of dressing, a singer or movie star, a place to visit, a way of looking at an issue, or anything else you think of that certain people like and approve of but you do not. Then make two lists. In the first, list the reasons for the popularity of this person, style, concept, or whatever. In the second, list your reasons for not liking it.

- Think of something that is unpopular right now among many people but that you like. Explain the reasons for this unpopularity and your own reasons for feeling differently.

- Look back to the essay you wrote in one of the writing assignments in Chapter 1. Begin your journal by commenting on what you think about that first assignment. What are you most satisfied with in your essay? Is there anything you would change or add if you were going to write it again?

- Begin your journal by writing about anything you want to write about.

INVENTION: HOW DO YOU BEGIN TO WRITE?

Hint 3: Before you begin to write a draft, explore your ideas freely with the help of invention techniques.

Writing is a solitary and demanding task. One way to make the task easier is to use *invention techniques*. These techniques will enable you to explore your ideas on a subject before you actually begin to write about it.

When you sit down to write, you probably know vaguely what you want to say but not exactly how to say it. Your ideas may seem chaotic; you have a lot of information and maybe strong feelings about a subject, but all this is stored in your brain in a complicated way. As soon as you write something down, twenty more ideas may come to your mind all at once, and all those ideas compete with one another for your attention. Invention techniques can help you get control of these chaotic thoughts and examine them one at a time to see which ones are worth developing.

In this section you will learn several invention techniques. You should experiment with each of these techniques just to learn how to use it. On your own, try each one again at least once to see if that particular form of invention is helpful to you. Different individuals have very different styles of creating. An invention technique that is extremely fruitful for one person may produce nothing of interest for another person. This is why you should try the techniques while you are actually trying to produce an essay. After you have experimented with each technique, select the ones that work best for you and use those.

In this section you will practice:

freewriting
listing

wh- questions
clusters or branches
looping
cubing
outlining

Freewriting

There are two kinds of *freewriting*. One type allows you to empty your mind temporarily of everyday concerns so that you can concentrate on the task at hand. The other type helps you begin to explore your ideas on a subject.

If you need to work on a writing assignment but cannot concentrate, the first type of freewriting may help you to clear your mind. Take a sheet of paper and begin to write about the thoughts on your mind at that moment. Write continuously for five minutes. This is usually enough time to rid your mind of distractions. If you still feel distracted, continue to write for another five minutes, or until you have gotten all distractions out of your system.

If you have chosen a general topic to write about but have not yet decided what aspect of that subject you wish to explore, the second type of freewriting should help you. Write your general topic at the top of a page. Then begin to write down everything that comes to your mind on this topic. Write continuously for ten minutes. Time yourself or have someone else time you. Do not let your pen stop moving. If you cannot think of anything to say, write "I can't think of anything to say" until something comes to you. Something will come, so relax and keep writing steadily. If you cannot think of the word you need in English, write the word in your own language or in some abbreviation or just leave a blank and keep going. The point is to get down as much as you can about the subject, no matter how disorganized.

■ STUDENT EXAMPLE: FREEWRITING

Here is an example of one student's freewriting.

Indonesia is not as popular as other places such as Thailand, Philippines, etc.—don't know the reason why—maybe it's not publicized that much—especially in America, almost nobody knows what or where Indonesia is. Sort of aggravating experience—feel embarrassed. Lots of interesting sights—Australian people go to Indonesia very often but seldom see American tourist. Bali is often visited—

most popular place, often called Paradise Island because of its beautifulness—many beaches—clean and refreshing. Java has many points of interest too. Yogya often called tourist city because of its many temples and again it has 3 beaches. Jakarta, capital city is metropolitan city—filthy side and beautiful side all together—island of Sumatra—mostly contains forests but on North side, Lake Toba—beautiful scenery.

Notice that this student did not worry about writing complete sentences or punctuating them correctly. She wanted only to get her ideas down on paper as quickly as possible. Here is a draft of the essay she eventually wrote based on her freewriting.

Although many people in America have never been to Indonesia, I think Indonesia is a place they must visit at least once in a lifetime. Part of the reason the Americans seldom visit Indonesia is because they do not know much about the place. Another reason is that they do not think there is anything worth going for. But they are wrong. In fact, there are many beautiful places in this country. For example, on the island of Bali there are two beautiful, white, and sunny beaches. Kuta is especially beautiful when the sun sets and Janur has a spectacular view when the sun rises. Another example is on the island of Java, where there are two cities that are very popular for their beautiful sites; they are the cities of Yogya and Jakarta. In Yogya, there are many ancient temples and in Jakarta there is a big playground similar to Disneyland. The last example of a tourist attraction is on the island of Sumatra; there is one most particular point of interest there and that is Lake Toba. When we see Lake Toba from the mountains surrounding it, it creates a breathtaking view. These are just three of the many beautiful places in Indonesia and I think it is a shame that more tourists don't know about them.

Pradanita N. Soepono (Indonesia) ■

Notice that this draft does not include everything that came up in the student's freewriting. Also notice that even this early draft contains things that did not appear in the freewriting.

When you do your own inventing, stop after ten minutes and reread what you have written. Underline or circle the ideas and expressions you like. If you find an idea that makes you think of something else you wanted to say, draw an arrow from that point and continue writing until you have written everything you had to say about that idea. Somewhere in what you have written you will probably find aspects of your topic you can write about. If not, go on to another invention activity.

WRITING PRACTICE: FREEWRITING
Imagine that you have decided to write a short composition about places of great natural beauty in your country. Do ten minutes of freewriting on this subject to see what ideas you come up with. When you finish, include this freewriting exercise in your journal.   ■

Listing

Once you have decided on an aspect of a topic to write about, you need to find out what you know about that topic and anything related to it. *Listing* is faster than freewriting but operates on the same general principle. When you list, you write down everything that comes to your mind about your topic, but you do not write sentences. Instead, you write only words or quick phrases. Once again, you are trying to get down quickly as much information as possible. Listing is particularly useful for getting examples or specific information about a topic. This technique is also one of the most useful ways for writers to get started again if for some reason their ideas dry up as they are writing a draft. Here is one example of a student's list.

■ STUDENT EXAMPLE: LISTING

SUNDAY NIGHT, MASSEY HALL LOBBY
Noisy: everybody returning from weekends
Crowded
Parents, boyfriends
Floor wet and white, snow
Coke machine noisy
R.A. at front desk bored, answers phone
Two guys playing Pac-Man
Others waiting
One guy on the phone for a long time
Two others waiting to call
Couples sitting in lobby, laugh, talk, forbidden to go upstairs in this
    dorm
Employees from pizza places delivering Sunday dinner
Snowball thrown in from outside, becoming a water hole
Someone playing piano, several voices singing a carol
Change machine broken, I have been asked for change twice
Girls come down for Coke, laundry tickets, sweets
Suitcases everywhere
Elevator broken

Cold as a bus station

R.A.'s pictures on the walls

On the opposite wall, announcements for parties, movies, free coupons, videos

Big blackboard in front of the doors, announcing that *Purple Rain* is playing

Poster saying "Happy Birthday, Linda. We love you." I don't know her

Garfield muppet on the table—forgotten by someone

From the window see white smoke from the heater system outside

Here is the final draft of an essay this student eventually wrote based on her list.

On Sunday afternoon, Massey Hall lobby looks as busy as a bus station. The place is really crowded because the students are coming back from their weekends away. Parents or boyfriends are carrying suitcases and standing around speaking with female residents. At one end of the lobby, two boys are playing a video game, "Pac-Man," while some others are waiting for their girlfriends. Other girls come down into the lobby very often to buy a Coke or laundry tickets. Every ten minutes, employees from Domino's Pizza or Mr. Gatti's deliver pizzas for Sunday dinner. As in every public place, the lobby is very noisy. Couples sitting on the blue sofas behind the front desk are laughing and speaking animatedly. The Coke machine next to them is terribly noisy, and it's difficult to hear the piano in the small room close to the lobby. The telephone keeps on ringing in the lobby office, and the R.A. has to answer it every minute. Everybody seems too busy to notice details in the lobby. Nobody is interested in the poster announcing Linda's birthday, nor in the announcements for parties and movies on the wall opposite the front desk. The blackboard in front of the doors, announcing the movie *Purple Rain* for Monday night, seems useless too. And people constantly open the doors to come in or go out, so it's cold. Just like in a bus station.

Anne Gouraud (France) ■

Look back at the student's list, and then answer these questions.

1. Did she include everything on her list in her essay?

_____

2. What categories of details from her list did she include in her

essay? _____

3. Can you detect a pattern in the details she included?

_____

4. What made her keep some details and eliminate others?

_____

WRITING PRACTICE: LISTING

Think of the first impressions you had of the community in which you now live in the United States. Make a list of everything that comes into your mind. Remember, try to get down as much as possible quickly. Keep this list in your journal. You may want to expand it into an essay someday. ▪

Wh- Questions

When reporters write newspaper articles, they usually try to write the first sentence so that it will answer the following questions: *who, what, when, where, why,* and sometimes *how.* These questions can be used to generate ideas for your compositions as well. Asking questions like these may help you to clarify exactly what subject you are going to discuss in your composition. This technique, like listing, is also good for finding details about your subject and for restarting your writing if for some reason you get blocked. You are the one who both asks and answers the questions. Think of as many questions as you can. Here is an example of one student's invention using wh-questions.

▪ STUDENT EXAMPLE: WH- QUESTIONS

What? Classical ballet, a stiff art form

When? Every time it is danced or when it is being performed or practiced

Where? In classes, in the theater, everywhere it is being done

Why? This question is a very ambiguous one. I could just talk and talk forever. But the very specific reason why is because it is done in a perfect placement of the body. Ballet is the only dance form that accentuates the body when it is performed so it needs to be perfect for the body to look right. This is the main reason why it is so stiff.

How? Taught at the barre. You have to take classes hanging on to a barre while the other side of your body is working.

From her invention writing, this student discovered that she wanted to explain why classical ballet is so stiff. Here is the final draft of her essay.

Classical ballet is the only art form that uses a perfect placement of the body when it is being performed and when it is being taught. Classical ballet is taught in a classroom with mirrors on all the walls. The main reason for this is so dancers can check their bodies to make sure they are standing straight up with their body weight well distributed, that is, not too much weight on one leg or the other one. Besides mirrors, there is a "barre" that goes all around the room. The main purpose of this barre is to help dancers learn how to control one side of the body when the other is moving doing an exercise. The dancer holds on to the barre with one hand while the other one is accompanying the leg that is doing the exercise. All of these facts make classical ballet a stiff art form. But the most beautiful thing about classical ballet is that all of this work can be hidden by the dancer when he or she is performing, and unless the people in the audience are familiar with the art form, they have no way of realizing how hard the dancer is really working.

Lucia Abbatemarco (Venezuela)   ■

WRITING PRACTICE: WH- QUESTIONS

Think of the last argument or disagreement you had with someone. Then write a list of questions about the argument and answer them. Write as many questions as you can (what kind of . . . , under what circumstances . . . , whose . . . , what cause . . . , what effect . . . , and so on). Did writing the questions and answers force you to consider any aspect of that argument you had not thought of before? Put this invention writing in your journal for possible future use.   ■

Clusters or Branches

The human mind seems to store information partly by associating new information with information already stored. As a result, calling up one piece of information may trigger a whole series of other memories. For example, have you ever been eating something you hadn't eaten in a long time and suddenly felt almost transported back to another time and place? That experience is an example of your associational memory at work. You can make good use of the mental capacity to associate when preparing to write essays. Write the subject of your composition in the middle of a piece of paper, and then write down all the things you associate with it. Then continue the process by finding associations for each of the things you have written down. Continue to do this as long as you can find associations. Then look at all the associations you have written down. Try to group items into *clusters* or categories. Here is an example of one student's use of clusters.

■ STUDENT EXAMPLE: CLUSTERS OR BRANCHES

The following is an early draft of the essay the student wrote based on the cluster shown in Figure 2.1. (Because it is an early draft, neither the grammar nor the organization is perfect.)

It is a great experience to be in a foreign country and trying to communicate with the local people even though sometimes it turns out to be a nightmare. First, the students, who are surprised to know where I am from and anxious to know more. That really is a good start, but soon I realize that they know nothing. They even expect people in Singapore to be staying in tree-houses. What a shame. Most of them expect my home country to be still very far behind in science and technology and still to have a lot of catching up to do. Therefore, when I explain to them what is really happening, they are surprised and say, "I don't believe it!" Second, the instructors who just don't care about where I am from when they first meet me. Anyway after some time when they start to know me well enough they start to get interested in me. They ask about what is going on in my home country, especially in the architectural field. They are surprised to find out how advanced we are. All these instructors are all very nice people, but there are a few instructors in the school who

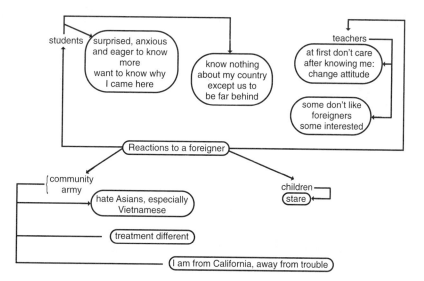

Figure 2.1.   Example of Clustering or Branching

don't like foreigners. If I signed up for their classes, I would be in a lot of trouble. I could expect myself to be deserted by the rest of the class and, of course, to get a low grade too.

Third, the community, which I consider to be the most interesting, because this is the group where I have all kinds of strange encounters. Generally, the retired army hate Asians, especially Vietnamese. Since all Asians look the same to them, I get in a lot of trouble when I try to communicate with them. As a result, when I meet a stranger and he or she asks me where I am from, I tell them I am from California. That really saves me a lot of trouble. Another interesting encounter I face is at a community gathering place like the Flea Market, where I am treated differently from all the others there. If an American could buy a used fan for ten dollars, I would have to pay fifteen dollars for it. Sometimes that really makes me frustrated because I am a human too.

Lastly, the children look at me in a very strange way. Maybe I'm special, unique, or even a rare species over here. From the way they look at me, I feel like they are trying to dig everything out of me just to satisfy their curiosity.

Even if some reactions are bad, I think this is a valuable experience for me because it helps me to be more mature in handling strangers and different types of people.

                                         Tai Herng Kong (Singapore) ■

WRITING PRACTICE: CLUSTERS OR BRANCHES
Try your hand at clustering or branching by thinking back to being sixteen years old. What associations does this age bring to mind? Cluster your associations, and keep pursuing them until you run out of associations. Keep this cluster with your journal entries.   ■

Looping

Looping is similar to freewriting, but it is more focused. It is especially useful when you have many ideas in your mind all at the same time. Looping can help you focus your thought on a subject, find the core or center of your thought, and pinpoint a main idea on which to elaborate.

To use this technique, begin by writing down the subject you want to consider. Keep that subject in the front of your mind as you write continuously for five minutes. It is important to keep the pen moving and to keep your mind focused on the subject. If you get distracted, just keep writing anything you think of until ideas on your subject come again. As with freewriting, do not worry about grammar or punctuation. If you cannot think of the word you want in English, write the word in your own language or leave a blank. Feel free to use abbreviations or your own personal shorthand forms of spelling.

At the end of five minutes (time yourself or have someone else time you), read what you wrote. Then write down one complete sentence that summarizes the essence of what you just wrote. You may find an actual sentence in your writing that seems to be the most important idea of the writing, or you may have to create one. In either case, write that sentence down. This is the end of your first loop.

Now begin a second loop by focusing on your summary sentence. Try to keep this sentence in your mind as you write continuously for another five minutes. When you finish the second five minutes of writing, read what you have just written. Look for the main idea or core toward which all the other ideas are turned. Summarize that core idea in one sentence, and write that sentence down. This is the end of your second loop.

Follow the same procedure for your third loop. At the end of your five minutes of writing, read the third text and summarize it in one sentence. For most writers, this last sentence usually captures the gist of what they have to say on their subject. If your last sentence is still not satisfactory, you should probably try another invention technique.

WRITING PRACTICE: LOOPING
At the top of a piece of paper, write the word *tradition*. Then write about that subject continuously for five minutes. When you have finished, summarize your text in a complete sentence and write that sentence down. Repeat this process twice more. If you find an interesting idea, keep it for later use in an essay.   ∎

This technique, like any invention technique, can be used at any time in the writing process. It can be especially useful when your ideas seem chaotic and you need to find a clear approach to your subject or an "angle" on the subject to write about.

Cubing

Cubing involves looking at an idea from six different points of view, each representing one of the six sides of a cube. You will look quickly at your subject from these six angles so that you have several perspectives on the subject available to you. You should spend three to five minutes examining your topic from each of the following angles:

1. Describe it. (What does it look like? What do you see?)
2. Compare it. (What is it similar to? What is it different from?)
3. Analyze it. (What is it made of? What are its parts?)
4. Associate it. (What does it remind you of? What do you associate it with?)
5. Apply it. (What can you do with it? What can you use it for?)
6. Argue for or against it. (Take either position. Give any reasons, even crazy ones.)

When you have finished, reread what you wrote to find ideas that you like. Write those ideas down and look them over. Perhaps one of them is particularly interesting and may be a good perspective for an essay on the subject.

WRITING PRACTICE: CUBING
To show you how powerful cubing can be in helping you find something to say, practice the technique using a candy bar as your subject. First, go and buy a candy bar. Then consider your candy bar from all six points of view. When you have finished, jot down the ideas you found that you like. Did cubing help you find anything interesting to write?   ■

Use cubing either at the beginning of a writing project (to find an angle for your essay) or during a writing project (when you run out of things to say on your subject).

Outlining

An *outline* is a structured method of exploring your thoughts on a subject. Some writers like to use the freer invention strategies to generate ideas. Then they make an outline to organize their ideas. Thus, outlining can be a transition between inventing and writing a first draft. When used this way, the outline functions as a plan for writing. It is extremely helpful in dividing up the big task of writing a formal paper into the much more manageable task of writing small parts that will eventually make a unified and organized whole.

Other writers like to make an outline of their paper after they have written a draft. When used this way, the outline is not a plan but rather a check to verify that the paper presents the ideas logically and covers all aspects of the topic the writer wants to cover.

In either case, the outline is not an end in itself. It is merely a tool to help you produce an organized discussion or to help you verify that the discussion you have produced is organized.

Basically, an outline helps you divide up a subject. Suppose you are going to compare conceptions of beauty in the United States with those in Greece. You can begin to figure out the structure of your paper by preparing an outline or structural sketch of one way to put your ideas together.

■ STUDENT EXAMPLE: OUTLINING

Beauty in the United States
In general: artificial
Face: makeup
Hair: any color is okay
Clothes: many colors, plaids, stripes

Beauty in Greece
In general: natural
Face: no makeup
Hair: blond, blue eyes preferred
Clothes: simple, European styles, single colors

Notice that the topic, concepts of beauty, is first divided into two parts, beauty in the United States and beauty in Greece. Each of these topics is then subdivided into subtopics or subheadings representing the categories that the author wants to cover. Each of the subtopics is further subdivided by comments the author wants to be sure to include in the essay (clothes in the United States: many colors, plaids, stripes; clothes in Greece: simple, European styles, single colors). Once the plan is written down this way, the author can easily rearrange material to make the plan symmetrical and the eventual essay logically presented. Also notice that the outline does not include many of the details that will eventually appear in the essay, but that all the details fit neatly under some subtopic or subheading in the outline.

Here is a draft of the paper the student wrote based on this informal outline.

One of the many differences between Americans and Greeks is what these two groups consider good-looking or stylish. Certain things that Americans seem to think look good would not be considered very attractive in Greece. In general the American look is somewhat artificial. Nearly all the women I see here wear makeup, even very young high school girls who do not need it yet. And the makeup is not always very subtle either, for example, red lipstick to class and dark purple fingernails. Although Americans do not seem to care much what color their hair is, they seem obsessed with washing it, many people washing their hair every single day, both men and women. In fact, men even get permanents and use hair spray. But the strangest thing about American style is the clothes people wear, stripes, plaids, polka dots on their shirts and even on their pants. I have also noticed to my surprise that many of the men wear polyester pants in very bright colors, like green and red. These are called golf pants.

In Greece we admire natural beauty more. Not many women, except over the age of 40, wear makeup and even then it is usually for a special event, not to go to school. Most Greeks have thick black hair and even though blond hair and blue eyes are considered ideal good looks, no one would think of changing their hair color; not many people have permanents either. Most people just wear their hair long or short but simply, naturally. Greek clothing styles are very much like European styles, natural fabrics, cotton or wool, in subdued colors and in simple styles. I cannot imagine seeing someone in Greece (besides a tourist) wearing red, green, or polka dotted pants. Perhaps when Americans look at Greek styles, they find them as strange as I find many American styles. I suppose I will become more used to seeing the American styles, too, and maybe next year I'll be the first in Greece to wear those golf pants.

Annabel Drousiotis (Cyprus)   ■

WRITING PRACTICE: OUTLINING

1. Take any of the invention writing you have already done and try to divide the ideas you generated into two or more broad, general categories. Then decide how each idea you generated in your invention might fit into these categories.

2. One possibility for your first journal entry was to create a "time line." Whether or not you chose to make this entry, write an outline dividing your life history into two, three, four, or more major sections. Can you see how each event in your life would fit into one of the sections?   ■

Discussion and Reading

One technique for generating ideas that has not been mentioned yet is simply talking to someone else about your ideas. *Discussion* is a powerful way to generate and test ideas. Unfortunately, it is also more restricted. You may not always be able to find someone willing to listen to you, or you may not be in a situation where discussion is appropriate (writing an essay exam, for example). But if you can, do discuss your ideas with others. The discussion may well help you clarify your thoughts.

Finally, perhaps the most common way of getting ideas is *reading* about a subject. Reading what others have written can both acquaint you with other people's ideas and stimulate you to think of new ideas of your own. If you use reading and research to find ideas, be sure to read more than one text on the subject so that you will not become excessively influenced by one writer. Also, be careful not to present the ideas of another writer as your own. (See Part III, Unit 4, for guidelines on using the ideas of others in your writing.)

USING INVENTION TECHNIQUES

Did any of your invention writing help you discover new ideas on your assigned subjects?

Invention techniques can help you start writing. But they can also be used after you have started to write a draft. Feel free to use one or more of these techniques whenever you cannot think of anything to write. Whenever you need to generate more ideas—as you begin a draft of a paper, in the middle of writing a draft, or after someone has read and commented on a draft—use one or several of the techniques you practiced here to stimulate the flow of new ideas from your mind onto your paper.

➤ *Writing Assignment 2.1: Sample Invention*

Writing
Assignment 2.1

Reread the essay you wrote for one of the Writing Assignments in Chapter 1. Choose at least two invention strategies, and apply each one to the essay you have already written.

Did you find any new ideas? If so, mark any that you would like to include in your original essay. Are there any sections of the original that you now want to eliminate? Mark those as well. Now rewrite your original essay to include the new ideas you discovered in your invention. Eliminate the sections of the original you have marked. See Chapter 4 for conventions to follow for writing essays.

Journal Suggestions

The following journal suggestions will help you prepare for the Writing Assignment in this chapter, which will deal with some feature of your culture.

- What do you think are the most difficult aspects of your culture for foreigners to understand? What do you feel is important for other people to understand about your culture? What do you find difficult to understand about other people's cultures?

- Are there expressions in your language or aspects of your culture that cannot be translated into English? Are there things in English or in North American culture that cannot be translated into your language or culture? Can you think of anything that you would find extremely difficult to explain to someone at home?

- What are the major tenets of your religion? Is religion in your culture considered a private or a public matter? Are people in your country religious or not?

- Here are some proverbs from different countries. Can you add any?

  > Japan: The nail that sticks up gets hammered down.
  > Ethiopia: When spiders unite, they can halt a lion.
  > Egypt: The man who is a mirror in front of you is a dagger behind your back.

  What do these proverbs say about human beings and society? Think of a proverb (or saying) in your language. What lesson is that proverb trying to teach? What does it show about your culture?

- Think of a technical term in your field of study. Define that term for someone with the same major as you. Then define it again for someone who has never studied your field and knows nothing about it.

- What machines or devices do you know how to operate? A typewriter, a computer, a fax machine, a car, a telephone, an airplane, a sailship, a dishwasher, a coffee percolator, a cash register? Write down as many as you can. What operations do you know how to perform, or what skills do you have? Can you ride a bike? Cook any foods? Braid hair? Knit? Change a fuse? Change a light bulb? Ski? Do you remember learning any of these skills? Write about any experiences you had learning a skill that you are proud of.

- Think of the classes you are now taking. Try to remember a significant process, piece of equipment, or concept that is related to one of the subjects you are studying. Describe that process, piece of equipment, or concept.

You might also consider reading one or more of the following Reading Selections in the Appendix. ◄

Readings
"Do Not Disturb," page 297
"Sacred Places," page 299
"The Japanese Funeral Ceremony and the Spiritual World after
    Death," page 307
"Japanese *Miai*," page 310
"Taking the Bungee Plunge," page 312

➢ *Writing Assignment 2.2: Invention for Cultural Artifact/Tradition*

Writing
Assignment 2.2

For this assignment, you will either describe something, explain how something works, or explain how to do something. Your readers will be your classmates and teacher. Try to think of an object, activity, tradition, or concept that is important in your home country but not well known outside your country. Choose something that will probably not be very familiar to your classmates and teacher. Don't choose something too common, like a holiday during which the whole family gets together, dresses nicely, and eats a meal together. Your readers will probably already be familiar with such holidays and will want to learn something new about your particular culture. Here are some topics students have used in the past.

> Wrapping a Sari
> Stealing the Henna (Traditional Tunisian Weddings)
> Sunday at a Dim Sum Restaurant
> Raising Singaporean Fighting Fish

Safaris in Kenya

France's "Système D"

Colombia's Salt Cathedral

Nigerian Scarring Ceremonies

Iranian Sigheh

Suhoor in Lebanon

Japanese Flower Arranging

Malaysian Pantun

Once you have decided on your subject for this assignment, find someone in your class who is not familiar with this subject. Then describe it to that person orally. As you describe it, notice when you have to use your hands to help your words. Also notice where your audience has trouble following what you mean and has to ask you for clarification. These parts will probably be the most difficult to describe in writing. If you find that your classmate has a great deal of trouble following or paying attention to your description, consider finding another topic.

When you have finished your oral description, use two or more different invention techniques to help you discover your ideas on your subject.   ◄

When you finish, your teacher may tell you to gather your ideas and write a paper on this topic based on the ideas you found through these invention techniques. If so, see Chapter 4 for help in writing a first draft.

See Chapter 4 to help you write a first draft.

Or you may be asked to put all the notes you have on this subject aside and save them until you work through the next chapter, on audience and purpose.

SEQUENCED WRITING PROJECT: CHOOSING A TOPIC

Sequenced Writing Project

If you choose to do the Sequenced Writing Project, you will write a total of five papers on the same subject over the course of this whole term. You will be given directions for each assignment in this chapter and the following ones.

You may write on any topic you wish with the approval of your teacher. However, to do the Sequenced Writing Project, you must select a topic that meets three requirements.

1. You must feel very interested in the topic and want to learn more about it, since you will spend much of the term writing five full papers on the same subject.

2. You must already have had some *personal* experience with the topic you will write on.

3. This must be a topic that will allow you to do all five parts of the project. (See the following description.)

Here are some examples of topics students have written on and their personal experience with their topics.

Topic	Experience
Financial aid for international students.	This student was having financial problems.
Making American friends.	The student had no American friends and wanted some.
The Iranian and American criminal justice systems.	This student's father had been imprisoned for political activity and she was taking a course in criminal justice.
The question of Puerto Rico's becoming one of the United States.	This student was from Puerto Rico and was going to have to decide on how to vote on this question.
Day care in the United States and China.	This student was sending his four-year-old son to day care while he and his wife attended classes.

As you can see, in each case the students had already had some *personal* experience with the subject of their project before they began the project. If you decide to do the Sequenced Writing Project, take your time deciding on an appropriate topic, one that will keep your interest through five complete writing assignments. You can think of this Sequenced Writing Project as gathering data for a research question. So consider choosing topics that you can and would like to do research on, perhaps related to your current school life (e.g., How are international students considered by departments where they enroll as majors?) or to the life of the community in which you now live (e.g., How does this community view international students?) or to any other topic you want to explore.

The five assignments for this project and the chapters where they are explained in detail are:

1. Explain the importance of the topic and your personal experience with it (Chapter 2 or Chapter 4).

2. Write a survey report (Chapter 5).
3. Write a report of an interview with an expert (Chapter 6).
4. Summarize three published items on the subject (Chapters 10 and 11).
5. Write a final report of all your findings (Chapter 12 or Chapter 14).

After you have carefully decided on a topic and your teacher has approved it, select two or more invention techniques to help you explore what you already know about this topic, its potential importance and interest to other people like your classmates and teacher, and your own personal experience with the topic.

Follow your teacher's directions about whether to use this invention writing to begin a first draft (if so, see Chapter 4 now) or to hold all your notes until you finish the work in Chapter 3.

The next assignment for the Sequenced Writing Project, the survey, appears in Chapter 5. ▬▬▬

> 3 <

Preparing for a Draft

Have you ever carried on a conversation that took place entirely in your head, perhaps while you were doing dishes or just walking down the street? This kind of internal dialogue often occurs after a disagreement, when you think of many clever and logical points you should have made while you were actually talking to the other person. In this kind of internal dialogue, you know very definitely whom you are talking to, what your relative social status is, just how polite or impolite you can be in your statements, and what kinds of points would be most persuasive. There may also be points you decide not to mention because you know that they would either offend or not be convincing to your audience.

AUDIENCE: WHO IS GOING TO READ YOUR WRITING?

If you have that same kind of awareness of your audience when you write, you will be better able to decide what would be convincing or informative. Thus, if you are writing for your compatriots, you do not have to explain anything you assume they already know. On the other hand, if you are writing for someone not from your country, you will have to give explanations that your compatriots would not need. In the same way, if you wrote an article on the advantages of having a vertical 90 degree 16 valve combustion engine on a Honda Interceptor motorbike for readers with no particular knowledge of or interesting this subject, those readers would probably feel you were wasting their time. They would not be able to understand all the technical terms or concepts you would be using. Yet the same article might be quite interesting to readers of a motorcycle magazine.

Concept of Audience

 The concept of audience is extremely helpful. If you identify clearly in your own mind who the members of your audience are, you will be better able to make assumptions about what they know, what they do not know, and what they want to know. This knowledge will help you make decisions about all aspects of your paper:

what explanations you must give to make your ideas clear to your reader

what types of explanations would be most helpful

how to organize your explanations

whether to write informally or formally

how careful to be of correct grammar, spelling, and punctuation

One special writing situation is writing for your teacher. Discuss these questions in class:

How is writing for teachers different from writing for other audiences?

What does your English teacher expect when she or he reads your writing?

What do other teachers expect from your writing?

Hint 4: Have an idea of the audience you are writing for and keep that person or group of people in your mind as you write.

When should you decide who the members of your audience are? There is no fixed time. Sometimes, such as when you are writing for a teacher, you will know your audience and purpose even before you begin any invention writing. At other times, your invention writing will help you discover the audience you are writing for and why. Sometimes, you will not really be sure of your audience until you are working on a draft. Your audience and purpose may even change as you write. Still, no matter where you are in the writing process, keep in mind that eventually your writing will be read by some specific readers.

As you can see, English-speaking writers are very conscious of their readers. If the communication between writer and reader breaks down, it is generally considered the writer's fault. It is up to the writer to accommodate the reader by explaining the ideas as fully and as clearly as necessary.

Writing for Different Audiences

Look at the following selections on the subject of friendships in the United States. Both were written by the same student, but each was aimed at a different audience. Each therefore has a slightly different emphasis, depending on the author's relation-ship with the particular audience and what she has decided that audience needs and wants to hear. The first example was writ-ten to a friend back home

■ STUDENT WRITING

You asked me if I have made any American friends since I've been here. To tell you the truth, I don't know. Americans seem to have an idea about friendship different from ours. First, everyone is very friendly. People smile and even sometimes say hello to me in the street—people I don't even know! Both boys and girls! And at the dorm everyone seems kind, friendly, smiling too. They say things like "We'll have to get together some time" or "Stop by some time." But they never have time just then to chat a little longer. They're al-ways in a hurry, on their way somewhere. Another thing is they'll ask about Egypt but they don't really seem to care about the answer, be-sides just noticing that our customs are different. And they really know nothing about Egypt or much of the rest of the world.

I think of you and Karima and the long discussions we had about our lives and about the world. That's what friendship means to me. I think of the many times I needed your help and even if you had your own problems, you always helped me. I haven't found that here even after one year of living here. I don't mean to complain, but you did ask. I guess I can say it's very easy here to make acquaintances but I'm not sure what friendship means in American terms.

The following was written for a class on social relations.

Polite social relations appear to be on one hand quite important in American society and on the other hand somewhat superficial. The cordiality may be seen in the typical American's behavior to-ward strangers on the street. A person will quite readily nod, smile, or even say hello to a stranger passing in the street. Americans smile easily and extend invitations to people they hardly know. On the other hand, there is a certain superficiality to this friendliness since Americans also tend to value the individual over the commu-nity. They drive to work in separate cars, each encased in his/her own private box. When they arrive at a crowded beach, they will head for solitude, isolation, a spot on the beach away from other people.

Furthermore, although friendships everywhere are necessarily based on a certain amount of trust, that trust is apparently condi-tional in American society. Thus, for example, an American would not find it strange to be asked to sign an IOU if he or she borrowed money from a friend. For an outsider, therefore, it is often difficult to see at what point an American considers another to be a friend and exactly what being a friend entails.

Fatimeh Ghazi (Egypt) ■

EXERCISE 1: AUDIENCE
Answer the following questions in class.

1. Consider the differences between these two examples from the following points of view:

   vocabulary _____

   examples used _____

   sentence structure _____

   use of pronouns _____

   specifics mentioned _____

   organization _____

   tone _____

2. What did the writer include in the first example that she left out of the second? Why? _____

3. What did she include in the second one that she left out of the first? Why? _____

   ■

EXERCISE 2: AUDIENCE
Read the following paragraph written by a student. Who do you think is this student's intended audience?

■ STUDENT WRITING

   Visiting American football games at the University of Tennessee is an exciting adventure because there are so many interesting things to watch besides the game itself, especially the spectators. First of all there are thousands of people in the stadium wearing orange clothes and shouting, "Go Big Orange." Orange is the color of U.T., and this is the reason Tennessee got the name "Big Orange Country." Compared to German soccer games, you find a lot more young people among the spectators, nearly as many girls as boys. But people seem to have quite different interests in coming to the game; while some of the spectators are really interested in watching the game itself, many of them seem to use this kind of meeting more as a social event and a chance to party. Some of the girls, for example, dress up very well, put on fresh makeup, and climb up all the rows of the stadium in their high heels! After a while some of these boys and girls just get tired and leave the game without waiting to find out who won. Isn't that strange? And also, during the game, nobody has to worry about food and drink; everything you need will be served directly to your seat: Coca Cola, popcorn, and hot dogs. Even though it is forbidden to drink alcohol on campus, you can smell the whiskey in the air. Watching the audience and their behavior, I feel more as if I were attending a public festival than a sports attraction. Because there are so many interesting things going on in the stadium, it's not that easy to keep concentrated on the game itself.

Karin Volkwein (Germany)   ■

Now answer these questions.

1. Does the intended audience attend the University of Tennessee? How do you know? _____

2. Is this intended audience American? How can you tell?

   _____

3. Does this intended audience know anything at all about American football? How do you know? _____

   _____

4. Describe the intended audience you think this student had in mind. _____

Turn to the end of this chapter for the answer to the first question.

Now answer these questions.

1. Is this paragraph appropriate for this audience?

   _____

2. What special information did the student include for the benefit of her audience that would have been irrelevant to someone from the United States? _____

   _____

3. What information would have been irrelevant to an audience from the University of Tennessee? _____

   _____

4. Do any sections of this composition strike you as inappropriate for the student's intended audience?

_____

■

EXERCISE 3: AUDIENCE

Probably most of your classmates have seen or eaten at a McDonald's restaurant either in the United States or at home. Discuss with the rest of the class what you would emphasize if you were an advertiser trying to persuade the following types of people to eat at McDonald's instead of another restaurant. Don't invent qualities for McDonald's; try to remember what you know.

Audience	Emphasis
1. a child under ten years old	_____
2. a high school student	_____
3. a graduate student	_____
4. a couple with three children	_____
5. a retired couple	_____

Try to decide on your audience early, somewhere between your invention writing and your first draft. But even after you have decided on a tentative audience, you may very well discover as you write that what you want to say is appropriate for some audience other than the one you originally chose. If so, feel free to change your perspective and write for your new audience. Just remember to read over what you have already written with your new audience in mind to make sure that this material is still appropriate.

Because your classmates and teacher will be reading your papers, they constitute a logical audience. However, they do not always have to be the audience you select. Perhaps you want to direct your writing to the members of the Ministry of Education back home who have created high school course requirements you do not like. Even though these ministers may never read your essay, they can still be your audience. The audience is merely a mental construct to help your writing stay on track even if that audience never actually reads it.

Whether or not your classmates and teacher are your intended audience, they will nevertheless be reading what you write. Think of them as coaches or critics (in the good sense of that word). Have you ever asked a friend to read over an official letter you wrote to make sure that it was clear and correct before you mailed it? Your classmates and teacher will be doing the same thing with your writing in class. They will be telling you if they think your work is clear, interesting, convincing, informative, and correct.

Look back at your notes for the Writing Assignments in Chapter 2. If you wrote about an object, process, tradition, or concept from your culture, your audience was your classmates and teacher. How would your invention writing be different if your audience was different—for example, a group of people your own age from your own culture?   ■

PURPOSE: WHY ARE YOU WRITING THIS?

Types of Purposes for Writing

Besides your audience, another important idea to keep in mind as you compose and revise a draft is your reason for writing, your reason for wanting to tell your audience about your subject. There are two basic reasons for writing (although one does not necessarily exclude the other): to express yourself and to communicate with someone else. When you keep a journal, your reason for writing is to express yourself; it doesn't matter whether anyone reads, understands, or likes what you have written. When you are writing to communicate, on the other hand, it is helpful to know not just with whom you want to communicate but also what you are trying to accomplish by writing your text.

Hint 5: Decide what your purpose is and what you want this piece of writing to accomplish. Will it inform? Persuade? Entertain? Will it help you discover your own ideas?

Asking yourself questions like the following ones may help you to discover your purpose:

1. Am I trying to inform my audience about a subject they do not know much about but would be interested in knowing?
2. Am I trying to show my audience a new way to look at this subject, a way they may not have thought of before?
3. Am I trying to persuade my audience to agree with my point of view on this subject?
4. Am I trying to demonstrate to my audience (to a professor, for example) that I know about this subject?
5. Am I trying to entertain by writing something funny or beautiful or dramatic?

For each of the following, write down what you think the author's purpose might have been in writing on this subject.

EXERCISE 4: PURPOSE

1. An essay in which the author discusses reasons against having only one child. Possible purpose: _____

_____

2. A short story. Possible purpose: _____

_____

3. An essay exam. Possible purpose: _____

_____

4. An essay about marriage customs in Tunisia. Possible purpose: _____

5. An essay in which the author discusses attitudes in the United States toward individuality versus community. Possible purpose: _____

6. An essay about how people in the United States mispronounce the author's Arabic name. Possible purpose:

_____

7. An article praising a new and unpopular state law requiring people to wear seat belts. Possible purpose:

_____

■

EXERCISE 5: PURPOSE

Your purpose in writing is related to the type of writing you are doing. The following are the first sentences of texts written by students in an English class. Can you figure out just from these first sentences what kind of text the student was probably writing? For each sentence, choose one of the following:

a letter home

an essay exam

an article informing readers about something they don't know about but might want to know about an article persuading readers to agree with the author

a text with no clear purpose

1. Non-engineering students often confuse computer pro-gramming with computer engineering, but these two areas of specialization are quite different. _____

   _____

2. My mother has always been kind and generous to all of her children. _____

3. The use of robots instead of human beings in certain work situations raises serious questions about the fate of workers in the affected industries. _____

   _____

4. Since bicycles are a popular means of transportation in many countries, most people have a fairly clear idea of what they look like. _____

5. Although this school is theoretically interested in educa-tional excellence, this goal is not obvious in certain classes here. _____

6. The hardest class I'm taking right now is United States history. _____

7. While it may make sense for North American students to take United States history, foreign students, who do not intend to become United States citizens, are forced to waste time and money when they are required to take United States history courses. _____

8. Erosion is the process by which the land surface of the earth is gradually worn away. _____

   ∎

EXERCISE 6: PURPOSE

Although an author may have one main purpose in writing, the text may sometimes fulfill other purposes as well. Read the fol-lowing texts written by students and try to determine each stu-dent's main purpose and any secondary purposes.

■ **STUDENT WRITING 1**

Cooking: A Rewarding Experience(?)

Did you every try to cook something impressive and new? I'm not talking about toast and coffee. I'm talking about the real McCoy, like, let's say, filet mignon or venison in butter with mushrooms. You never tried it? Let me tell you then how cooking things like that becomes a "rewarding" experience.

First, you can become the envy of all your friends, but it's very important that you announce your meals to your guests properly. Don't tell your friends they'll be able to enjoy a "Cordon Bleu" when it might turn out to be a "Cordon Noir." No one will be really delighted; no one enjoys a piece of crispy charcoal. But if you announce something special or exotic without exactly saying what it is, your friends will enjoy their tasty black meat balls and probably they'll tell you that you're a very fine cook. You can even use your leftovers to heat your kitchen. So, even if nobody wants to eat the specialties, you can help to save energy.

Another very important advantage of cooking is the fact that you really learn something. It is like reading the book "How to get to know your kitchen in two hours." You'll discover this reward if you search for all the stuff you need to prepare your delicious meal. You have to open every single drawer and door and remove everything. You'll find things you never dreamed of—ancient ketchups and dressings, lots of sticky stuff, and . . . little animals. You may come to love this private kitchen life and finally recognize that the kitchen is not simply a place to cook in. There's really something happening; your kitchen is rockin' 'n' rollin'. It's alive!

After the discovery that your cooking impresses others and is really fun, you may get your final "reward." This happens when your meal is in the oven too long and starts smoking and steaming. A mushroom cloud immediately fills your kitchen with smoke. You're not able to see anything. While you're trying to find your stove, you burn your fingers on the hot pan and stumble to the sink to get some relief from cold water. But instead of reaching your goal, there's a chair in your way. You fall down, not without banging your head on the corner of the cupboard, while the butter in the pan on the stove catches fire and destroys the nearby microwave, which causes an incredible explosion, and you are sent to heaven.

All this shows that cooking can not only make you feel like you are sitting on a cloud but it can actually put you on one. It is one of the last real adventures in our hectic times. Just open your kitchen door. You'll find the place where dreams are made.

Uwe Lehmann (Germany)   ■

1. Main purpose: _____

2. What makes you think so? _____

_____

3. Secondary purpose(s): _____

_____

4. What makes you think so? _____

_____

■ STUDENT WRITING 2

One Day on the Battlefield

The worst thing that happens in our world is war. War is a disaster that humans can avoid. We cannot avoid a tornado or an earthquake, but we can avoid a war. War is not like what we see in the movies. War is the biggest crime against human nature conceivable. The only obvious result of war is death and misery.

My country has been at war for six years. The war is spread over a 600 mile border between two countries, and I have seen how terrible the battlefield is. Most of the year the weather on the battlefield is so hot that you cannot touch your rifle or your helmet. In that high temperature, the water of your body vaporizes very fast. Your body needs more water, but usually there is no sign of the water truck when you need it.

If you are on the front line, you usually live in a reinforced concrete fortress with two or three other soldiers. The fortress is usually so small that you cannot lie down to rest. Early in the morning your alarm clock is the roar of the enemy's jet fighters. You start to shoot at them, but they are so fast that you usually miss them. If there is not a major attack from the enemy, the jet fighters' aim is to scare you. Suddenly, you are aware that your own army's jet fighters are chasing the enemy's jet fighters. First, you feel excited and hope that they can hit the enemy's jets, but the battlefield is not like a movie where good always defeats evil. You can see a 40 million dollar aircraft vaporize in the air. You cannot put any price on the pilot's life. Before noon, the cannons start shooting at each other. They remind you of a dragon with flame breath. The difference is the cannon is real and deadly, but dragons only live in fairy tales.

Your food is usually bread, cheese, and potatoes. In fact, in that high temperature you cannot eat anything else. At lunch time, everybody complains about the quality of the food, but there is no other choice. When you realize that this food might be your last meal, you lose your appetite anyway.

In the afternoon, it is the army's turn to move its units and attack the enemy's units to discover new details about the enemy's situation. These attacks are really dangerous because the airforce never supports the army in small attacks. In these attacks you learn to act like a wild animal. You have to kill to stay alive. If you look at the battlefield from a long distance at night, it looks like sparkling fireworks, but the difference is that each bright light you see in the sky is meant to kill you or your friend. Suddenly you realize that the nice fireworks look more like the entrance doors to hell.

There are always different points of view between the governments of different countries. For the country that wins a war, maybe there is glory. But for the individual soldier there is only misery and horror.

Farzad Ghannadian (Iran) ▪

1. Main purpose: _____

2. What makes you think so? _____

    _____

3. Secondary purpose(s): _____

    _____

4. What makes you think so? _____

    _____

▪ STUDENT WRITING 3

Music and People

Almost everyone on this earth listens to music. Each person spends countless hours listening to music. People spend lots of money on albums, musical instruments, and record-playing equipment. We can hear people whistle, dance, and sing at parties and even on the streets. It is rare to find a person who dislikes music although not everyone likes the same type of music or uses it the same way. People have different reasons for listening to or making music.

Music provides a background for activity. Some people want music around them almost all the time. For instance, I have a friend who listens to music almost twenty-four hours a day. Music is just a part of him. Everyday, when he returns home from school, he will turn on the radio first before he changes his clothes. He even turns on the radio before he starts cooking and studying. Music soothes his nerves and puts him in a good mood so that he can go on with his daily routine. For some people if their portable radios or record players were taken away, they would feel uncomfortable, and thus their activities would be disrupted.

Another use of music is to provide a special atmosphere for a non-musical situation. Music is used in motion pictures to increase the attractiveness of the pictures. Sentimental music during sad scenes makes the audience feel very emotional or haunting music during scary scenes makes the audience jump off their seats. In short, music is very important in films to attract the audience's attention; without music the audience may lose interest in the film.

Music must be appreciated because besides the enjoyment it brings to us, music also brings people closer together. For instance, people go to discos, parties, and concerts to enjoy music and at the same time they make new friends. Music as one of mankind's great accomplishments yields much meaning and enjoyment to every person who can hear and understand it.

Zailani Mohamad (Malaysia)   ▩

1. Main purpose: ———————————————————————

2. What makes you think so? —————————————————

3. Secondary purpose(s): ———————————————————

   —————————————————————————————————

4. What makes you think so? —————————————————

   —————————————————————————————————

5. Did you have trouble determining the purpose of this essay? ———————————————————————————

   —————————————————————————————————

6. Who do you think was the intended audience for this essay? ———————————————————————————

   —————————————————————————————————

Turn to the end of this chapter for one analysis of this essay's audience and purpose.   ■

A writer's purpose in writing is closely connected to the audience for which the writer is writing. When you write a letter to your parents describing a typical day here or how your studies are going, your purpose is to inform because you know that your parents are interested in what you do. If you wrote the same letter for your English class, however, your purpose would not be clear. It would not be obvious that your readers have any reason for wanting to read about your typical day.

Deciding on a tentative purpose before you write will help you decide what to write and how to write it, just as deciding on a tentative audience will. Once again, however, you may find as you are writing that your original purpose is no longer what you want to convey. In that case, change your purpose and reorient your discussion. Reread what you have written to make sure that everything you have said fits your new purpose.

Focusing on the Subject

One part of determining your purpose is clarifying to yourself exactly what your subject is. Again, as you are writing a draft, you may change your mind about what you want to write. Look at the following student essay. As you read the essay, think about what subject the student was focusing on in this draft, and his probable purpose in writing about this subject.

■ STUDENT WRITING

Teenage Suicide in Japan

A thirteen-year-old girl leaped off the roof of her four-story school building just before afternoon classes just three weeks ago. This is the most recent incident in a rash of teen suicides in Japan over the past few years. The note she left said that she could stand the taunting of classmates no longer.

Young teenage suicide is becoming one of the most tragic social problems in Japan. About forty suicides have been reported this year already. Some of them were even elementary-school children. There are many pressures on Japanese schoolchildren, and the causes of their suicides are related to these pressures and the way Japanese society has developed. When the students cannot stand the pressure, they commit suicide. In many cases, the reasons for suicide seems to be linked with victims' treatment by peers.

Victims were often isolated and teased by groups over a long period of time. In a school community, sometimes kids are very cruel to a quiet or different student without any other reason than his or her difference. Research shows most students who committed suicide were very calm, gentle, silent students. Obviously, they were good targets of bullying groups because they tended not to complain or fight back, especially since groups of bullies can be quite large — ten or more students. Teasing is more mentally abusive than physically. Taunters may make fun of their target every day, hide his or her school materials, and even force the individual to provide slave-like service. If they disobey the orders, bullies sometimes "discipline" them. Unfortunately, bullying groups are close-knit and represent a large portion of a class, and non–group members allow their actions. This problem is perplexing because not only are students' actions involved but also their attitudes, and these are difficult to reform. Sometimes, discipline by a teacher can cause a counterresult, by promoting more subtle and wicked revenge.

Surely a reason behind this problem is the lack of time spent in moral and ethical education in Japan. Morals, ideally, should be taught by parents, but it has seemingly not been done. Perhaps in the increasingly industrialized society of Japan, a large number of children feel insecure. Their society promotes a "busy-ness" in their parents which can rob children of the attention and affection which are needed to build their self-worth. According to some surveys, parents spend an average of three hours a week in interaction with their children. In order to make themselves feel better, they often isolate a particular student and attempt to make him or her feel worthless. Also, traditional Japanese religious teachings are all but ignored in most homes. When the children feel isolated, they confine themselves to their room instead of sharing the problem they are facing with someone. Committing suicide is the only way that they can find to escape the pains of being isolated, ridiculed, rejected, or ignored.

EXERCISE 7: FOCUSING ON THE SUBJECT

Answer the following questions and then compare your answers with those of your classmates.

1. What reasons does the writer give to explain why many teens commit suicide in Japan? _____

   _____

2. What reasons does the writer give for the behavior of the bullying groups? _____

3. How do the reasons in questions 1 and 2 overlap?

   _____

4. What topic besides teenage suicide in Japan is the writer interested in discussing? _____

5. In the last section of the third paragraph, which attitudes does the writer mean when he refers to attitudes that are "difficult to reform"? _____

6. According to the last paragraph, which children suffer from lack of attention from their parents? _____

_____

■

In analyzing his purpose in this essay, this student wrote: "I wanted to show the reasons why many teens have committed suicide recently in a highly industrialized country, Japan." But when he looked more carefully at his first draft, he realized that his paper had taken a slightly different direction. He found that he was also interested in writing about how and why gangs of high school students terrorize other students. In order to accomplish this new, slightly altered purpose, the student wrote this second draft.

A thirteen-year-old girl leaped off the roof of her four-story school building just before afternoon classes just three weeks ago. This is the most recent incident in a rash of teen suicides in Japan over the past few years. The note she left said that she could stand the taunting of classmates no longer.

Young teenage suicide is becoming one of the most tragic social problems in Japan. About forty suicides have been reported this year already. Some of them were even elementary-school children. Like the case mentioned above, in many cases the reasons for suicide seem to be linked with victims' treatment by peers.

Victims were often isolated and teased by groups over a long period of time. In a school community, sometimes kids are very cruel to a quiet or different student without any other reason than his or her difference in appearance, behavior, manner of dress, or even accent. Research shows most students who committed suicide were very calm, gentle, silent students. Obviously, they were good targets for bullying groups because they tended not to complain or fight back, especially since groups of bullies can be quite large—ten or more students. Teasing is more mentally abusive than physically. Taunters may make fun of their target every day, hide his or her school materials and even force the individual to provide slavelike service. If they disobey the orders, bullies sometimes "discipline" them. Unfortunately, bullying groups are close-knit and represent a large portion of a class, and non–group members allow their actions. Changing the behavior of these group members is a perplexing problem because not only are students' actions involved but also their attitudes, and these are difficult to reform. Sometimes, discipline by a teacher can cause a counterresult, by promoting more subtle and wicked revenge.

What might prompt children to such cruelty to peers? Perhaps in the increasingly industrialized society of Japan a large number of children feel insecure. Their society promotes a "busy-ness" in their parents which can rob children of the attention and affection which children need to build their self-worth. According to some surveys, parents spend an average of three hours a week in interaction with their children. In order to make themselves feel better, the school bullies isolate a classmate and attempt to make him or her feel worthless, thereby somehow increasing their own feeling of self-worth. Another reason behind this problem of bullying gangs is the lack of time spent in moral and ethical education in Japan. Morals, ideally, should be taught by parents, but morals have seemingly not been taught. The traditional Japanese religious teachings of Buddhism, for instance, are all but ignored in most homes.

This same busy-ness and lack of religious convictions are also likely responsible for the rash reaction of some children to teasing. These children confine themselves in their rooms and do not share the problems that they are facing at school with their parents. They also do not seem to believe in a "higher love" more important than acceptance by their peers, the love their parents have for them. Committing suicide, they reason, is the only way that they can find to escape the pains of being isolated, ridiculed, rejected, or ignored.

Taisuke Akasaka (Japan)   ■

EXERCISE 8: FOCUSING ON THE SUBJECT
Describe what you think this student's purpose was in his second draft. Was he just exploring his own ideas? Was his purpose to inform, persuade, convince, or entertain?

1. This author's purpose was to _____ on the

subject of _____ .

2. What changes can you find in his second draft that reflect

his new purpose? _____

_____

3. Notice that the original title was "Teenage Suicide in Japan." Can you think of a title for the second draft that more closely reflects the student's new purpose

_____

Turn to the end of this chapter for the answer to the first item.   ■

✰ When you ask yourself "Why am I writing about this?" you should also ask yourself the following two questions:

1. Do I know enough about this subject, or do I need to learn more about it?
2. Why am I interested in writing about this subject?

You may find that you are not yet ready to write on your subject for an audience. Therefore, you must think, read, discuss, and/or write privately some more before you begin to write. You may also find that you are not really interested in writing about your subject. If that is the case, change the topic if you have that option. It is more difficult to write about something if you are not interested in writing about it. Therefore, if you ever get an assignment in which you are not interested, try one of these strategies:

• Discuss your situation with the teacher of the course. Together you may be able to find an alternative topic that interests you more.
• Try to find an aspect of the subject that you *are* interested in.
• Try to find more information on the subject. By learning more about a subject, you will often develop an interest in it.

If none of these strategies works, focus your attention on your audience. Analyze what you want your audience to do or to know about the subject or about *you*, the author, after reading your text. Concentrate on that aspect as you write.

➤ Writing Assignment 3.1: Invention for New Audience/Purpose

Writing Assignment 3.1

To help you see how a different audience and purpose can change your writing, look again at Writing Assignment 2.2 in Chapter 2. You were asked to think of an object, process, tradition, or concept in your culture and to use an invention technique to describe it to someone unfamiliar with it. In this assignment, you are to gather ideas on the same topic once again through whichever invention technique you choose, but your audience will be a group of people your own age from your own culture. Before you begin, discuss with your class what purpose you might have for writing about this subject for your new audience.

How will your new audience and purpose change the focus of your invention writing? For example, instead of focusing on the description of a tradition, you might focus on how that tradition has changed in your lifetime, how it compares with similar traditions in other countries, what the significance of the tradition is or has been, what the origin of the tradition is, what impact the tradition has had on modern life, or any number of other angles.

When you have finished, compare what you wrote in this assignment with what you wrote in the previous one. How did the change in audience and purpose affect the focus of your invention writing?   ◄

➤ *Writing Assignment 3.2: Invention for New Audience/Purpose*

Writing
Assignment 3.2

If you prefer, choose some invention writing you have done on any subject up to now. In this assignment you are to gather ideas on the same topic once again through whichever invention techniques you like, but this time keep a different audience and purpose in your mind as you invent. When you finish, compare your invention writing for this assignment with the one you did before. How did your new audience and purpose change the focus of your invention writing?   ◄

SEQUENCED WRITING PROJECT: INVENTION FOR NEW AUDIENCE/PURPOSE

Sequenced Writing
Project

If you are doing the Sequenced Writing Project, ask yourself who you assumed would be reading your writing, choose another audience and purpose as explained above, and again do some invention writing on the same subject. Did the new audience/purpose affect the ideas you found through the invention writing?

ANSWERS TO EXERCISES

- *Answer to Exercise 2: Audience.* The student who wrote this essay is a physical-education major. Were you able to guess that her intended audience is a friend from back home who knows in general about American football?
- *Possible answer to Exercise 6: Purpose.* The last essay was

written for an English class, but the student's purpose and audience were not clear. As a result, his paper is not very effective. If this student's purpose was to inform, it is difficult to see what audience he was writing for. For example, did you learn much from this essay, or did you know most of this information already?

- *Answer to Exercise 8: Focusing on the Subject.* The student's purpose in his second draft was to inform his audience about the behavior of bullying gangs and their victims and the probable causes for this behavior.

Writing a First Draft
and Getting Feedback

FROM INVENTION TO DRAFTING:
PREPARING TO WRITE A FIRST DRAFT

Now that you have experimented with getting ideas and writing with a particular audience and purpose in mind, you can put your skills into practice by writing a draft.

➤ *Writing Assignment 4.1: First Draft*

Writing
Assignment 4.1

Choose one of the following as the subject for your draft.

1. Look again at Writing Assignment 2.2 in Chapter 2 and reread the invention writing you did for a paper on an object, process, tradition, or concept from your culture for an audience of people unfamiliar with it. Add any ideas or comments that come to mind as you read.

2. Think of an object, process, piece of apparatus, or concept in your major field or from any other class or subject area you have studied that you know enough about to describe fully. Use one (or more) of the invention techniques you have learned to generate ideas on this subject. It may help you to first review any class notes you have on the subject you choose. You may also want to see an example of other writers' explanations of a concept. Look at the following articles in the Reading Selections in the Appendix.

Readings
"Darwin Revisited," page 315
Excerpt from *Black Holes and Baby Universes*, page 318

When you have finished, reread your invention writing and add any ideas or comments that come to mind as you read.

Now, with a different color pen, circle any sections of the invention writing that you want to be sure to include in your draft.

Next, if you can, number the sections you circled according to the order in which you want to mention them.

Now answer the following questions:

Self-Analysis (Pre-Draft)

1. Who is your audience right now? What does your audience already know about this subject? What special terms or concepts might you use that you will have to explain to this audience?

   Note: Remember that you may eventually change your mind about your audience.

2. What is your purpose in writing about this subject? What do you want to communicate to your audience? Why do you want to communicate this information to this audience?

   Note: Your purpose may be to inform your classmates and/or teacher about a subject you think they do not know about but should; or you may want them to know about an experience you have had; or you may want to show what you have learned about the subject you are discussing. Your purpose may change eventually, but try to decide what you want to accomplish right now.

3. Read your invention writing again. List what you think you will have to concentrate on to shape that invention writing into a good draft.

   Note: Think in terms of which ideas you want to express, how much you want to say, and in what order you want to present your ideas. Don't worry about grammar, spelling, punctuation, or finding the exact word in English. You will have time to worry about all that later. For now, if you cannot find a word in English, write it in your own language or leave a blank. Think: To make this into what I think is a good draft,

   a. What must I be sure to mention about my subject?

   _____

   _____

   _____

b. What should I discuss first, second, third, and so on to make this easy for my audience to understand?

_____

_____

_____

c. What background information may I have to give in order to help my audience understand what I am saying?

_____

_____

_____

d. What special terms may be unfamiliar to my audience that I will have to explain?

_____

_____

_____

What else will I have to keep in mind as I write?

I'll have to _____

I'll have to _____

I'll have to _____

Continue the list.

Your invention writing is probably a mixture of general and specific statements and ideas. Before you write your draft, it may help you to consider what English-speaking readers generally expect when they read a text. These are not rigid rules, but they may help you find a way to approach your draft. (You will consider these ideas in more detail in the next chapter.) English-speaking readers, particularly in academic writing, seem to expect this typical three-part pattern:

1. A brief but definite beginning that serves two functions:
   a. announcing the subject of the paper, and
   b. announcing the direction the discussion will take.
   This beginning is a kind of general summary statement of what the whole paper is about and what it will discuss.
2. A longer middle section. Here the writer usually
   a. explains,

   b. illustrates, or

   c. proves

   what the beginning announced or asserted by describing, comparing, giving examples, or showing supporting evidence.

3. A relatively brief conclusion. Here the writer

   a. states the implications of the discussion,

   b. links the specific discussion to broader issues, or

   c. summarizes the most important ideas in the text.

Look at your invention writing again. Now answer these questions as completely as you can:

Part 1: What is the subject of this draft? What is the main thing I want to say about this subject?

Part 2: As I explain the subject, what kinds of things do I want to be certain to bring up? (See the circled sections of your invention writing.) Can I group these ideas in some way so that I can discuss them one group at a time? What would be the clearest or most logical order in which to discuss these ideas?

Writing Assignment 4.1 continues on page 64.

Part 3: What conclusions do I want my reader to reach about my subject after reading my draft? ◄

SEQUENCED WRITING PROJECT: FIRST DRAFT

Sequenced Writing Project

Reread the invention writing you did for the Sequenced Writing Project assignments in Chapter 2 and in Chapter 3 with a new audience and purpose. Add any new ideas that occur to you as you reread. Remember that your goal in this paper is to explain what the topic is, why the topic is significant for your intended audience, and what your personal experience with the topic has been. It is not necessary to follow this order in your presentation. Select the order that explains your ideas best.

Now follow the directions for writing a first draft beginning back on page 59. ▄▄▄

FORMAL FEATURES OF A PAPER

Although this is not the final draft, there are certain formal conventions you usually must follow when writing in English.

Indentation

Sections of writing are marked off into paragraphs signaled by indentation. A new paragraph normally signals to the reader a shift in perspective. It means that the writer will now begin to discuss a different aspect of the subject at hand. Look, for example, at the composition on reactions to foreigners on page 27. Note that this student changed paragraphs with each new category of person he discussed. But in English not every sentence should begin a new paragraph, even though in a sense every sentence is a new idea. Instead, group sentences into categories of ideas; each paragraph is a group of sentences on a related idea. Paragraphs in English vary in length, but most are several sentences long, rather than just one or two. Each time you begin a new paragraph, indent, that is, leave blank about an inch of space from the left-hand margin (five spaces if you are typing).

Margins

Left-hand margins are usually printed on lined paper. Do not write beyond that margin. There are no right-hand margins marked on the paper, but maintain an imaginary margin of one-half to one inch on the right side. Do not try to squeeze words in; they will be too hard to read. Do not squeeze words into the bottom line of your paper either. In typed papers, keep a margin of about one inch on all four edges of the paper.

Paging

The first page typically has the title in the middle of the top line, then a blank line, then the beginning of the text (with the first line indented). Usually the first page is not numbered. Subsequent pages may be numbered at the top or the bottom of the page, either in the middle or on the right-hand side. After the first page, most people skip the very top line and begin writing on the next line. In formal papers, write only on one side of the page. Your papers should look something like those shown in Figure 4.1.

It is not necessary to follow this format in a first draft, because you will be rewriting the draft later anyway. On the other hand, some people like to see neat copies even of their first drafts. If you are such a person, you may want to follow this format now and become accustomed to writing this way. If not, you may refer to this section when you are writing subsequent

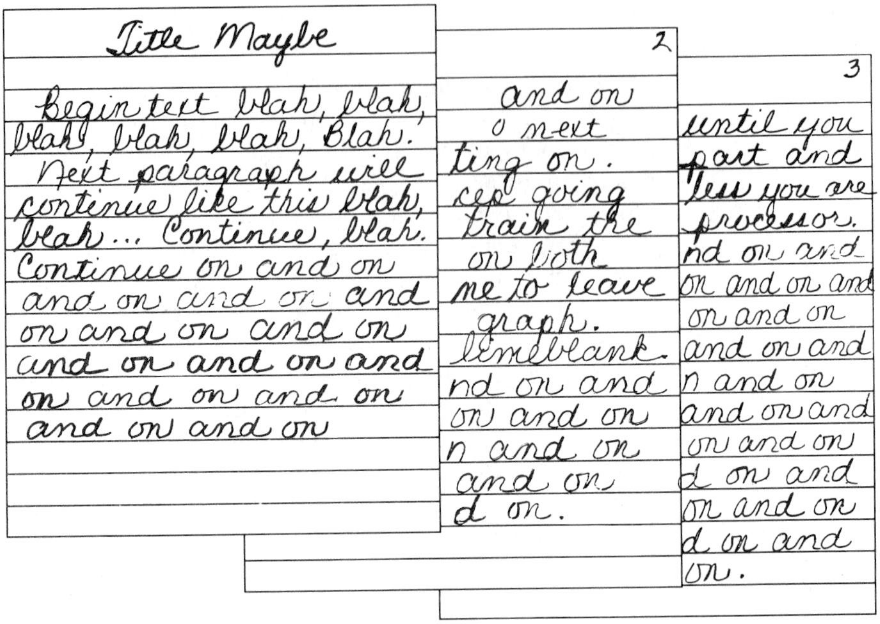

Figure 4.1 Example of Paper Format

drafts. Whatever you do, be sure to leave plenty of room in a first draft for later alterations. It is a good idea to leave larger margins than usual and perhaps to skip every other line.

WRITING THE FIRST DRAFT

Continuation of Writing Assignment 4.1 and Sequenced Writing Project

Hint 6: Don't worry about detail in your first draft. Try just to get your ideas down on paper. You can shape your ideas later.

Now gather all your material together, including your answers to the pre-draft questions, and write your first draft. Try to follow the three-part pattern most English-speaking readers expect. Write legibly so that your classmates can read your draft easily, but don't worry too much about correct grammar, spelling, punctuation, or vocabulary. Just try to get your ideas down on paper. You will have plenty of opportunity later to change this draft. If you get stuck or blocked as you are writing and find that you don't know what else to say or exactly how to say it, try any of the invention techniques you learned to start you up again. If you need to define an object or concept in order to discuss your subject, you may want to look at Unit 6, Chapter 16, on writing definitions.

When you have finished, reread your draft and your answers

to the pre-draft Self-Analysis questions. Then answer the following questions:

Self-Analysis (Post-Draft)

1. Who was in the back of your mind as you wrote? Did that audience change as you wrote?

2. Reread your draft as though you were your intended audience reading the draft for the first time. In a different color ink, make any comments or questions you think your audience might have on any part of the draft, especially comments or questions asking for more or clearer information.

3. As you were writing, did your purpose change? Did you change your mind at all about what you wanted to communicate?

4. How does the draft you wrote compare with the ideas you had about it before you began to write?

5. Do you feel that you did what you set out to do? Go back to the list you made in the third pre-draft question and put a check next to the items that you carried out in your draft. Did you find as you wrote that you didn't need or want to do some of the things you set out to do?

6. Did you write enough in your draft to be able to answer questions 1 through 5 here, or do you perhaps need to gather more material and expand your draft?

Writing
Assignment 4.1
and Sequenced
Writing Project resume on page 72.

7. What was easy about writing this draft? What was difficult about writing it?

8. Do you feel satisfied or disappointed in your draft? Explain why.   ◄

Don't be worried if your audience, purpose, or goals changed as you wrote. Writers very often realize what they really wanted to say only in the middle or even at the very end of a draft. Except in special situations like essay exams, you will have the chance to revise your draft to fit your new audience or purpose or to express ideas you thought of as you were writing. Remember to make use of invention techniques *as* you write, if you need to, as well as before you write.

Hint 7: Reread your own writing frequently. Try to read objectively, as though you were not the author and you were seeing it for the first time.

As you wrote this first draft, you did invention writing, then considered audience, and then purpose. It is not necessary to follow that particular order each time, as the parts of the writing process are interrelated. But it is important to consider each part of the process. Refer to this section whenever you are having trouble preparing to write a paper.

GETTING FEEDBACK: CRITERIA FOR RESPONDING TO WRITING

In this section, you will learn to comment on your classmates' writing. But how will you be able to recognize good writing, especially since what is considered good writing varies somewhat from culture to culture and from one writing situation to another? It may help to read some writing other students have done, to see how you react to this writing, and to compare your reactions with those of your classmates and teacher.

The following three essays were written for an English class like yours. The audience in each case was the student's classmates, and the purpose was to inform them about the subject mentioned in the title. Read the three essays and rank them in the order of your preference. Then rank them in the order you think your teacher would prefer. Discuss with your classmates and teacher the criteria you used in deciding how to rank the essays.

Recognizing a Good Paper

▪ STUDENT WRITING 1

The Best Ways to Learn a Foreign Language

Learning a foreign language can intrigue one person while it can frustrate another. Why is this so? One reason is the method involved in learning the foreign language. Students in class can benefit greatly if they have an excellent teacher. The teacher can, through innovative teaching, make lectures interesting and this in turn can motivate the students further to excel in the language. Classmates can be another source in learning a foreign language. If everyone in class is enthusiastic and cooperative, students will find learning the foreign language a great thrill. Besides learning a foreign language in class, one can also pick up the language outside the class. This can be done through conversing with native speakers. Students can listen, observe, and lip-read how native speakers talk by watching television. A student can also find additional material in books or magazines on the specific language. The best way to learn a foreign language is a combination of both in-class and out-of-class learning as these two involve different methods.

Poh Choo Tan (Singapore)   ▪

■ **STUDENT WRITING 2**

What Makes a School Good

Although all the years of high school were very good, for certain reasons the last two years were the best years I have ever had. For one thing, the teachers were very good. For example, my biology teacher was the best one I have ever had. His class never got boring and almost all the students had good grades in exams. We really enjoyed that class. But he wasn't the only good teacher in those years. Almost all our teachers were good. But the teachers weren't the only factors making up such good times. The friends that I had during those two years were also very good friends. For example, Mahasti and I used to study together and she is still one of my best friends even though I cannot see her very often anymore. My other friends like Shole, Mandana, and Mojgan were also very nice and we all had a very good time in school. Having good teachers and good friends were the most important things that made those two years the best years of my life.

Keihan Mani (Iran)   ■

■ **STUDENT WRITING 3**

Cultural Differences in Nonverbal Communication

Although France and the United States belong to the same kind of Western civilization, some nonverbal aspects of social behavior can be different and even opposite depending on the country. For example, I was surprised by the fact that Americans who are in a public place wait in a straight line with free space between each person. In France, everybody tries to be the first in line and consequently stands very close to the other people. French lovers walk in the street hand in hand, and their close physical contact shows their intimacy. I don't remember having seen such behavior in the United States. These two examples might suggest that French culture allows a closer social space, but that is not a universal rule. For instance, Americans who hug their friends accept closer contact than French, who might kiss a friend in greeting but will not take them in their arms. Social behavior in public places is different too. In France, one is allowed to look at strangers but not to say "Hello" to them because that would make them feel threatened. On the other hand, most Americans feel so uncomfortable when they have eye contact with strangers that they feel they need to smile and to say "Hi." So, each country has its specific rules of social behavior and a foreigner has to become used to nonverbal communication if he wants to get integrated into a different culture.

Anne Gouraud (France)   ■

- Which do you think is the best essay? _____

  Second best? _____

  Third best? _____

- Which essay do you think your teacher would like best?

  _____

  Second best? _____

  Third best? _____

- Which does your teacher actually like best? _____

  Second best? _____

  Third best? _____

So, what makes good writing? Certainly, the writer must have ideas to communicate and must express these ideas well. But what does it mean to express an idea well? One essential quality of good expository writing in English is clarity—that is, expressing an idea clearly, completely, and explicitly so that the reader can understand it easily. Remember that in English academic writing it is the writer's responsibility to make the reader's work easy. Here are some ways to find out what the reader needs:

1. Get feedback from readers.
2. Become a reader yourself and notice what you as a reader need in order to understand you classmates' work.

Hint 8: Let others read what you have written and give you feedback.

From now on, you and your classmates will read and comment in writing on one another's work. Not all the suggestions or comments you receive from your classmates will necessarily be helpful to you. Don't react to your classmates' comments immediately; take time to think them over. If one classmate didn't understand something, get another student's reaction. If several people say that part of your paper needs to be explained more, this is useful information. Then it is up to you to decide whether or how to strengthen that section. The ultimate responsibility for your work is yours.

When you give feedback, try to be as specific as possible. Keep in mind that part of your work is to help your classmates improve their writing as they help you improve yours.

Finally, of course, your teacher will also give you feedback. When you get your teacher's comments on a draft of your writing, notice the kinds of things he or she is looking for: more specificity, clearer links between ideas, more sophisticated approaches, for example.

PRACTICE RESPONDING TO WRITING

"What do you mean when you say _____?"

"Give me an example of _____."

"Explain the part about _____ more clearly."

"Give more information. I cannot follow your train of thought."

"Prove what you say about _____."

"Be more specific. Exactly how does _____ operate?"

These are typical comments from readers trying to understand the ideas in a text. Through such comments, readers express their needs that your essay has not filled. Try to anticipate these needs. When you finish a draft of a composition, put yourself in the reader's place. Ask yourself if you need to give an example of what you mean, if you should give more information to make your point clearer or stronger, or if you need to be more specific. Don't make your reader guess.

Look at one of the drafts you have written for this class and try to transform yourself into a reader instead of the writer. As you read the draft, stop after each sentence and write in the margin in a different color ink any questions that sentence raises. Good questions to ask yourself are:

Why is this the case?

How does this happen?

So what; why are you telling me this?

Then look at the next sentence to see if they answer these questions. If not, your reader may have trouble following your train of thought.

Now practice responding to someone else's writing. Look back at the paper selected as the best of the three compositions at the beginning of this section and answer as a class each question in the following analysis guide. Listen carefully to your classmates' and teacher's responses.

PRACTICE PEER RESPONSE: STUDENT WRITING

1. What was the best/most interesting part of this composition? Why do you think so?

2. What was the most important point the writer made? Write it in your own words as specifically as you can and then compare your answer with your classmates' and teacher's answers.

3. Was there any part of this composition where you wanted more information because you were interested? What else did you want to know?

4. Was there any part of this composition where you needed more information just to understand? What did you need to know?

5. Who do you think was the intended audience for this composition? How do you know?

6. Did the draft seem to follow the typical English three-part pattern?

7. Were the explanations sufficient for you to understand easily and accept the points the author made?

8. Name two things you learned from this composition that you either didn't know before or had never thought of in this way before.

9. Note everything you liked about this composition.

10. Note anything you feel was not successful in this composition.

11. Do you have any other comments or suggestions?   ■

You may want to go back now to the essay you like the *least* and answer these same Peer Response questions about that paper. This may help you see more clearly what you, your classmates, and your teacher value in writing.

Bring to class one of the drafts you have written for this course. Form groups of three or four with classmates who have not already read your draft. Then do one of the following:

1. Take turns quickly (not more than about a minute or two) telling the group what you said in your draft. Then exchange papers and read and analyze one another's drafts.

2. Exchange papers without discussion. If you choose this option, proceed as follows:
   a. Read the title (if there is one), the first sentence, and the last sentence of the paper.

b. Begin at the beginning, and read the whole paper quickly. Don't worry if there are parts you don't quite understand. In this reading you need only to get a general idea of the discussion.

c. Begin at the beginning once again, and this time read carefully to the end.

Choose the method your group feels comfortable with. Keep a pencil in your hand as you are reading and mark places you especially like and places you have trouble understanding. Don't hesitate to ask the author about words you cannot read, but don't spend time discussing or debating the paper.

When you have finished reading, take a full-sized, clean sheet of paper, and prepare it as shown in Figure 4.2, "Example of Peer Response Form."

```
Author's name

Reader's name

Date and name or subject of paper
```

Figure 4.2   Example of Peer Response Form

You will now answer questions on your classmate's paper similar to the ones you answered on the sample essay. Answer the questions as fully, honestly, and specifically as you can. If you do not understand something in the paper, say so. If you need or would like more information from the writer, say so. (*Caution*: The point of this procedure is to help, not to criticize, one another. Be honest but not harsh or unkind. Remember that you too are only an apprentice reader, not an expert critic.)

Peer Response: First Draft of Writing Assignment 4.1 or Sequenced Writing Project

Continuation of Writing Assignment 4.1 and Sequenced Writing Project

1. What was the best/most interesting part of this paper?
2. If your classmate described an object, device, or machine, did you understand what it looks like and/or how it functions? If your classmate described a process or concept, did you understand it?
3. Was there any part of this paper where you wanted more information because you were interested? What else did you want to know?
4. Was there any part of this paper where you needed more information just to understand? What else did you need to know?
5. Who was the intended audience for this paper? How can you tell?
6. What was your classmate's purpose in communicating these ideas? Did he or she want you to know something that you did not already know?
7. Did the draft follow the typical English three-part pattern?
8. If you had to reduce the length of this paper, what would you eliminate?
9. List everything you liked about this draft.
10. Do you have any additional comments or suggestions?

◄

When everyone in your group has read all the drafts, give your classmates the comments you wrote analyzing their papers. Read the comments you receive and respond to them. Note what you agree with, what you do not understand, how you might change something a reader commented on, or any other reactions you have.

When you have finished reading the comments on your

draft, ask your readers any questions you may have about their comments, especially if they make comments that contradict one another. Even contradictory comments can be useful.

The following is a student's first draft of an essay on Islam. Read the essay, and then read the comments of two of the student's classmates.

■ **STUDENT WRITING**

Islam is divided into two main branches, Sunni and Shiite. This division is according to differences in the basic faith. The Sunnis believe the first four caliphs of Islam to be the rightful heirs of the Prophet. They give the caliphs due respect and reverence but do not consider them to be sacred or holy. Sunnite is further divided into four sects, Hanafites, Hanbalites, Shafites, and Malikites. This division is not according to faith but according to jurisprudence and methods of performance of different tasks. Since the Prophet performed a few tasks in more than one way, each one of the sects follows the ways its scholars had chosen arbitrarily. The name of each sect is the adjective of the names of the originators.

On the other hand, Shiites believe the Prophet's daughter Fatima and her husband, the Prophet's cousin Ali, and their descendants to be the rightful heirs of the Prophet. The Shiites are also divided into two branches, the Isna Ashemis and the Fatimids. The Isna Ashemis believe in the 12 Imams or leaders, the first one of them being Ali. The rest are his eleven direct descendants. The belief in these Imams is part of the faith and they are considered to be holy and sacred. After the Imams, the Isna Ashemis also believe in a living vice-Imam called Rooh Allah. There are two Rooh Allahs in the world today, Khomeini in Iran and Aga Khan in Iraq. The Fatimids do not believe in all the 12 Imams. They are the most secretive group in Islam and not much is known to outsiders about their faith and practices. Though these are the main branches and sects of Islam, there are many other smaller sects and branches totaling to about 72, the largest number of Muslims being Hanafite Sunnis.

Anis Kwaja (Pakistan)   ■

Here are two responses to this composition.

> I had a hard time understanding your paper because I am not a Muslim. You mentioned many names and special concepts which I don't know about. Maybe this is a good paper for another Muslim to read.

> This was a totally clear, well-organized, and developed essay. Since I am a Muslim, I already knew all the information

in this paper, but it is a very good paper for a student who does not know about Islam.

These two contradictory answers told the student indirectly that the audience for this paper was not clear. What he had written was confusing to non-Muslims but obvious to Muslims, and therefore not worth writing about for them. Thus, the student knew he had to rethink his audience and purpose for the paper.

➤ *UNIT TWO*

Working with a Draft

≻ 5 ≺

Focusing on Main Ideas

Later in this chapter, you will either recount a personal experience that revealed something to you and/or conduct a survey on a question of interest to you. To prepare for these writing assignments, consider writing on one or more of the following journal suggestions.

Journal Suggestions

- How do people in the community where you are now living react when they find out where you are from? Try to think of all the different types of reactions you have seen. Is there any pattern that you can see in the types of people who have various reactions?

- What kinds of stereotypes do people here have about your country? Did any of these stereotypes surprise you? Do any of them correspond at all to reality?

- What do you find difficult to understand about U.S. culture? What would your friends and family back home find difficult to understand about this culture?

- What did you imagine the United States would be like before you arrived here? What is it actually like? How is it different from your expectations?

- If you were a student at a university in your home country, how would your life be different from the way you are living now?

- Tell the story of the strangest (or funniest or most frustrating) experience that you or someone else has had with English.

- Think of advice your parents or someone else gave you when you were a child that you still follow. Do you have any advice to offer, perhaps on the subject of family, strangers, friends, money, sex, or education? Have you had any experiences that show the wisdom of this advice?

THESES AND TOPIC SENTENCES

As you have learned, a finished academic paper usually begins with a general idea, gives the details that support that generalization, and finally returns to another general statement on the same topic.

Generalization

Specifics that allowed you to make the generalization

Return to a general, more abstract level

The three student essays in the last chapter illustrate this typical movement from general to specific. These essays follow the typical three-part blueprint or pattern that English-speaking readers seem to expect. Look at each essay and indicate where you might separate the beginning from the middle. Where do general comments end, and where do the specific cases begin? Then divide the middle section from the end. Where do the comments become general again? Finally, how might you divide the middle section?

These kinds of divisions often correspond to paragraphs, but not always. Whether or not you begin a new paragraph depends on how long each section is and how great a shift of perspective occurs between the sections. Most English-speaking readers would probably expect the student examples you just reread to consist of only one paragraph because they are short and explain only one main idea.

Look back at the drafts you have written for this class. Reread the one you like best and try to write in one sentence the main idea of the whole draft. What were you trying to show in that composition?

Main idea:

Without looking back at the three student examples you just reread, try to write the main idea of each one in one sentence. Compare your sentences with those of your classmates and decide which ones best express the main points of each essay.

Main ideas:

1. _____

2. _____

3. _____

Definitions

The main point or central idea of a piece of writing in English is often explicitly, or directly, expressed near the beginning of the text. This statement is traditionally called the *thesis*. In addition, if the article has several paragraphs, the main point of each paragraph (traditionally called the *topic sentence* of the paragraph) is often expressed somewhere near the beginning of the paragraph. You can think of these explicit statements of the main ideas in a composition as labels. To help you understand how these labels function, imagine that you are moving to a new apartment and must pack all your belongings in boxes. In order to remember which box contains kitchen utensils, which box contains books, and which box contains clothes, you might label the outside of each box with a statement of what is inside. Similarly, a thesis helps the reader understand immediately what the basic content of an essay will be, and a topic sentence near the beginning of a new paragraph helps the reader see in which direction the author intends to move in that paragraph. What you say in a thesis or in a topic sentence will make your reader expect to read certain things in your discussion, and English-speaking readers trust you to meet their expectations.

Figure 5.1 shows the usual pattern of a typical academic essay.

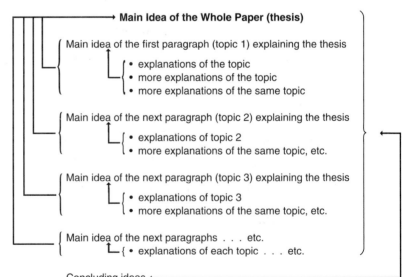

Figure 5.1   Possible Organization of an Essay

The following sentences express the main ideas of several paragraphs.

1. For years scientists have tried to discover exactly what causes headaches, but they have had little success. Although the exact cause is still unknown despite today's great advances in medicine, a few facts have emerged.

   Most English-speaking readers would expect a discussion of the facts that are known about the causes of headaches.

2. As a first step toward understanding headaches, scientists distinguish among several types.

   The rest of this discussion will probably cover each of the different types of headaches.

3. Although nearly all adults suffer from headaches, one type of headache is most common in women while another type is more typically experienced by men.

   Here most English readers would expect a comparison of these two types of headaches.

4. The most common type of headache experienced by most men is called the cluster headache.

   This sentence leads the reader to expect a description of the characteristics of this type of headache.

5. Migraine headaches are always painful, but the case of Joan Didion is an extreme example of how a simple headache can disrupt an otherwise normal life.

   The writer will probably tell the story of Ms. Didion's case.

In each of the previous sentences, the writer made a kind of promise to the reader about the content of the paragraph to come. English readers tend to trust the writer to fulfill this promise. If the writer goes off in another direction and discusses something else, the reader becomes confused and even frustrated, finding it difficult to follow the writer's "train of thought."

EXERCISE 1: MAIN IDEA

Suppose you are under stress from your studies or your job. You need to find a way to relieve that stress, and you find the following article.

Psychologists working together with medical doctors have developed a number of ways to relieve tension and stress caused by overwork and anxiety. When people are under stress, they may be anxious and irritable. They become difficult to deal with because they often feel intolerant of other people's mistakes. In addition to these psychological symptoms, people under stress often show physical symptoms. They may experience headaches, muscular tension, stomach disorders, even ulcers. If you have had any of these symptoms, you should find a way to relieve your stress as quickly as possible.

Answer these questions with your class.

1. What did the first sentence promise? _____

_____

2. Was that promise fulfilled? Explain. _____

_____
                                                                                    ■

EXERCISE 2: MAIN IDEA

Read the following sentences. If each was the topic sentence in a paragraph, what do you think a reader would expect that paragraph to explain or prove or illustrate?

1. The meaning of the expression "black hole in space" is fairly easy to explain even to non-astronomers.

   Reader's expectation: _____

   _____

2. My interest in International Studies comes from both my personal experience and my educational background.

   Reader's expectation: _____

   _____

3. A picnic area on a Saturday afternoon in summer in the Great Smoky Mountains National Park is like some picture of a typically American scene.

   Reader's expectation: _____

   _____

4. Since I have been in the United States, I have noticed basically four types of reactions to foreigners.

   Reader's expectation: _____

   _____
                                                                                    ■

An explicit statement of the main idea of an essay is most helpful to the reader when it is:

1. *general* enough to indicate the basic content of the essay, but
2. *specific* enough to give the reader the clearest idea possible of where the discussion will lead.

EXERCISE 3: MAIN IDEA

■ STUDENT WRITING: EXAMPLE 1

Read the following paragraphs in which the topic sentences have been deleted. After each paragraph are three possible topic sentences. Select the one that is both general and specific enough for that paragraph, the one that will give the reader the clearest idea of what the paragraph is about. Compare your selections with those of your classmates. If your selections do not agree, discuss the merits of your choices.

_____ . For instance, it is obvious that all objects will fall and a lot of people before Newton had seen an apple falling from a tree. But Newton's penetrating mind used the simple fact that things fall to the ground to develop one of the most stable theories in physics, the Universal Gravitational Theory. An even more difficult task than inventing a new theory is disproving a generally pervasive public belief. Before the Renaissance it was believed that heavy objects fall faster than light objects. But Galileo's keen mind disproved this misconception and started a new era in physics. We now believe that all objects will reach the ground at the same time in a vacuum no matter how heavy or light they are. Finally, the most difficult task for a scientist is to go against theories that are popular with the scientific community. Newton's theories were regarded as clearly true by scientists until Einstein's genius succeeded in refining Newton's theory into the law of relativity. As these examples demonstrate, scientists may invent new theories but it takes the insight of a genius to help us see the world in a radically different way.

Ali Keshavarzi (Iran) ■

Select from the following the sentence that best expresses the main idea.

1. At different times in human history, people have believed

in explanations of natural phenomena which were ultimately proven untrue by great scientists.

2. Although everybody has intelligence and dedication to some extent, it takes the creativity of a genius to develop exciting new theories in physics.

3. Many scientists have changed our views about the laws of physics.

■ STUDENT WRITING: EXAMPLE 2

_____

_____ . The first difference between Arabic and English is in grammar. For instance, there are about twelve tenses and eight pronouns in English, but there are only three tenses and about sixteen pronouns in Arabic. In English there are only singular and plural sentences, but in Arabic sentences are singular, plural, and double. For example, in Arabic we never say about two people, "They are nice." Instead, we must say, "Both are nice." The second major type of difference between English and Arabic is that the Arabic writing system is totally different from English writing. In Arabic one writes from right to left, but in English one writes from left to right. Furthermore, in Arabic if one misplaces a dot on a word, the whole meaning of the word changes. In English misplacing a dot is not particularly important because no matter how people dot their i's, the meaning of the letter is the same. These are some of the big differences between Arabic and English, which show up especially in grammar and writing to make life hard for poor language students.

Fadi Zakaria (Jerusalem) ■

Select from the following the sentence that best expresses the main idea.

1. Although different languages are spoken all over the world, all languages are equally useful to the people who speak them.

2. Learning a different language can be quite difficult, especially if you must learn to write accurately in the new language.

3. Learning to write English presents particular difficulties for a speaker of Arabic because of wide differences between English and Arabic.

Look at the first few sentences of at least two essays you have written. Then answer the following questions for each.

1. Do these sentences express the main idea you developed in your essay? Yes _____ No _____

2. What was the main idea you wanted to develop in the essay? _____

3. How well do the sentences predict what appeared in the rest of the essay? _____

■

Making Main Ideas and Text Fit

As you have seen, the main idea of an essay is usually expressed somewhere near the beginning of the text. However, you do not need to know exactly what the main idea is before you begin to write. Although you will probably know the topic you want to write on, you may not know exactly what you want to say about it until you have done some invention writing and seen your ideas on paper. Formulating a thesis or a topic sentence that exactly fits your discussion is a form of revising, of focusing more clearly and sharply. Once you know more or less what your main idea is, that is, once you know what you intend your essay to explain or prove, keep this idea in mind as you gather information and write or reread your draft.

On one hand, the way you state or even think of your main idea will have an important effect on what you then write about your main idea in your paper. Keeping your main idea in mind will help you to select what to include in your paper and also to recognize what is irrelevant. On the other hand, you may find as you gather information or write your draft that your main idea changes or becomes clearer to you in different terms. That is fine. Just change your thesis or topic sentences so that they become good summary statements of the ideas you discuss in the essay or paragraph. Then reread your paper and remove any statements that are now irrelevant to your new main idea.

Benefit of Explicit Theses and Topic Sentences

Explicitly stating your main idea is useful for two reasons:

1. For the writer: It helps you control your writing by helping you decide what to include in your essay and how to organize your ideas. Writing down on paper a clear statement

of your main idea forces you to think through fully what you want to say and to crystallize it into a few words.

2. For your reader: A clear, explicit statement of the main idea helps your reader know quickly what direction you intend to take in the essay and within the paragraphs of the essay. This efficiency and clarity are especially important in business or industry, where your audience may be an administrator who wants a quick overview of what you will communicate in a report you submit. In fact, in some situations, particularly in technical writing for business or industry, readers will request a statement like this at the beginning of a piece of writing: *"In this report I am going to define (or explain or compare X to Y or show or analyze) . . ."* However, this kind of blunt announcement violates the conventions of academic writing in some situations. You should avoid such a statement unless you are specifically asked to include one.

There is no rule of English that says a statement of the main idea must appear near the beginning of a paper. In fact, while there is always a main idea in published writing, it sometimes appears at the end of the piece, especially in editorials in newspapers and journals. Sometimes, the main idea is not explicitly stated at all in the article. In most academic writing, however, readers appreciate being told early what the main idea will be, and it is probably a good idea for you to meet that expectation.

The ability to produce a clear summary statement of your main idea is a valuable skill to develop for your school work. Look at the following question and answers from an essay exam in a U.S. history course. The specific answers to the question are the same, but the second one is more powerful intellectually and gives a better impression because the generalization or topic sentence at the beginning suggests that the writer is in control of all the ideas.

Question: What were the main causes of the U.S. Civil War?

Answer 1: One cause of the Civil War was that the North was developed industrially while the South was mainly agricultural. Another cause was that the South wanted to expand the number of slave states. Another cause. . . .

Answer 2: The main causes of the U.S. Civil War fall into two distinct but interlinked categories: economic causes and political causes. Economically, the North was developed industrially while. . . .

Notice that in the second answer the general statement of the main idea is not long or elaborate. It is a straightforward one-sentence general answer to the exam question. The general answer is then followed by a specific explanation of the main idea expressed in the topic sentence. Because the main idea is not explicitly expressed in the first answer, it is hard to tell if the student is in control of the information. This answer gives the impression that the student's ideas are listed in a random order, not analyzed logically.

(For further discussion of essay exams, see Chapter 15.)

In this section, you have learned about the concept of the thesis, topic sentence, or main idea of a piece of writing. The following assignments will give you practice identifying and extracting the main idea from a body of data.

➤ *Writing Assignment 5.1: Extracting the Main Idea in Recounting a Personal Experience*

Writing
Assignment 5.1

For this assignment, recount an incident you have witnessed or have been a part of since you came to the United States that reveals some insight about life in the United States, people in the United States, or yourself. Notice that the assignment is not just to tell the story. You must also extract from the story the lesson you learned or the significance of the incident. That lesson will be your main idea.

Begin this assignment by thinking about incidents that have occurred since your arrival. Look through your journal and at the invention writing you did on page 23 to see if you have recorded any revealing incidents there. Look also at the student essay by Tai Herng Kong in Chapter 2 (pages 27–28). He did not write about one incident; he wrote about types of reactions people in the United States have had toward him. But he might have considered just one reaction and recounted how one teacher reacted to him, for example, or how one vendor treated him at the Flea Market.

You may want to jog your memory by using an invention technique to note as many of the events, happy or sad ones, as you can remember that have occurred since your arrival. Then choose one of them to concentrate on.

You may also want to look at the following articles in the Appendix to help you think about this topic.

Readings
"The Quality of Mercy," page 322
Excerpt from *Eight Little Piggies*, page 327

Audience Analysis

For this assignment, choose one of the following audiences:

Your classmates in your English class
Americans in the community where you now live
Friends and family back home

To help you analyze this audience, answer the following questions:

1. How well do these people know you?
2. Why might they want to read about an incident that reveals something about you personally?
3. Why might they want to read about an incident that reveals what any non-native might experience in the community where you are living?
4. Why might they want to read about an incident that reveals something about the United States?
5. Is your audience likely to have had similar experiences?
6. Is your audience likely to interpret your experience in the same way you have?
7. Where will your audience read your article? In your presence in the English class? In an article in the local newspaper? In a letter home?

What you eventually write will be affected by which audience you choose to write for and how you analyze that audience.

Keep in mind that your purpose is to reveal something about the United States or about yourself. Do not include information in your paper that does not fit this purpose.

Finally, when you are ready to begin your draft, consider how you will arrange your material. For this particular paper, explain your insight (main idea) near the beginning of the paper. Depending on your audience, you may need to give some background information about the setting of the incident. Then explain the incident that led you to your insight by telling your story one step at a time. Conclude your paper by restating your insight in other terms, by explaining that insight more deeply than you did at the beginning of the paper, or by suggesting the effects of the character trait that your experience revealed.

Self-Analysis

After you have written your first draft, answer the following questions.

1. Did you find this assignment difficult or easy to do? Why?
2. Did you think of your story first and then figure out the point of the story, or did you have a generalization in mind first and then look for a story to explain it?
3. How do you expect your audience to react to your paper? To laugh? To feel sorry? To be surprised? Something else?
4. What are you most satisfied with in your essay?
5. What are you least satisfied with?
6. What will you change in your next draft?

Now give your draft to at least one classmate to read and comment on.

Peer Response

1. State the main idea in your own words without looking back at the paper.
2. Which audience do you think the writer was aiming at? How do you know?
3. Do you feel that the story explains the writer's main idea convincingly?
4. If you had to eliminate any part of this paper, what would you eliminate?

5. Do you feel that you are led logically through the ideas in this paper? If not, where do breakdowns occur?
6. Considering this paper as a whole, what are its strengths?
7. Can you suggest any improvements?

Revision

Using your first draft, your self-analysis, your classmates' responses to your draft, and what you have learned in this chapter, revise your first draft. ◄

▪ STUDENT WRITING

Here is an example of one student's draft on this subject.

How the American Way of Life Has Affected My Behavior

When somebody moves to another country it is natural for that person to adapt to the new culture by altering some parts of his or her behavior. When I came to America, I knew that I had to adjust to the American way of life if I was going to enjoy my stay here and really understand the American people. But I never realized that I also would abandon some of my ideals and beliefs that formed the basis of certain parts of my behavior back in Sweden.

In my home country people are generally more concerned about the environment than Americans are. We try to buy "green products" and recycle our waste. For example, I always use soft soap when I clean my apartment back in Sweden because it is not harmful to the environment. Consequently, I was really disappointed when I only could find atomizer products to clean my apartment with here in America. But after living here for a couple of months I'm getting used to a product that I would never dream about using in Sweden. I don't even reflect on it. Another example of my decreasing concern about the environment is the way I have totally adapted to using paper mugs. Americans seem to love paper mugs. You can find them in every cafeteria and fast-food restaurant, and as far as I know the degree of recycling is very low. But even though I realize what an environmental waste it is, I have accepted it. And I use as many paper cups as a native American, who doesn't have the slightest idea about how this affects the environment, would use.

My first impression of the American food culture was superfluity, fattening and sloppy foods. And even if that still is my opinion, I'm beginning to get more American-like in my eating behavior. When I first got here I was amazed that people could eat muffins for breakfast, nachos for lunch, and a hamburger with French fries every day. Of course, I had eaten this kind of food back in Sweden before but never as frequently as is customary here. I have always considered this kind of food unhealthy and not appropriate for a basic meal. But after some time in this country I find myself eating pancakes for breakfast, for example (in Sweden, we eat them for dessert), and I would gladly have dinner at Taco Bell. And I don't feel bad if I cannot eat all the food I have taken in the cafeteria. I just throw it away as all the Americans do. In Sweden such behavior is looked upon as very impolite, as well as a big waste. . . .

It is most likely to believe that I have changed my behavior because I don't want to be different from anybody else, and that I want to fit in. But that cannot be the explanation in my case because I don't mind being different. Instead I think that when the majority behaves in a certain way and justifies that behavior, it is very easy for a person to just follow along without thinking. I believe that is the reason I have started to eat more unhealthy food, for example. Even though one's ideals and beliefs conflict with the behavior of the majority, as my belief that one should use "green products," one might adopt the behavior of the majority because it feels like one person's behavior won't make any difference. If the majority doesn't care about the environment, for example, it feels like my concern about it won't make any difference. I have always viewed myself as an independent person who is resistant to negative influences on my behavior. But now I have realized that it is not always so easy to behave in a different way from the majority, even though you strongly dislike that behavior.

Cecilia Lennartsson (Sweden)   ■

➤ *Writing Assignment 5.2: Extracting the Main Idea from Survey Data*

Writing
Assignment 5.2

Collect data on a subject of interest to you by surveying a group of people. Then analyze your data by generalizing from the information you collect.

For this assignment, you will work with another student to gather facts and statistics by conducting a survey or interviewing people on a subject of interest to you. Once you have collected the data, you will generalize from those specifics and reach a conclusion about people's opinions on a certain issue. That conclusion will be the main idea of your report.

Once you have your general results and before you write up the details of your inquiry, your teacher may first ask you to briefly report the results orally to the class.

Choosing a Subject

Find a partner with whom to work and together decide on a question about a subject currently of interest to you and to your classmates. Following are some topics students have used in the past. You may choose one of these or come up with one of your own.

1. How do you feel about cross-cultural marriages? Would you marry an American? Why or why not?
2. How do you feel about a law requiring you to wear a seat belt in your car?
3. How do you feel about laws restricting smoking to designated areas only?
4. How do you feel about being required to take English at this university? (Indicate if you are an international student or a native student.)
5. What languages have you learned or failed to learn? What helped you to learn or prevented you from learning?
6. How do you feel about surrogate mothering? Is it a valid way for an infertile couple to have a baby of their own, or does it allow rich people to exploit poor but healthy women?

In addition to these questions, consider recent events on your campus that have caused controversy or issues being discussed in your major field. Be as specific as possible in your questions. For example, rather than asking

How do you feel about taking English?

ask:

How do you feel about international students' being required to take a year of freshman English?

or ask:

How do you feel about international students' getting extra time to write essay exams in classes where they are mixed with native speakers?

If you choose a question that can be answered yes or no, prepare follow-up questions asking for more details:

Why do you feel that way?

Do you think this should be the case under all circumstances?

If not, when should this be different?

Sometimes the number of people answering yes or no to a question is interesting in itself. However, asking people *why* they feel as they do may yield even more significant information.

Choosing the Sample

There are two types of people you can question. The first type is the "man or woman in the street." These are people who have no special reason for being interested in or knowledgeable about the subject. They can give you the average person's opinion on the subject. This sample might include students in your classes or in your dorm. The second type of people are those who are particularly interested in the subject, perhaps an expert in the area you are exploring, someone who has been affected by the issue, or someone who has simply thought a great deal about the issue. These people may be particular students, professors, or members of the community.

Whichever type you choose to survey, it is important to get your participants' cooperation. Do the following for all the people you question:

1. Ask for their participation.
2. Make sure they have time to talk to you. This may mean contacting people ahead of time and making appointments for times when they will be free to talk to you for a few minutes. This is particularly important if you intend to survey people while they are at work (for example, professors or administrators).
3. Explain what the survey is and why you are doing the survey.

4. Tell participants that their answers will remain confidential.

5. Be sure to be prepared yourself. Have your questions ready, and take notes or use a tape recorder to collect your information.

6. When you have finished, thank the participants for their cooperation.

Both you and your partner should speak to as many people as you can (at least ten for each of you). Then, analyze your sample:

Who are the people you questioned?

What characteristics do they have in common? Consider their age, sex, nationality, occupation, or any other feature that you think may influence their answers.

What is their interest in the subject of the survey?

What is their knowledge of the subject of the survey?

How does the issue you raise in the survey affect them personally?

Analyzing the Data: Main Ideas

Combine what you and your classmate found and analyze your data. Look for patterns in the data. What responses were given? What reasons were given for those responses? Did the responses vary depending on the type of people you asked? Perhaps most students felt one way about an issue, for example, while most people in the community felt another way. Group similar reactions together. (For a discussion of classification of information in a piece of writing, see Chapter 16.)

Arrange your information systematically—for example, by response (yes, no, maybe, sometimes), by reasons for the response, or by types of people surveyed. As you look over your data, come to conclusions about the opinions of the group of people you questioned. For example, from your findings you may conclude that a large majority of participants in your survey oppose the freshman English requirement for international students in universities in the United States. This general conclusion will be the main idea of your entire paper, the thesis statement, which you will explain or prove by referring to the data you collected through your survey. In addition, extract a general statement from each group of similar responses, the topic sentences of your paragraphs.

If you make a brief oral report to the class on the results of your survey, write down any questions your classmates ask you. You may decide to include answers to those questions in your written report.

As you write up the results of your data gathering, remember that writers normally interpret data for their readers. This does not mean that you must give your own opinion. It does mean, however, that your reader will expect you to explain what the raw data means. For example, suppose you find that eight out of ten international students prefer an American roommate but that eight out of ten American students are neutral about having an international roommate. You might conclude that international students are looking for contact with Americans whereas Americans do not seem to be actively looking for an international experience. This is not just your opinion; it is an interpretation you make for the reader based on the evidence you have collected. Be sure your data justifies your generalization.

Arranging the Data

Keep your purpose in mind as you write your report. Perhaps you simply want to inform your classmates about a group of people's opinions on an issue of interest to you and presumably to them. On the other hand, you may have been surprised by your findings and may want to share your surprise with your classmates. Perhaps your results expose a situation that you would like your classmates to try to change. Decide what reaction you want your audience to have to your report, and keep it in mind to help you decide which of your findings you will report and in how much detail.

Begin your report with a statement of the general results of your survey and a description of your sample (how many questioned, what type of people). Then discuss your data in any order that seems logical to you. For example, if you ask the question on cross-cultural marriage, you might organize your information like this:

All those favoring cross-cultural marriages
   Reason 1
   Reason 2

All those opposed
> Reason 1
> Reason 2
> Reason 3
All those with no opinion

Note: If you refer to percentages, avoid beginning a sentence with a number. Rewrite the sentence to begin with a word instead. For example, instead of writing

40% of the people polled . . .

you might write:

Of the people polled, 40% . . .

or:

In their answers, 40% of the people polled . . .

If you have a fairly small sample (fewer than twenty responses), avoid using percentages. The use of percentages implies a large sample and therefore might be misleading to the reader. Instead, use the numbers: "The survey showed that four out of the twenty people questioned/polled/surveyed felt/said/agreed that. . . ."

To see how others have used objective data, you may want to read the following selections in the Appendix.

Readings
Excerpt 1 from *Savage Inequalities*, page 331
"History Proves It: Other Systems of Naming Work," page 337

When you have collected all your data, drawn your conclusions, and decided how much information to include and how to organize that information, write your first draft. When you have finished your draft, answer the following questions.

Self-Analysis

1. What did you learn from this survey that was interesting to you or that surprised you? Or did you expect the results that you got?
2. Why did you select the group of people you questioned?

3. Was everyone you asked willing to talk to you?

4. Why did you select the topic you did? Why is it of interest to you?

5. In what way was the topic of particular interest to the people you questioned?

6. How did you come to your main idea from the opinions you gathered?

7. How did you arrange your data for presentation in your draft?

8. What was difficult about writing your report?

9. For whom did you write this report? That is, what audience was in your mind as you chose your subject and sample and wrote your report?

Now give your draft to at least one classmate.

Peer Response

1. Why do you think the writer chose this topic?

2. Why do you think the writer questioned the category of people surveyed? What special interest might they have in the topic?

3. Which of the findings surprised you?

4. How did the writer organize his or her findings?

5. Can you think of some other possible ways to organize these findings?

6. What conclusions did the writer reach about the answers to the survey? What are the implications of those answers?

Here is an example of the survey report one student wrote for a class like this one.   ◄

▦ STUDENT WRITING

Americans' Idea of Foreign Students at UT

As a foreign student in this country, I have often wondered how Americans think about us, international students, especially in school. From our survey about Americans' ideas of foreign students, we found out that all participants in this survey had positive ideas toward international students. The result was different from my expectation that there must be a number of people who have negative ideas about international students.

In this survey, we asked eighteen Americans about their ideas toward foreign students around them. There were ten questions including three questions of hypothetical situations (what would you do if . . . ?). These three questions assessed how the person would react to specific situations. The purpose of one question was to figure out whether Americans have stereotypes of foreign students. I also included a question about the participant's background which might affect their attitude toward international people.

We learned that all our participants have a favorable impression of international students. All people answered that they would help foreign students when they needed some help from an American even if the foreigner's English was imperfect. Although one participant expressed his frustration with talking to non-native speakers, he also answered that, like other participants, he would try to talk with foreigners using easy words. Our participants told us various ways of helping international students, such as using gestures and drawing, and even finding another person who came from the same foreign country as the student to interpret his explanation.

The participants in our survey did not care when many foreigners got together and talked in their own language. One day I heard an American say that he did not like to see international students gather together and speak only their language. I wondered if this idea was common among Americans. However, most of our survey participants answered that it did not bother them at all. Several people kindly recommended international students use English as much as possible in order to improve their language skills.

Among eighteen participants, fourteen people did not have a chance to be with a foreigner when they were a child. Most of the people met their first international friends in high school. These students answered that there were one or two exchange students around them. My expectation that only those people who had foreigners around them when they were children would have positive attitudes toward foreigners in general was false. However, the experience of exchange students in high school may have helped Americans' positive attitudes toward international students.

Contrary to my conjecture, many Americans have positive attitudes to foreign students. However, because the survey conditions were not perfect, we need to consider the survey results. The survey condition limited the number of participants and kinds of people (all are UT students). In addition, the fact that the questioners were foreigners might have affected the results. There may be some who have negative attitudes to foreigners. Still, the results of our survey indicate there are many people who are interested in the sound of another language, or in learning about another culture or language, or who think it is good to have international students at UT for cultural exchange. At least we can say that most Americans who are in UT have positive ideas about foreign students.

Momi Yamanaka (Japan)   ▨

Revision

Using your first draft, your self-analysis, your classmates' responses to your draft, and what you have learned from this chapter, revise your first draft.   ◄

SEQUENCED WRITING PROJECT: SURVEY

Sequenced Writing Project

Follow all the directions from Writing Assignment 5.2 beginning on page 89, except for the references to working with a partner and to selecting a subject, since you already have a topic.

The next assignment in the Sequenced Writing Project, the interview report, appears in Chapter 6.   ▬▬▬

⊱ 6 ⊰

Developing and Shaping Ideas

The Writing Assignments in this chapter will ask you to discuss forms of nonverbal communication, to describe a scene, or to interview an expert for your Sequenced Writing Project. To prepare for these assignments, you may want to write on one or more of the following journal suggestions.

Journal Suggestions

- Besides using spoken language, people also communicate a great deal of information through body language. Have you noticed that the gestures of people from other cultures are different from the gestures people in your country make? Think of hand gestures and their meanings, facial expressions, and distances maintained between people having a conversation. In your country, what movements of which parts of the body indicate the following: *yes, no, I don't know, I don't care, Come here, Leave me alone*? What gestures do you make to indicate someone making a phone call, eating, drinking? What gesture do you make when someone has made you furious? In a conversation, whom can you touch as you talk? Where can you touch another person? Are there people you cannot touch? Find out how your friends and classmates answered these questions.
- Have you noticed that there are different attitudes toward time in different parts of the world? If you are invited to dinner in your home country at seven-thirty, at what time would you probably arrive? How would your hosts react if you came at seven-fifteen? At exactly seven-thirty? At quarter to eight? At eight-thirty? At what point would you feel obligated to call and say you were going to be late? If you came at quarter to eight, would you feel embarrassed for being late? What if you came at eight-thirty?
- What specific gesture or speech patterns are used in your

country to show respect for a new acquaintance, a parent, an older person, a teacher, or a boss?

- Have you felt happy, sad, embarrassed, lonely, or self-confident lately? Think of a scene you associate in your mind with that feeling and describe it in detail. In your description, try to include sights, sounds, smells, feelings, and tastes.

- Think of places that are important to you in your home country. What places are they? Describe them in as much detail as possible. What makes these places so special?

- What is the most important place to you here in the United States? Where do you spend the most time? Where do you have the most fun? Describe these places in as much detail as you can.

Doing the following invention activities will further prepare you for the Writing Assignments in this chapter.

INVENTION FOR WRITING ASSIGNMENT: USING PERSONAL EXPERIENCES

A Writing Assignment later in this chapter will ask you to write a draft of a short paper discussing some aspect of body language or nonverbal communication. To get some examples of how body language and nonverbal communication work, you may want to read the following texts in the Appendix and in this chapter.

Readings
"The First Four Minutes," page 341
"Nonverbal Communication," page 344
"How to Spot a Liar," page 349
"Primate Studies and Sex Differences," page 353
Student Writing by Anne Gouraud, page 67
Draft by Chi Kin Cheng, page 103

Gestures, body language, and people's sense of personal space vary widely from culture to culture. Make a list of forms of nonverbal communication common in your country that might not be understood in the United States and/or examples of body language common in the United States that might not be understood by people in your country. As part of your invention writing, ask other people from your country what differences they have noticed, and add these to your list. Or you might question people from other countries about gestures they use. Try grouping examples according to some system (different parts of the body used, different meanings of the gestures, or the different people who may use the gestures, for example). As your list grows, keep trying to come to some conclusion about body language. What does all this information about gestures and body language tell you about how people communicate? Continue to collect material for this assignment and save your invention writing for later.

INVENTION FOR WRITING ASSIGNMENT: USING OBJECTIVE DATA

To give you some examples of how writers use objective data to support their ideas, read the following articles from the Appendix and in this chapter.

Readings
Excerpt 1 from *Savage Inequalities*, page 331
Student Writing by Anne Gouraud, page 67
Student Writing by Son Sang Kong, below

■ STUDENT WRITING

Eating at the crowded and noisy Strong Hall Cafeteria, one of my school cafeterias or canteens, as we say in Hong Kong, can be a really entertaining experience if you just relax and watch the scene. Because of its large size and central location on campus, more than three hundred students crowd there during each eating time. Different noisy groups are formed, like the basketball players, football players, and especially the punks and the freshman kids, occupying the long tables in the bright yellow main hall. The noisiest group is the punks, who laugh rudely every ten seconds. Wearing red, pink, green, and yellow T-shirts, those punks have peculiar hair styles, like the one who has the mushroom-shaped hair on top of his head but has no hair on the lower part. They probably major in fine arts or rock bands. The second noisiest group is the freshman kids, who look and act like high school kids. They like throwing French fries at each other and giggling and screaming all the time. As for me, I just sit in my corner, enjoy my American hamburger, and watch this American rock concert-like scene.

Son Sang Kong (Hong Kong) ■

In a Writing Assignment later in this chapter, you will practice using specifics as well as generalizations by describing a scene in detail. To gather material for this assignment, walk around your campus or neighborhood and find an interesting place to describe. When you have found a place, sit down for twenty minutes and list everything you see, smell, taste, hear, and feel there. You do not necessarily have to take these notes in English. At the end of twenty minutes, your list should be fairly long. Reread the list, circling the details you find most vivid or memorable or unusual. Save this invention writing for later.

USING SPECIFICS

The typical pattern that English writers follow is to say something fairly general and then to give more specific information to prove, illustrate, or explain that general statement. Student writers have trouble with this seemingly easy pattern because it is not always so obvious to them what is more general and what is more specific.

EXERCISE 1: SPECIFICS

Look at the following pairs of phrases. In each pair, which item is more specific?

A	B
nervous	hands shaking, voice quivering
smell of baking bread	good, sweet smell from the oven
reds, blues, and greens	many beautiful, brilliant colors
a huge, strong dog	a full-grown German shepherd
a room with white bare porcelain walls	a room that seemed completely sterile
the kind of people who never quite got over the youthful hippie culture of the 1960s with its emphasis on country naturalness and simplicity and on rebelliousness against authority and propriety for its own sake	the kind of people who wear bib jeans with a hole in the seat, and have long, straggly hair with a red bandanna around their head

■

EXERCISE 2: SPECIFICS

Arrange each of the following groups of phrases from most general to most specific. In the space following each phrase, enter *a* for most general, *b* for in between, or *c* for most specific.

1. waving hands _____

   using gestures _____

   using hands _____

2. giving money to charities _____

   being generous _____

   donating one hundred dollars to the March of Dimes

   every year _____

3. Casa Gallardo _____

   an ethnic restaurant _____

   a Mexican restaurant _____

4. communicating with more than just words _____

   using gestures while talking _____

   talking with more than just words _____ ■

As you can see, *general* and *specific* are relative terms. In the first example, "using gestures" was the most general of the three phrases listed. In the last example, however, "using gestures" was the most specific of the three phrases.

EXERCISE 3: SPECIFICS

In each of the following pairs of statements, mark the more specific one.

1a. She arrived at the dentist's office and sat in the waiting room looking nervous.

1b. She arrived at the dentist's office and sat in the waiting room biting her nails.

2a. A North American professor visiting Brazil soon realized that Brazilian attitudes about time were more flexible than his own.

2b. When you visit a foreign country, you may find that what you consider polite or impolite behavior is not the same as what the people from that country consider polite or impolite behavior.

3a. When you visit a foreign country, you may be surprised to realize that many attitudes which seem natural or inherent in human beings differ from one culture to another.

3b. When you visit a foreign country, you may find that what you consider polite or impolite behavior is not the same as what the people from that country consider polite or impolite behavior.

4a. At the restaurant last night, the salad dressing was rancid and the buns were like rocks.

4b. The food at the restaurant last night was as bad as I have ever tasted.

5a. A good language class is one in which students are not afraid to ask questions.

5b. A good language teacher knows how to create the right atmosphere for learning. ∎

EXERCISE 4: SPECIFICS

Answer the following questions. Be as specific as you can.

1. How can you tell when someone is embarrassed?

2. How can you tell when someone is angry?

3. How can you tell if a language classroom has a good atmosphere for learning? ∎

EXERCISE 5: SPECIFICS

∎ STUDENT WRITING

Read the following paragraph on nonverbal communication in Taiwan.

(1) Every culture has its own rules about nonverbal communication among the members of its society, and the Chinese are no exception. (2) The Chinese believe that they have to keep a distance between people, whether they are strangers or friends. (3) For example, the Chinese consider that it is rude to stare at a stranger because this will make the stranger feel that he must have done something wrong. (4) On the other hand, the Chinese seldom smile at a stranger they meet either because they believe that they should never trust a stranger. (5) This distance among people carries over to nonverbal forms of communication among friends. (6) Thus, according to old Chinese traditional culture, the Chinese do not accept embracing as a way to show friendship or kissing as a way to show love. (7) Although Chinese have the same kinds of emotional rela-

tionships as people do in any other culture, the Chinese are careful to maintain physical distances among themselves.

Chi Kin Cheng (Taiwan) ▪

On the following scale, rank each sentence of this composition by number according to how general it is. Is the sentence more general, more specific, or about the same as the sentences before and after it? The first two sentences have been done for you.

Most general: sentence 1 _____

More specific: sentence 2 _____

Most specific: _____

▪

Did these sentences become increasingly more general or increasingly more specific, or did specific and general ideas alternate in some pattern?

You should see from your ranking that the student began with a general assertion. His discussion then moved back and forth between more specific ideas and even more specific ideas. Finally, he ended with a statement more general than the discussion but perhaps not quite as general as the first sentence. Notice that more specific sentences are often comments on more general statements made earlier.

Sometimes student writers think that writing well means writing general and abstract statements. They are afraid that explaining what they mean specifically will sound too informal or too inelegant. In the following draft, the student was answering the question: What is the best way to learn a new language?

▪ STUDENT WRITING

Talking to native speakers gives the language learner a good chance to practice the language in real life. In other words, being in another environment gives the learner the need to communicate with the native speakers. That need comes from the necessity of buying food and other things. Furthermore, talking to native speakers makes the student capable of speaking the language fluently. In addition, outgoingness and curiosity are good qualities in the learner's personality in order to communicate and learn fast.

When this student exchanged papers with a classmate who had written on the same subject, he realized that because they both had written abstract, general statements about learning a language, the two papers were almost exactly the same. In order to make his paper different from his classmate's, the student tried in his second draft to provide more concrete support for his ideas. Once again he began with a generalization, but this time the following sentences were much more specific.

> Talking to native speakers gives the learner a good chance to practice the language in real life. Being in another country and among native speakers gives the learner the need to communicate. That need comes from the need for food and for buying and selling things. Gradually, the learner will start to catch new words and new expressions. He will also start to pronounce the language the way he hears it. For example, I usually go to Philadelphia every summer and run an ice cream truck in Philadelphia's streets. Last summer I worked in a Black neighborhood, and I gradually started catching the Black accent. After four or five weeks working in the same area, I found myself speaking the customer's accent, which was great because they started to understand my English much faster. This real example shows how native speakers will help a learner practice a language and learn new words, expressions, and accents.
>
> Mohammad N. Obeissy (Syria) ▩

In English writing, the writer is usually expected to do the work of explaining, showing, and proving. Except in works of fiction, the English-speaking reader, especially at the university level, rarely expects to have to draw conclusions or make generalizations based on the specifics mentioned in the text. The reader expects the writer to draw the conclusions and make the generalizations. Without specific support or proof or explanation, however, the English reader is unlikely to believe a writer's generalization or assertion. English writing moves back and forth between telling the reader something (an assertion) and then showing the reader that the statement is true (the evidence). *Telling* alone is not believable; *showing* alone is too hard on the reader.

SELECTING SUPPORTING MATERIAL

Types

The use of specifics makes writing easier to understand. Writers explain their generalizations in the following ways:

> using examples to illustrate a point or to show how a generalization works in a representative or typical case

using reasons, causes, or effects related to the generalization
to make it understandable

using descriptive details to allow the reader to imagine the
generalization better

using the familiar to explain the unfamiliar

discussing a subject step by step

Examples and anecdotes are meant to help a reader understand a generalization by showing how it operates in a specific
instance. Understanding a specific instance makes the abstract
notion easier to understand. Think of the classes you are taking.
Students often ask professors for examples in order to make concepts clearer.

But it is not enough for writing to be clear. Perhaps more important, a writer must convince the reader of the validity of his
or her assertions by giving evidence to support those statements.
Typically, writers support their generalizations with data:

facts or statistics that bring objective evidence to prove a
point

personal experiences, representative cases, observations, or
anecdotes meant to prove that a generalization is true because it is based on a specific, real incident

references to recognized authority or experts in the subject

These types of support—facts, statistics, real incidents, or references to authority—are objective pieces of evidence used to support and prove a generalization.

EXERCISE 6: SUPPORT

Look back at the second draft by Mohammad N. Obeissy on page
105. What kinds of support did he use to prove or explain his
general statements in the first few sentences about learning a
language?

Support _____

■ STUDENT WRITING

Now look at the following two paragraphs. What kinds of support does each one use?

Young teenage suicide is becoming one of the most tragic social
problems in Japan. This year alone, some forty deaths of Japanese
children have been confirmed as suicide. The most recent incident in

a rash of teen suicides in Japan over the past few years occurred three weeks ago, when just before afternoon classes, a thirteen-year-old girl leaped off the roof of her four-story school building. The note she left said that she could stand the taunting of classmates no longer.

Taisuke Akasaka (Japan)   ■

Support ─────────────────────────────────────

■ PROFESSIONAL WRITING

Much of our folklore and many of the essays in popular and scholarly journals and books are full of information which suggests that women and men have many different experiences. Or at least women and men are *thought* to possess many gender-linked interests and behavioral characteristics that lead them to different experiences. Women, for example, are thought to be more talkative, more religious, and more sensitive to others than are men. Men are thought to be more knowledgeable about business, more objective, independent, aggressive, active, adventurous, and more likely to think men are superior to women. By itself alone, the constant reaffirmation that we are one gender or the other means that we have somewhat different experiences. Cultural customs also serve not so much to acknowledge the (relatively slight) biological differences but actually *to produce* a sense of them: e.g., traditional courtship patterns, courtesy systems (protecting females from spiders, rain, cold, and other dangers), separate toilet facilities, and job placement (women in housekeeping and mothering jobs). These customs call for frequent expressions of genderism and make gender *appear* "natural" and highly significant; they are not expressions of natural differences, but they do mean that women's experiences differ somewhat from men's.

(Adapted from Cheris Kramarae, Women and Men
Speaking, Rowley, Massachusetts: Newbury
House, page 39).   ■

Support ─────────────────────────────────────
■

Deciding which specifics to include depends very much on your audience and purpose as well as on your main idea. For example, if you were writing a term paper for a sociology class on racial discrimination in housing in your community, which of the following types of support would you be *least* likely to use?

facts or statistics

personal experience or anecdotes

references to authority

examples

reasons or effects

descriptive details

familiar situations to explain unfamiliar ones

step-by-step explanations

On the other hand, which of these types of support might be appropriate for an editorial for your school paper or for a letter home or for an essay on the evils of discrimination?

In your choice of how to approach an explanation of your ideas, you must consider your particular writing context. Is it formal or informal? Public (a newspaper article) or relatively private (a letter home)? Will your audience consider you an authority or will you need more objective evidence to make your point? Keeping your answers to these questions in mind will help you select the most effective support for your ideas.

Unity

The following are the two most important requirements for selecting material to prove or explain your point:

1. The support must be pertinent.
2. There must be sufficient support.

Pertinent means that the support must be directly related to the generalization or the main idea you are trying to explain. One common problem student writers have is making irrelevant statements, ones not directly pertinent to the main idea. In the following composition, the student was explaining the origins of certain restrictions on Japanese women, but he included information about his subject that was not related to his main idea. Read the article, and then write the numbers of the irrelevant sentences in the space provided.

EXERCISE 7: SUPPORT

▪ STUDENT WRITING

(1) You may have seen on television or in the movies that Japanese women cover their mouths when they laugh. (2) Why do

Japanese women do this? (3) This is a dying mannerism traceable to the feudal concept of women in Japan. (4) Older women, more than forty, have this mannerism, but most young women don't care. (5) Before the Meiji modernization about a hundred years ago, a well-brought-up woman had a set of prescribed mannerisms to observe. (6) Until the Meiji modernization, feudal Japan tried to shut all the Western countries out. (7) The basic feminine characteristics expected of a woman were self-restraint and self-effacement. (8) Any display of assertiveness was strictly frowned upon, and laughing in public was considered such a display. (9) What was considered particularly offensive was for a young woman to laugh revealing her teeth.

(10) In feudal Japan, people's social status was indicated by the kind of dress they wore. (11) The married status was revealed by their teeth. (12) That is, a married woman painted her teeth black (with special herb preparations) while a young girl kept hers natural and unpainted.

(13) In either case, for a woman to laugh out loud was considered unlady-like and ill-mannered unless she made a little show of self-restraining modesty by making an attempt, however symbolic, at covering her mouth when laughing.

Taisuke Akasaka (Japan) ∎

Irrelevant sentences _____

∎

Because this student's intention was to discuss the origins of certain social regulations for Japanese women, sentence 6, for example, does not belong. Sentence 6 makes a comment on sentence 5, but it has nothing to do with the social restrictions on women. Sentence 10 also gives information that does not relate to the main idea. If the student wants to keep the same main idea, he must remove the irrelevant sentences or rewrite them somehow to fit his main idea. On the other hand, if he wants to keep these sentences, he must alter the main idea. One possibility might be to reorient the entire discussion to focus primarily on different aspects of life in feudal Japan, which might include a discussion of social prescriptions for women. In any case, the supporting material the student selects must fit the main idea he expresses.

Sentences 4, 11, and 12 present other problems. They are more closely related to the student's topic, but sentence 4 seems out of place where it is. Can you suggest another place to include the information in sentence 4? Sentences 11 and 12, on the other hand, have not been interpreted for us by the author. As a result, the connection between revealing teeth and revealing marital status is not clear.

EXERCISE 8: SUPPORT

Look at the following main idea and each statement given to support it. Which statements are most pertinent? Which do not seem to support the main idea directly? Mark each sentence P (pertinent) or I (irrelevant).

Main Idea: Chicago offers good recreational programs for children during the summer in its many city-run parks.

_____ **1.** The first recreation programs began just after World War II.

_____ **2.** Swimming pools are open every day and swimming lessons are available for children more than 4 years old.

_____ **3.** Of the 100 neighborhood parks run by the city of Chicago, over 70 hire special recreation directors in the summer for their children's programs.

_____ **4.** In the bigger parks, children can take dance, sports, or craft lessons.

_____ **5.** The parks run morning camps for children under 7 and day camps for children between 7 and 14.

_____ **6.** All recreation directors are trained in first aid.

_____ **7.** Dance classes are also offered for adults for a minimal fee.

_____ **8.** A park is one of the few places in the city where the air is relatively fresh and clean.

_____ **9.** The park system sponsors athletic teams.

_____ **10.** In the field houses of bigger parks, children can use the gym for basketball or volleyball.

Look at the pieces of evidence you found unconvincing. What makes each of them weak support for the main idea?

_____

■

Sometimes student writers try to include every detail they know about a topic, even though that information may not be relevant to their particular audience or purpose. Or they may include irrelevant information because they have gone in another direction from the one they originally set out on. Or sometimes they have simply lost sight of their main idea and have forgotten what it was they set out to discuss, for whom, or why. At other times, what seems like irrelevant information might actually be relevant, but the writer has failed to interpret it and to show how it is linked to the main idea or is significant for the audience or purpose of the text.

In other words, the writer must not only give pertinent supporting information but also interpret that information for the reader when necessary to show exactly how it helps explain or support the main idea. Look at statements 6 and 7 in the preceding exercise, for example. Even though they are weak support for the main idea, can you see why a writer might have included them as support for the generalization? Although statement 7 is related to recreational programs, it gives information on adult recreation, not children's recreation. The problem with statement 6 is somewhat different. The fact that the recreation directors are trained in first aid is irrelevant *as written* because it is not interpreted; that is, the writer failed to explain why this fact shows how good the recreational programs are. Can you rewrite statement 6 to link those two ideas and make the statement relevant to the main idea?

_____

Here are some ways you might rewrite statement 6 to make it fit the main idea:

1. In addition to the variety of programs offered, the children can play in safety because all recreation directors are trained in first aid.

2. Because they are all trained in first aid, recreation directors are able to handle any accident that might occur in the pools, playgrounds, or gyms.

3. Should a child be injured while taking part in one of the recreational programs, the child will receive professional help since all recreation directors are trained in first aid.

Any of these revisions makes clear the significance of the fact that the recreation directors know first aid. Can you rewrite any of the other statements that do not seem relevant (for example, 8 or 9) so that they are more directly linked to the main idea? _____

_____

Amount

How much support is enough? This question cannot be answered precisely because the answer depends very much on who the audience is and what the purpose of the text is. Sometimes a single example or an especially striking anecdote is enough to explain a point clearly. Sometimes three or four are needed in one paragraph for a point to be convincingly made.

In the preceding example, how much evidence would be the minimum amount necessary to convince *you* that Chicago has good recreational programs? The answer depends both on you and on the type of evidence offered. If you come from a city with no recreational programs for children, perhaps one single example would be enough for you. On the other hand, if your city has more to offer, perhaps even five or six pieces of evidence would still not seem convincing. Furthermore, perhaps one particular piece of evidence may be so convincing that it outweighs three or four pieces of less convincing evidence.

As a writer, you must judge your audience and use your intuition and feedback from your readers to determine how much support is needed to explain your point. Furthermore, you will need to decide what type of support (fact, statistic, example, anecdote) or combinations of types will be most effective in accomplishing your purpose with a specific audience.

ARRANGING SUPPORTING MATERIAL

Once you have enough pertinent, specific material to support your point, you must decide how to arrange it.

EXERCISE 9: ARRANGING SUPPORT

In the list of evidence used to show that Chicago offers good recreational programs for children, can you find supports that seem to belong together naturally? Which ones? Group the pieces of evidence and write down the numbers of the sentences you have grouped together.

Group _____

Group _____

Group _____

What is the common feature linking the items in each group? Write down the common feature for each group as a subtopic or subheading.

Subtopic _____

Subtopic _____

Subtopic _____

■

Now compare your labels with those of your classmates. Did you find different systems for grouping the evidence?

A sample diagram or outline of this subtopic approach is presented in Figure 6.1. By dividing your composition into sections, using transitions to mark where each section begins, and stating what each section covers, you are helping your reader to grasp more easily what you are trying to communicate in your writing. The more complex your subject, the more helpful these aids are to the reader.

Once you have selected and grouped your material, you still must decide in what order to present the material. English-speaking readers are accustomed to seeing the following types of arrangements:

> Least to Most: Begin with the least significant or powerful information, and then move to the more convincing or important ideas.

Main Idea
        Subtopic 1:
            Example, and/or
            Illustration, and/or
            Fact, and/or
            Personal experience, etc.
        Subtopic 2:
            Example, and/or . . . etc.
        Subtopic 3:
            Example, and/or
            Statistic, and/or
            Reference to authority, and/or . . . etc.
Conclusion from all the supporting material given

Figure 6.1 Diagram of Organization by Subtopic

Most to Least: To get your reader's attention quickly (in an essay exam, business report, or newspaper article), begin with the most striking information and move toward less important points or facts.

Known to Unknown (or Accepted to Controversial): Begin by establishing common ground with the reader, and then move to the new material you are trying to explain or prove.

Step-by-Step: Use chronological order (what happens first, second, and so on) or spatial order (describe one part at a time).

By Categories or Divisions: Divide your subject into parts or separate your supporting material into categories, and describe one part or category at a time.

For Comparisons: Discuss all the features of one item first, then all the corresponding features of the other item. Or discuss one feature of each item, then the next feature of each item.

In any piece of writing, keeping in mind the audience and purpose of the text, the author must decide on an overall organizational plan and on some arrangement for the ideas in each paragraph. Most texts include some combination of the methods described here. For more detailed discussion of certain patterns of organization (division/classification, cause/effect, definition, and comparison), see Chapter 16, Practicing Taking Essay Exams.

 Finally, keep in mind that English-speaking readers expect to be led systematically from one point to the next. They expect a writer to present all the evidence and the conclusions drawn from that evidence. They do not expect to have to draw their own conclusions about the material or to accept unsupported generalizations. In the next assignment, you will practice:

using specific supporting material;

relating that material to the main idea;

and arranging that material appropriately.

➤ *Writing Assignment 6.1: Nonverbal Communication and Personal Experience*

Writing
Assignment 6.1

Your assignment in this section is to write a paper on some aspect of body language or nonverbal communication.

Audience and Purpose

Read through all the invention writing you did as you gathered material for a paper on nonverbal communication. Now consider your audience and purpose for this assignment. To whom do you want to communicate the information you have discovered through your invention writing?

> To people from your country?
>
> To Americans who have not spent much time with people from other countries and are not aware of differences in body language?
>
> To your classmates from all parts of the world?
>
> To anyone who knows little about your country but perhaps plans to travel there?
>
> To some other audience?

You also have several options in deciding your purpose for writing.

> Will you inform your audience of customs in your country to help them understand the meaning of gestures used in your country that might seem strange to them?
>
> Do you want to help your audience avoid the embarrassment of using inappropriate gestures in your country?
>
> Do you simply want to educate others you assume do not know about the existence and meanings of body language?
>
> Will you compare gestures in two or more countries to show how surprisingly different people's communication patterns are?

If you uncover some particularly amusing or strange information about body language, you may set as part of your purpose to entertain while informing your audience. Whatever approach you take, ask yourself what you are trying to accomplish by sharing this information with your audience. The information you decide to select will depend on the following:

1. the audience for which you are writing
2. the purpose you have set for your writing
3. how you express your main idea

Once you have searched your own mind, questioned others, thought about your findings, and have some idea of your audience and purpose, review the information in the previous section on possible ways to arrange your supporting material.

You should now be ready to begin your first draft. Write this draft quickly. If you spend too much time, you will be reluctant to alter anything you worked so long to produce. Also, consider writing more than you think you will eventually need. You may find, like some writers, that it is easier to remove material than to add it.

Main Idea

When you have finished writing your first draft, reread it and ask yourself what the main idea seems to be. Write that main idea near the beginning of the paper; word it so that it is general enough to cover the entire paper and specific enough to convey the content of your paper.

Supporting Material

Next, consider the specific support material in your discussion. Read each sentence and ask yourself:

Is this sentence clearly and directly related to the main idea?

Do I make any statements that must be interpreted in order for my reader to make the connection between that statement and the main idea?

The following questions will help you explore your options for explaining your ideas more specifically and completely. Keeping in mind the audience for which you are writing and what you want to accomplish by communicating this information, ask yourself:

Are there any examples/facts/statistics I could add to my discussion to make it clearer or more forceful for my audience?

Have I had any personal experience I could mention that might help to explain my point?

What are the causes of the situation I am describing? What are the reasons for the behavior I am describing? Are there any significant effects of this situation or behavior?

Can I make my explanation clearer by describing how something works/looks/feels?

Could I compare my subject to something my readers are likely to recognize that would help them understand better what I am saying? (For example, a gesture unfamiliar to your readers may resemble another one more familiar to them.)

Is there anything I need to define more completely in order to explain what I mean?

In a different color ink from that in the original draft, put an asterisk at any places in your draft where you know you can add more specific information. Then write at least one of those examples or explanations on another sheet of paper. Reread the composition with your additional, more specific information. Did your addition improve your original?

Arrangement

Ask yourself the following questions about the arrangement of the material in your draft:

How did I arrange this information?

Is there any other way to arrange the information, considering my audience and purpose?

Would another arrangement be better or worse for my particular audience and purpose?

When you have finished writing, rereading, and analyzing your draft, answer the following questions.

Self-Analysis

1. What is the main idea of the paper (thesis)?
2. Where is that main idea expressed?
3. What is the main idea of each paragraph?
4. What kinds of things does your reader probably already know about your main idea?
5. What did you assume your reader did not know or might want to know about your topic?
6. What kinds of specifics did you use to develop and support your main idea?
7. In general, are you satisfied with what you have written?
8. What would you change if you wrote this paper again?

Now give your draft to at least one classmate to read and comment on.

Peer Response

1. Who do you think was the audience for this paper?
2. What do you think the writer's purpose was in writing this paper? That is, what do you think the writer expected the audience to learn from reading the paper?
3. What ideas or examples in this paper struck you as the most interesting?
4. Is there any part of this paper where you felt a need for additional or clearer information?
5. How would you describe the way the writer organized the material?
6. What suggestions can you offer that might improve the paper?

Revision

Revise your paper, incorporating any suggestions from your classmates that you found useful.   ◄

➤ *Writing Assignment 6.2: Description and Objective Data*

Writing
Assignment 6.2

In this assignment, you are to describe in detail the scene you observed in your invention writing.

Main Idea

Your audience for this assignment is your classmates. Your purpose is to give your classmates such a sense of this place that they can almost imagine themselves there.

Reread your invention writing and write one sentence that generally describes the place you observed. This will be your main idea. Do not describe how you feel; describe the place. Another person should be able to write virtually the same summary statement from the details you noted.

Avoid describing the place as nice or beautiful or comfortable or peaceful. Try to find a word to describe the place that is more specific than these words. Push yourself to look for a way to generalize about the place so that the generalization will *not* apply to very many other places. Rank the following three statements from least specific to most specific.

1. As the moving truck loaded with all my possessions moved away from the curb, I stepped back one last time into the apartment where I had lived for so long and in place of my warm cozy living room I found a kind of hole, hollow, sterile, and unfamiliar.
2. From the balcony of my old apartment I could see the beautiful scenery stretching to the horizon and making me feel comfortable.
3. On Sunday afternoon, Massey Hall lobby looks as busy as a bus station.

Which of these three sentences gives you the best idea of the description that would follow? Which one would apply to many other places?

Supporting Material

You have collected a great deal of material, and now you must select which details from your list to include. To help you decide, ask yourself the following questions:

Which details fit the main idea?
Which details are most interesting, striking, lively, or impressive?
Can I present or interpret each of these details so that it clearly helps to explain or prove or develop my main idea?

Arranging Supporting Material

When you have selected the most striking details, ask yourself the following questions to help you decide how to arrange them:

Can I group these details according to any logical categories—for example, according to the five senses or according to location?

What order should I use to describe this place: The order in which I noticed the details? An order corresponding to how much the details affect each of the five senses? The order of least interesting to most interesting?

Now write your draft quickly, using your invention writing and your notes. When you have finished, answer the following questions.

Self-Analysis

1. Why did you choose this place?
2. Do you think your readers would be able to recognize the place you described just from your description?
3. What are you most satisfied with in this paper?
4. What do you think your paper still needs?
5. Did you enjoy this assignment?

Now give your paper to at least one classmate to read and comment on.

Peer Response

1. What details from this paper best supported the generalization?
2. If you had to eliminate any information or description from this paper, which would it be?
3. How did the writer group the details in this paper?
4. In what kind of order did the writer present the material in this paper? Is this order effective?
5. Do you think you would be able to recognize the place described if you came across it?
6. What is the best part of this paper?
7. What suggestions do you have for improving this paper?

Revision

Revise your paper, incorporating any suggestions from your classmates that you found useful.   ◄

SEQUENCED WRITING PROJECT: INTERVIEW

Sequenced Writing
Project
In this section of the Sequenced Writing Project, you will write a report of an interview with an expert on the topic you selected.

Choosing the Expert

Depending on your topic, the expert can be a friend, a teacher, a university administrator, or anyone else who knows a great deal about your topic. Following are some examples of experts whom other students have interviewed.

Topic	Expert
Financial aid for international students	The university's director of financial aid
Making American friends	A Chinese student with a lot of American friends
Iranian/U.S. criminal justice systems	A professor of criminology
Puerto Rican independence	A newspaper journalist in Puerto Rico (by *phone*)
Day care in United States/ China	Director of a local day-care center

If you interview a friend, you can make informal arrangements for the interview. But if you are interviewing, for example, a university official, prepare for the interview by following the directions you followed for the survey you did. (See page 89.)

Writing the Report

After the interview:

- Write notes for yourself on everything you remember about the place where the interview took place, any body language your expert used, and your own impressions of the interview.
- Review your notes or listen to your tape recording several

times, making notes on important comments your expert makes.

- Decide what the Main Idea is that you want your report to get across to your audience.
- Select the information you find most interesting or useful for your purposes. You do not need to report everything the expert said because the idea is not to present a portrait of the expert but to report on information about your topic.
- Also select details about the setting and the expert's body language that you think will make your interview report most lively.
- Read the suggestions for determining the Main Idea, selecting support material, and analyzing support material for Writing Assignments 6.1 and 6.2.

Now write your draft quickly, using any invention writing you did and all your notes. Be sure to include information on the expert, such as why this person could be considered an authority on your topic. If you use the exact words that your expert used, be sure to put quotation marks around those words. When you have finished your draft, answer the following questions.

Self-Analysis

1. How did you make contact with your expert?
2. What was your reaction to doing this interview? Do you feel that it went well and that you gathered good information?
3. In your report what is your main idea?
4. What is the most interesting information you learned from this expert?
5. How did you decide what to include in your report and in what order to include it?
6. What do you wish you had done differently in the interview?
7. In general, are you satisfied with the interview and with your report?

Now give your draft to at least one classmate to read and comment on.

Peer Response

1. Who was the apparent audience for this report?
2. Was there anything included in this report that the audience probably already knew and so could be eliminated? What?
3. What questions are still left unanswered by this report?
4. Is there any part of this paper you felt was unclear? Which part?
5. Is there any part of this paper that seems irrelevant? Which part?
6. How would you describe the way the writer organized the material?
7. What suggestions can you offer that might improve the paper?

Revision

After reading your classmates' comments, look again at your interview notes and revise your paper, using your classmates' suggestions and anything from your notes that you think might strengthen your paper.

The next assignment in the Sequenced Writing Project, summaries of published material, appears in Chapters 10 and 11.

➢ 7 ≺

Beginning and Ending Drafts

Term papers, formal essays, articles, theses, dissertations, and books typically include an introduction and a conclusion set apart from the discussion of the topic. In this section, you will look at introductions, conclusions, and titles and practice writing them.

INTRODUCTIONS

You may find it strange to learn that many writers do not begin writing with the introduction at all, even though the introduction is the first part the reader reads. In fact, some writers write the conclusion first, then develop their ideas, and write the introduction last, after the draft is already finished. You too may find this order easier in your own writing.

Nearly all introductions perform three functions:

1. hooking readers and convincing them to take the time to read the article, essay, or book
2. giving whatever background information may be necessary to understand the article
3. stating the information or argument the reader will find in the article, essay, or book (and sometimes how it will be discussed)

We will discuss these functions in this order, even though the parts of the introduction may be written in any order and even though one sentence can sometimes perform more than one of the functions.

Getting Attention

The first sentence (or first few sentences) in a short introduction is usually meant to be the hook that will entice or interest as many readers as possible to continue reading. The following are the beginnings of several articles published in newsmagazines and textbooks.

■ PROFESSIONAL WRITING

1 Help from the Hotline

It is 4:30 in the afternoon in Los Angeles. At station KLCS-TV, Channel 58, the show is ready to roll. A phone rings and the man before the camera picks it up. "Welcome to *Homework Hotline*," he says. "I'm Ira Moskow . . . I have John from Hughes Junior High on the line."

(Time 31 December 1984, p. 69) ■

2 AIDS: Testing Insurance

"No man really knows about other human beings," John Steinbeck wrote. "The best he can do is to suppose that they are like himself." Not many Americans suppose that anyone at risk of AIDS is like himself. Yet the precedents established for supporting these sick will soon touch many others.

(Jane Bryant Quinn, Newsweek 8 June 1987,
p. 55) ■

3 One Miracle, Many Doubts

The dying heart was an ugly yellowish color when Dr. William DeVries finally cut it loose, tore it out of the Mercurochrome-stained chest cavity, and put it to one side. For the next three hours, while a nearby heart-lung bypass machine kept the unconscious patient alive . . . DeVries' sure hands carefully stitched into place a grape-fruit-size gadget made of aluminum and polyurethane.

(Otto Friedrich, Time 10 December 1984,
pp. 70–77) ■

4 An Unsung Czech Slams Martina

Tennis fans had come to think of her as unbeatable. She had won 74 consecutive matches and needed only a win in the Australian Open to sweep all four Grand Slam events in a calendar year. But last week, Czech defector turned Texan Martina Navratilova lost the semifinal of the Australian Open.

(Newsweek 17 December 1984, p. 67) ■

5 The Using of Baby Fae

The placing of a baboon heart into the chest of little Baby Fae caused indignation in many quarters. For some, who might safely be called eccentric, the concern was animal rights.

(Charles Krauthammer, Time 3 December 1984,
p. 87) ■

6 Meaning in the Child's Language

How do children learn the meanings of words? The words they hear are all new to them. Adults faced with unfamiliar words can consult dictionaries, or ask other people, or try to guess the meaning from the context. Adults face this problem only occasionally, but young children face this problem all the time. One- and two-year-olds obviously cannot consult dictionaries or ask other people, but they can and do make use of context.

(Adapted from H. H. Clark and E. V. Clark, *Psychology and Language.* New York: Harcourt Brace, 1977, pp. 485–86) ■

7 Racism and Cross-Racial Hostility

Racism is all around us. We eat, sleep, speak and breathe it. We see it everywhere. We feel it inside us. We are discouraged by it more often than not—discouraged because fewer and fewer perpetrators of racism are even conscious of their racist behavior—or perhaps they don't care

(Virginia R. Harris and Trinity Ordona in Gloria Anzaldua [eds.], *Haciendo Caras: Making Face, Making Soul*) ■

EXERCISE 1: INTRODUCTIONS
Now answer these questions.

1. How did each writer try to get the reader's attention? That is, what words or images were meant to be particularly interesting or dramatic?

1. _____

2. _____

3. _____

4. _____

5. _____

6. _____

7. _____

2. Which of these introductions were successful? That is, which of them would motivate you to read at least a little

more of the article? _____

■

As you can see, the writers of these introductions have used dramatic description, narration, striking words, a quotation, and a question to attract the reader's attention.

Most writers believe that they have something worthwhile to say and will try to get the reader at least to begin reading the article. The writer may ultimately be unsuccessful in getting the reader to read the entire article, either because the reader is not interested in the subject or because the writing itself is not interesting enough. The writer does usually try, however, to show in the introduction that reading the article will be worth the reader's trouble.

EXERCISE 2: INTRODUCTIONS

In small groups or as a class, make a list of ways to begin a piece of writing that are likely to attract a reader's attention.

_____

_____

_____

_____

_____

■

Although the hook is often fun to write because it is short and sometimes dramatic or entertaining, it is probably the least important part of the introduction. In fact, the hook is missing altogether in many, if not all, academic papers. If a hook appears, it will usually be fairly serious: a quotation, statistic, or interesting fact, rather than an exclamation, joke, or story, for example. There is little need to entice your teachers to read your papers; they will do so whether you use a hook or not.

Giving the Background

After getting the reader's attention, the writer now wants to move toward his or her main purpose for writing the essay, but the reader may first need some background information to be able to follow the author's thoughts. Sometimes that background information is simply a reminder of information the reader probably already knows. It therefore establishes a common ground of understanding between the writer and the reader. In the following introduction, the writer quickly reviews the points of view of

two groups opposed to the implanting of a baboon heart in Baby
Fae. (Baby Fae was an infant who was born with heart problems. Doctors knew that she would die without a heart transplant. For the first time in history, doctors attempted to use an
animal's heart instead of a human being's heart for the transplant. This experiment caused a great deal of controversy. Baby
Fae lived for only a short time after her operation.)

■ **PROFESSIONAL WRITING**

The placing of a baboon heart into the chest of little Baby Fae
caused indignation in many quarters. For some, who might safely be
called eccentric, the concern was animal rights. Pickets outside
Loma Linda University Medical Center and elsewhere protested the
use of baboons as organ factories. Dr. Leonard Bailey, the chief surgeon, was not impressed. "I am a member of the human species,"
he said. Human babies come first. It was unapologetic speciesism.
He did not even have to resort to sociology, to the argument that in a
society that eats beef, wears mink and has for some time been implanting pigs' valves in human hearts, the idea of weighing an animal's life equally against a human baby's is bizarre.

Others were concerned less with the integrity of the donor than
with the dignity of the recipient. At first, before Baby Fae's televised
smile had beguiled skeptics, the word ghoulish was heard: some sacred barrier between species had been broken, some principle of
separateness between man and animal violated. Indeed, it is a blow
to man's idea of himself to think that a piece of plastic or animal tis-
sue may occupy the seat of the emotions and perform perfectly well
(albeit as a pump). It is biological Galileism, and just as humbling.
Nevertheless it is fact. To deny it is sentimentality. And to deny life to
a child in order to preserve the fiction of man's biological uniqueness
is simple cruelty.

(Charles Krauthammer, *Time* 3 December 1984,
pp. 87–88) ■

Because this issue was so controversial at the time, most
readers were probably familiar with the objections to the im-
plant. The introduction reminds them of the issues and leads
them toward the last sentences of the introduction, which are a
statement of the argument the writer plans to make.

This introduction was relatively long. In some writing situations, such as in academic writing, the introduction is likely to
be much shorter. In an essay exam, for example, there might be
no more of an introduction than a simple direct answer to the
exam question. (See Chapter 15, "Preparing for an Essay
Exam.") In deciding on the length of your introduction, you will

have to use your own judgment, based on your audience's needs and likely reaction.

Establishing a Viewpoint

The third part of an introduction is usually a fairly clear statement of the position the writer will take in the paper. Traditionally, this statement appears toward the end of the introduction, although it may appear at the beginning as well, particularly if the introduction is quite short. Look at the excerpt from the article on Baby Fae. Does the writer agree with those who object to the heart transplant? Can you state what position the writer will probably take in this essay?

Writer's position _____

⭐

See Chapter 5 for help with topic sentences and thesis statements.

This section of the introduction is traditionally called the thesis statement. Because the thesis statement is a one- or two-sentence summary of the entire article, it is meant to enable the reader to anticipate quickly just what the writer plans to show or argue or discuss, and perhaps how the writer plans to organize the discussion. Therefore the thesis statement is most helpful to the reader when it is specific enough to summarize that particular essay and no others. You may want to review the discussion of topic sentences and thesis statements in Chapter 5.

The following hints will help you sharpen your ability to write a clear statement of your main idea, particularly when you are writing an argument. To synthesize the basic idea in your essay, use this formula:

Although _____ X _____ , _____ Y _____

because _____ Z _____ .

In the Baby Fae essay, the author's basic argument is:

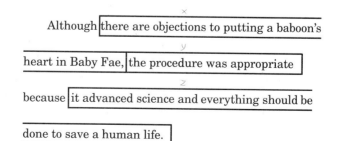

Although there are objections to putting a baboon's

heart in Baby Fae, the procedure was appropriate

because it advanced science and everything should be

done to save a human life.

Notice that the writer did not use these words or this statement anywhere in the article, yet the statement expresses his main idea and suggests that he will support his main idea in two ways:

1. by explaining how this procedure advanced science
2. by arguing that human life is precious and that everything possible should be done to save it

EXERCISE 3: VIEWPOINT

Review the compositions you have done for this class. Can you restate your main idea for any of them in terms of the "Although X, Y because Z" formula? Complete that formula here for any that you can.

1. _____

2. _____

3. _____

∎

Remember that this formula usually works best when your article states and defends a particular position. In that kind of writing situation, use the formula as one way of testing whether you have a strong thesis.

Now choose a paper you have already written and write a new introduction for that paper. Try to include:

1. a hook that will entice the reader to continue reading
2. whatever background the reader may need to understand your ideas, to be reminded of the issues surrounding your topic, or to see your topic in its context
3. an explicit statement of your main idea or thesis

CONCLUSIONS

The last of the three parts of a typical essay in English is the conclusion. As with the introduction, the conclusion may be reduced or nonexistent in some writing situations, particularly once again in an essay exam. Normally, however, an article, essay, or research paper without a conclusion sounds strange. Read the following example.

Doctors have known for over 100 years of the power of hypnosis to alleviate pain. Now increasing numbers of medical schools are teaching doctors to use hypnosis to end suffering from toothaches, migraine headaches, childbirth, and even extensive burns. Hypnosis works by distracting the patient's attention so powerfully that, although the pain remains, the patient no longer notices it. Amazing as it may seem, some patients can be so deeply hypnotized that they could undergo open heart surgery without anesthetic.

Do you have the feeling that there should be more information about this subject or that something is missing here? What else do you expect? _____

_____

 A good conclusion leaves the reader feeling that the writer has discussed all the important points on the topic laid out in the thesis statement and that everything promised at the beginning has been said. The conclusion often begins either with a comment referring to the last point made or with a transitional expression announcing the conclusion. A conclusion may:

1. quickly summarize the main ideas or main points made in the discussion
2. interpret the discussion or explain why the discussion is important and what it suggests
3. link the main idea of the text to the future or to some broader issues not specifically covered in the article

The conclusion in a short composition may be one sentence; in a longer essay, the conclusion is often a paragraph of several sentences; in a book the conclusion is often a separate section or chapter.

Here are examples of how the article on hypnosis might conclude.

Doctors have known for over 100 years of the power of hypnosis to alleviate pain. Now increasing numbers of medical schools are teaching doctors to use hypnosis to end suffering from toothaches, migraine headaches, childbirth, and even extensive burns. Hypnosis works by distracting the patient's attention so powerfully that, although the pain remains, the patient no longer notices it. Amazing as it may seem, some patients can be so deeply hypnotized that they could undergo open heart surgery without anesthetic. **Thus, by helping sufferers intensely fo-**

> cus their attention elsewhere, doctors now have one more
> weapon in the fight against pain.

This conclusion restates or summarizes the main idea of the
paragraph.

> Doctors have known for over 100 years of the power of hypnosis
> to alleviate pain. Now increasing numbers of medical schools are
> teaching doctors to use hypnosis to end suffering from
> toothaches, migraine headaches, childbirth, and even extensive
> burns. Hypnosis works by distracting the patient's attention so
> powerfully that, although the pain remains, the patient no
> longer notices it. Amazing as it may seem, some patients can be
> so deeply hypnotized that they could undergo open heart surgery
> without anesthetic. **In other words, hypnosis offers the
> enormous benefit of natural pain relief without the side
> effects or the possibility of addiction inherent in drugs.**

This conclusion interprets the meaning of the information given
in the report.

> Doctors have known for over 100 years of the power of hypnosis
> to alleviate pain. Now increasing numbers of medical schools are
> teaching doctors to use hypnosis to end suffering from
> toothaches, migraine headaches, childbirth, and even extensive
> burns. Hypnosis works by distracting the patient's attention so
> powerfully that, although the pain remains, the patient no
> longer notices it. Amazing as it may seem, some patients can be
> so deeply hypnotized that they could undergo open heart surgery
> without anesthetic. **The medical establishment's gradual ac-
> ceptance of hypnosis is just one more sign that doctors
> are recognizing the benefits of a more holistic approach
> to medicine.**

Here the writer linked the use of hypnosis to the future and to
the broader issue of a more naturalistic approach to medicine.

Here are the concluding statements from some student essays you have already read. Notice that conclusions have a particular sound to them. Can you characterize that sound?

1. So, each country has its specific rules of social behavior
   and a foreigner has to become used to nonverbal communication if he or she wants to get integrated into a different culture.
2. These examples demonstrate that the greatest advances
   in physics are most likely to be made by geniuses.

3. These are some of the big differences between Arabic and English, which show up in grammar and writing to make life hard for poor language students.
4. Although Chinese have the same kinds of emotional relationships as people do in any other culture, the Chinese are careful to maintain physical distances among themselves.

Concluding statements often begin with a reference to something previously stated (as in examples 2 and 3) or with a transition (as in example 1). In a long essay or speech, the writer may use a transitional phrase such as "In conclusion," but in short essays or paragraphs the conclusion is announced less dramatically with expressions such as the following:

Thus
Therefore
As we have seen
In short

These expressions signal the beginning of the conclusion, particularly when the conclusion summarizes, repeats, or shows the results of whatever has been discussed.

Conclusions also commonly begin by simply repeating a key word or phrase from the beginning of the text to link the beginning more closely to the last sentences. Look at the essay on Japanese women in Chapter 6 (page 108–109). Which important words did the student use in the conclusion that appeared at the beginning as well?

Read the following concluding paragraphs.

▪ PROFESSIONAL WRITING

1. Whether economic resurgence was another factor which saved the treasures of Tutankhamun's tomb is not certain. Two tunnels were found to have been dug through the entrance hall debris, but fortunately for all of us the thieves were not successful.

("Tutankhamun: The Golden Pharaoh," *Horus: Inflight Magazine of Egyptair* Spring/Summer 1985, pp. 11–12) ▪

2. Anyone with a feeling for nature must regret this. Crocodiles may not make good pets, but they are an essential ingredient in a whole interlocking life-system. They certainly no longer pose a

threat to man and it would be a pity if, for anything as unimportant as a pair of shoes or a purse, 80 million years should go for nothing.

("Crocodile," *Horus: Inflight Magazine of Egyptair* Spring/Summer 1985, pp. 16–17) ◼

3. (This article discusses a computer-based language developed for the study of chimpanzees that may help deaf and/or mute people learn to communicate.)

Buoyed by success, the scientists now want to extend their reach. This fall 27 retarded students in the Clayton County, Ga. public schools will study Yerkish, and Rumbaugh hopes that within the next decade a lightweight, economical version of the Yerkish keyboard (which now costs $2,500) will be developed to aid the speech-impaired in homes and schools. "Ten years from now," says Rumbaugh, "I hope this looks like a very primitive beginning."

("Scaling the Walls of Silence," *Newsweek* 8 July 1985, p. 46) ◼

4. Hamilton's remarks about how we'll deal with earthquakes in the future may be a modern echo of John Milton's words written more than 300 years ago: "Accuse not nature! She hath done her part; do thou thine."

(F. H. Forrester, "Finding Faults: Earthquakes," *USAir* June 1985, pp. 46–64) ◼

5. That attitude, added to peer pressure and more discretionary income, almost guarantees a very profitable decade for companies selling children's goods

(Pamela Ellis-Simons, "Bringing up Baby: A New Kind of Marketing Boom," *BusinessWeek* 22 April 1985, pp. 58–65) ◼

6. Still, researchers realize that they now face their toughest adversary. Roaches have been plodding though human kitchens since the dawn of cooking. And through 250 million years of evolution, they have so far remained a jump ahead of the best efforts to eradicate them.

(Andrea Gabor, "Planned Parenthood for Roaches," *BusinessWeek* 22 April 1985, p. 92) ◼

7. But for patients such as Robert Etter, the ability to see normally without glasses is well worth the risk. Two weeks after his surgery, an enthusiastic Etter said he was "going round doing everything I couldn't do before without glasses. When I go to night clubs now, I don't have to get so close to see what the ladies look like." That same morning, Etter received a letter from the Los Angeles Police Department inviting him to take its physical, including an eye test he now can easily pass.

(Joan M. O'Connell, "The Radical Eye Operation
That's Becoming Routine," *BusinessWeek*,
22 April 1985, pp. 90–91)   ■

EXERCISE 4: CONCLUSIONS
Now answer these questions.

1. What do you think the discussion in each article covered?

   1. _____
   2. _____
   3. _____
   4. _____
   5. _____
   6. _____
   7. _____

2. Does each conclusion seem to summarize main points of the article, to look to the future, to suggest the significance of the material in the article, or is it a combination of the three?

   1. _____
   2. _____
   3. _____
   4. _____
   5. _____
   6. _____
   7. _____

3. Which words in each conclusion establish a link to the preceding paragraph?

   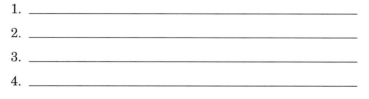

   1. _____
   2. _____
   3. _____
   4. _____

5. _____

6. _____

7. _____

■

Here are some things to avoid in any conclusions that you write:

1. Avoid bringing up new points to support or illustrate your main idea or thesis. If you have such new points, add new development paragraphs and then write the conclusion.
2. Avoid awkward concluding announcements such as:

    In conclusion (This sounds like a politician's speech.)

    From the above (Instead, briefly state what "the above" was.)

Now choose a draft of a paper you have already written and add one paragraph of conclusion. In your concluding paragraph, try to mention the significance or the implications of what you discussed in the paper.

If you have trouble writing your conclusion, write whatever you can on a separate page. Then give the rest of the essay, without the conclusion, to at least three classmates. Ask each of them to write a concluding paragraph on a separate sheet of paper. Look at all four conclusions, your classmates' and your own, and do one of the following:

1. Choose the conclusion you like best of the four, and add it to your essay.
2. Combine the elements you like of each one into a new conclusion.
3. Together with your three classmates, decide on the best conclusion or best way to combine the elements of the four conclusions.

Student writers sometimes find it helpful to think of an introduction, discussion, and conclusion in diagram form. In a typical essay, the pattern is something like that shown in Figure 7.1.

"Nonverbal Communication" (page 344) follows this basic plan. Try to identify each part of that essay using the plan.

Introductory paragraph
- hook
- background or connecting/linking material
- statement of the thesis of the entire paper

Development/Explanation of the first point
- topic sentence expressing main idea of the paragraph and showing how it is connected to the thesis
- explanation of the main idea just expressed
- (sometimes) a concluding sentence or a look toward the next point

Development/Explanation of the second point
- same pattern as above

Development/Explanation of the third point
- same pattern as above

(and so on)

Concluding paragraph
- first sentence = some comment on the previous idea discussed
- (sometimes) a summary statement referring to all the main points made
- (often) a look toward implications or significance of the discussion in the paper

Figure 7.1   Diagram of an Essay

TITLES

Even more so than the first few sentences of an introduction, a title is meant to attract a reader's attention. Of the following titles, which ones most attract your attention?

The Using of Baby Fae
Tutankhamun: The Golden Pharaoh
Scaling the Walls of Silence
Finding Faults: Earthquakes
Bringing Up Baby: A New Kind of Marketing Boom
Planned Parenthood for Roaches

EXERCISE 5: TITLES

The title should also help the reader to know at a glance what the article, essay, or book will discuss. What do you expect to read about from each of these titles?

1. _____

2. _____

3. _____

4. _____

5. _____

6. _____

                                                    ■

EXERCISE 6: TITLES

What do you notice about all the titles here? List what you notice about the following:

1. capitalization _____

2. punctuation _____

3. length of title _____

                                                    ■

In writing a title, remember:

- Titles are usually short—a phrase rather than a sentence— although a question or sometimes an exclamation may also be used.
- Capitalize the first word and all the others except articles (*a, an, the*), conjunctions (*and, but, or*), and short prepositions (*in, at, on, of*).
- Do not put a period at the end of a title.
- Do not underline the title or put quotation marks around it.

EXERCISE 7: TITLES

Write three possible titles for a composition you have written. Then give your composition to a classmate. Your classmate should choose the title he or she likes best of the three, and add one more of his or her own. ■

➤ *UNIT THREE*

Reworking the Draft

➤ 8 ◀

Revising

You now have several first drafts and reactions to your drafts from your classmates. What will you do with these? Getting feedback is helpful in itself, but you can improve your writing skill faster by acting on the feedback and revising your first draft.

WHY REVISE

Even professional writers revise, rereading what they wrote, crossing out sections, rereading again, moving sections from one place to another, constantly comparing what they have on paper with an image in their minds of what they want to communicate.

Revising is *not* a punishment for writing a bad text. All experienced writers revise. In fact, revising can be quite pleasurable, even easier and more interesting than writing the first draft. Think of revising as a game or puzzle that you control and manipulate.

Here is a summary of what you have studied so far about approaching a writing task.

1. Gather your thoughts on paper by doing one or more invention activities.
2. Using your invention notes, write a first draft. Exhaust your subject by writing even more than you may need. Later you can take out any sections that you decide are weak or irrelevant.
3. Reread your draft several times, and analyze it as you read. Keep a pencil in your hand to mark any sections you may want to change. Look at the ideas you expressed. Ask yourself if you have said everything you wanted to say, if the ideas flow smoothly and logically from one to the next, if everything you said fits your audience, your purpose, and your main point. Change whatever you want to.
4. Give the draft to one or more people to read and comment on.

5. Read the comments; then set the whole pile of papers aside for a while.

6. After a day or two (or even just an hour if that is all you have), reread the draft, your readers' comments, and perhaps your own self-analysis.

7. Begin to revise.

Revising is as much rereading as it is rewriting. This rereading is very important because it allows you to compare what you wrote with your sense of what you want to communicate. Furthermore, rereading is necessary because each section of the essay that you cross out, add, or move around must be smoothly reconnected to, or integrated into, the text around it. When you reread, begin at the beginning of your paper or at least *several* sentences before the spot you want to change so that you can get a clear mental picture of the parts you are fairly satisfied with before you get to the part you want to improve.

WHAT TO REVISE: REVISION STRATEGIES CHART

Hint 9: Don't be afraid to add ideas, delete them, or move them around.

Different writers have different styles of composing and revising. Some find it easier to write a great deal in their first drafts and to revise by cutting material out. Their drafts are often long and disorganized, going off in many directions. Other writers prefer to get basic ideas down in sketchy drafts and then to expand on the ideas. These writers may have a hard time taking material out. Which type of writer are you? Becoming conscious of your own writing habits will help you focus on specific problems you have and on possible solutions. Whatever type you are, do not be afraid to experiment by adding ideas, deleting them, or moving parts of your text around. As long as you do not throw anything away, you can always return to your invention writing and drafts, if you do not like your alterations.

When you are ready to revise, analyze your draft by looking first at its broad features. First, remind yourself who your audience is and what your purpose is in writing. You might want to write a short note to yourself stating clearly for whom and for what purpose this draft is being revised. Next, this is a good time to outline your draft. (Refer to the section on outlining in Chapter 2, page 30.) In the margin, write down the main idea for the entire paper and then extract the main idea of each paragraph. Check to see that the main ideas of the paragraphs fit with one another and with the main idea of the paper. Reread each paragraph with its main idea in mind, checking to see that what you express in that paragraph fits the main idea.

Then use the chart of revision strategies presented in Figure 8.1 on pages 143–144.

Responses from your classmates and teachers should help you see where a draft needs revision. One approach is to collect several reactions to your draft and then to fill out a sheet summarizing all the responses you have received. Other approaches:

- When you are trying to add ideas to a draft, remember that you can always generate ideas through invention techniques.
- When you are trying to clarify your ideas, discuss the idea with someone; some people find that even talking into a tape recorder helps to clarify ideas.
- When you want to shorten a section or to delete material, put the original aside and try rewriting the same section from memory. You might also ask a friend to read or to listen to you read that section and then to write down whatever he or she remembers.

HOW TO REVISE: ADDING, DELETING, AND MOVING TEXT

The following exercises illustrate three common forms of revision: adding text, deleting or substituting text, and moving text around.

Read the following first draft of a student's paper.

■ STUDENT WRITING

The way I felt about the United States and expected it to be was different from the way I found it and the way I look at it now. Everything I knew about America was only from what I had seen from the TV. I thought that people were hostile; I assumed walking alone at night was extremely dangerous. I thought that big cities seemed to be very dirty.

When I came here though, I realized that people are very friendly and they help you if you need something. They are also very kind and they respect someone's privacy. It is not so dangerous to walk at nights, but maybe this is because I live on campus, where everybody is young and has the same interests as I do. Also I never lost anything even if I left something somewhere and went back later to

Problem	Solution
When the main idea of the paper is missing, inadequate, or not clear,	reread your paper and try writing the main idea in different ways; look again at your statement of audience and purpose.
When the main idea of any paragraph is inadequate,	reread the paragraph and try to extract the main idea.
When there is not enough support,	look for places where you can add material by asking yourself the questions on page 116 in the section "Supporting Material."
When the discussion is not balanced (i.e., too much or too little for the importance of the idea),	shorten too much discussion of an unimportant idea by extracting the most important part of it and by deleting the rest; expand too little discussion by asking yourself what you might add to clarify the idea (see the section "Supporting Material" on page 117).
When the support is not specific enough,	review the section "Using Specifics" in Chapter 6.
When the support is not clear enough,	try writing that section in a different way without looking at the original.
When the support is not clearly linked to the main idea or not clearly interpreted,	review the section "Unity" in Chapter 6.
When the support is not clearly linked together,	look again at your sketchy outline to see if you can reinterpret the support to link it better.
When parts need to be rearranged for logic or clarity,	study the sketchy outline again for ways to rearrange.
When irrelevant material appears,	review the section "Unity" in Chapter 6.
When the introduction is not clearly related to the body of the text.	either reinterpret the material in the introduction or delete whatever does not fit.

Figure 8.1   Revision Strategies

Continued

Problem	Solution
When the introduction does not give enough background discussion for the intended audience,	add to the introduction by gathering material through invention techniques.
When the introduction is too long,	rewrite it without looking at the original, trying to concentrate on the most important features.
When the conclusion introduces new support material,	begin a new development paragraph, include the new support material there and write a new conclusion.
When the conclusion is not clearly connected to the main idea and development,	reread the main ideas of the entire paper and of each paragraph, review the section on writing conclusions in Chapter 7, and try writing a new conclusion without looking at the original.
When the conclusion is too long,	delete material or create a new development paragraph and use the extra material there.

Figure 8.1   *Continued*

get it. No one stole anything from me. The most surprising thing, though, is how clean the campus and this city is.

I find a lot of similarities with my country, which I thought was the only place which was not dangerous and people were friendly.

Another student read the draft and made the following comments.

I wish you included more details like explanations about why you thought it was dangerous to walk around at night and now you think you are never in danger. . . . I don't think you need the part about living on campus and that people there have the same interests as you. Also, how do people respect your privacy and how do they show their kindness?

The student used her classmate's comments to help her decide what to revise. Here is her first revision.

The way I felt about the United States and expected it to be was different from the way I found it and the way I look at it now. Everything I knew about America was mostly from what I had seen on TV: cowboys, murderers, hippies. I thought that people were hostile, that they didn't talk to strangers because they didn't trust them. I assumed walking alone at night was extremely dangerous because of the high risk of being robbed or attacked for a few dollars or even being killed for no reason, especially after watching the film "This is America." People seemed to be tough and the big cities very dirty.

When I came here though, I realized that people are very friendly: they talk to you even if they do not know you and they help you if you need something. They are very kind and they respect a person's privacy. For example, if you are studying, nobody disturbs you. It is not so dangerous to walk outside at night, being afraid of being raped or robbed. I never lost anything even if I left something somewhere and went back later to get it. Nobody ever stole anything from me. The most surprising thing though is how clean this city is. There is always someone cleaning the roads, courtyards, dorms, everything.

I find a lot of similarities between the United States and my country, which I thought was the only secure place to live in.

EXERCISE 1: REVISING
Compare the two versions of this student's paper and point out the changes that she made.

Additions:

_____

_____

_____

Deletions/Substitutions:

_____

_____

_____

Other Changes:

_____

_____

_____

■

The student responded to her reader's suggestion to add some details and to delete one section. For example, she added an explanation of why she thought it would be dangerous to walk alone at night, mentioning a film she saw. But she does not make an explicit connection between the film and the reason she thought walking alone would be dangerous. The mention of this film is not well integrated into the paper and therefore seems somewhat artificial, as if the writer herself was not sure why she had added it. What do you think is the connection between the film and the danger she believed existed in the streets?

1. Using this student's first draft, try to respond to her reader's need for additional explanation by integrating her example of "This is America" into the text better. Use a separate sheet of paper. Try to imagine what she was trying to accomplish by mentioning this movie. Feel free to make any necessary changes in order to integrate this addition. Now compare your work with that of your classmates; decide on the best revision. Why is it best?

2. The reader commented that the paper should include more details. Which parts of the first draft do you think the reader was referring to? Circle these parts.

3. Now circle any sections of the second draft where *you* want more details.

Here is the final revision of the student's paper.

The way I felt about the United States and expected it to be was different from the way I found it and the way I look at it now after being here for eight months. Everything I knew about America was from what I had seen on TV: mostly cowboys and murderers. I thought that people were hostile, that they didn't talk to strangers because they didn't trust them. I was afraid of walking alone at night because of the high risk of being robbed or attacked for a few dollars or even being killed for no reason. I had seen such crimes committed in the film "This is America," which shows Mafia, drugs, all the murders that were committed for money. Americans seemed to be tough and dangerous. I also noticed in movies that big cities like New York, Los Angeles, and Chicago seemed to be very dirty. The subway in New York looked dark and somehow greasy; big avenues like Fifth Avenue had extra garbage falling out of garbage cans on the street.

When I came here though, I realized that people are very friendly; they talk to you even if they do not know you. Since I had the idea that Americans were hostile and selfish, I was surprised to see that they are kind and respect a person's privacy. For example, if they know you are studying at the dorm, they won't leave the music loud and nobody disturbs you. People realize that sometimes a person needs to be alone. I also found that it's not so dangerous to walk outside at night. Since I've been here no one has been raped or robbed. I've never even lost anything. In fact, once I forgot my purse in the South Carrick Hall lobby and later I went back to see if it was there and nobody had taken it or touched it. The most surprising thing though is how clean Knoxville is. There is always someone cleaning the roads, sweeping the pavement, emptying the trash cans. Courtyards, dorms, and all the buildings are always clean.

Before I came to the States I thought that Cyprus was the most secure place to live in. After having lived here for eight months, I realize that the United States has a lot of similarities with my country.

Annabel Drousiotis (Cyprus) ■

EXERCISE 2: REVISING

What kinds of changes did the student make this time?

Additions:

_____

_____

_____

Deletions/Substitutions:

_____

_____

_____

Other Changes:

_____

_____

_____

■

Do you think that the final version is better in general than the second draft? Circle the sections that are more effective in the final version than they were in the previous versions. How do the changes improve these sections?

■ STUDENT WRITING

Here is another example of the first draft of a student's paper.

There is a surprising amount of difference between the American and foreign students at the University of Tennessee in their activities.

The Americans in general love to play games like football, tennis, baseball, and other outdoor sports. On the other hand, foreign students are less involved in outdoor games. Instead they prefer to watch the TV. During the football season, big groups of American students go to the stadium to support the home team. They appear to be very enthusiastic about it. Very seldom can you find foreign students at football games. Most of the foreign students must be at home doing some studying. In the off-campus area, especially on Friday night, groups of Americans have parties and barbecues, with loud music being played till late at night. For the foreign students, there seems to be little cause for any celebration. Though there is a marked difference in our involvement in various activities, we are all fun-loving people.

Were there any parts of this paper where you wanted further explanation? Circle those sections.

Here are some comments the student received on this draft.

Why do you say there is no cause for celebration for the foreign students? I think it depends because I am a foreign student and I go to parties. Also I think it is a contradiction when you say "we are all fun-loving people."

Your paper is very good but I disagree with one thing. Americans stay home and watch sports on TV, not foreign students. I play on the university soccer team and most of the other players are foreign students. I think the Americans watch TV all the time.

Did you have questions in any of the same places?

Because his readers objected to his generalizations, the student knew that he had to make his argument more convincing. These responses made him realize that his audience's experience and information on his subject contradicted his own experience and knowledge. The student decided to revise the paper using his own situation as an example of how at least some foreign students live. His purpose became to convince his audience (other foreign students) that American students have more fun than foreign students and to explain the possible causes. Here is the revised version.

There is a surprising amount of difference between my American neighbor and me in our attitudes towards studying. The attitude is reflected in our daily activities. He loves to play games like football, baseball, and other outdoor sports. Quite often in the evening, he is outside his apartment playing catch with his other friends. In the late evening, he strums his guitar together with his friends. He loves to watch football and is there at the stadium to support the home team whenever there is a game. He appears to be enthusiastic about it and encourages me to join him. On Friday night, he has a barbecue or a party with music being played till late at night. During the weekends, he is out washing his car and doing some other minor adjustments or repairs. Being a student seems relaxing for him and he is able to pursue his non-academic interests. I, on the other hand, am having quite a tough time with my studies. I study till late at night every day as I am taking many courses. I seldom have the time to play games as I have to put in a lot of time studying for the numerous examinations. I love to play games and to party till late at night, but I can't do that as I am restricted by my workload. The only time that I can enjoy myself thoroughly is during the break. Being a foreigner, I have to struggle hard to get my degree and achieve good grades within the shortest possible time. Time and money are not on my side as it is very hard on my parents to pay my fees, which are very high. I have to graduate as I will need to support my family in the near future.

My American neighbor does not have the same problems as I have. He can take his time completing his undergraduate program. Being an American, he does not need to do well in his studies if he chooses not to. This is because he can get a job easily without getting good grades in his school work. If I were like him, life as a student would be very interesting and exciting for me too.

Tiong Kheng Loo (Singapore)   ■

EXERCISE 3: REVISING
What changes did the student make in his second draft?

Additions:

_____

_____

_____

Deletions/Substitutions:

_____

_____

_____

Other Changes:

_____

_____

_____

                                                                              ■

Do you think that the second version is better than the first? Does the second version seem to fulfill the purpose the student set out for himself better than the first version did? Why or why not?

    In the second version, the student comes to some conclusions about his own experience as a student and the experience of his neighbor. Do you think that these conclusions are justified based on his description of his own activities and those of his neighbor, or do you think that they are unsupported generalizations?

➢ *Writing Assignment 8.1: Revision*

Writing
Assignment 8.1

Choose one of the drafts you have already written and received feedback on. Reread the draft and your classmates' feedback. Are you satisfied with this draft, or are there sections that you could improve by adding, deleting or substituting, or moving ideas around? Analyze your draft once again, using the following questions as a guide.

1. First answer these questions about your *audience*:
   Who is your audience? What interest do they have in this subject? What do they already know about this subject?

2. Then answer these questions about your *purpose*:
   What did you want to accomplish by writing this paper? To entertain your audience? To educate them? To inspire them to do something? To help them understand something new? To help them see something familiar from a new point of view? To change their minds about something?

3. Next write the *main idea* of your draft in a complete sentence. Ask yourself these questions:
   Is the main idea stated somewhere near the beginning of the paper? If not, would the paper be more effective if you did state the main idea? No matter where the

main idea appears in your draft (or even if it is only implied), is the main idea clear to *you*? Do you think it is clear to your audience?

4. Considering the audience you are writing for and your purpose, analyze the *development* of your paper:

a. Support material: type and amount

Do you need to develop any ideas more fully? Do you need to be more specific or concrete in your explanations? Look again at the questions you asked yourself on page 116. How would you answer them now? Did you include all the information you needed to discuss your topic as fully as you wanted? Should you add anything to your discussion?

b. Support material: relevance

Did you give your readers enough background information for them to understand not only your ideas but also the relevance of your discussion? Is there any irrelevant information, information the audience either already knows or does not need to know in order to understand your explanations? Should you delete any sections of your discussion?

Have you said anything your reader is likely to disagree with? Have you answered those anticipated objections? Have you said anything your reader may not understand?

c. Support material: arrangement

Does your discussion move smoothly and logically from one idea to the next? Is each new idea explained sufficiently before you move on to the next one? Are the ideas clearly linked together? Do you lead your reader step by step to understand your ideas? Should you rearrange any sections of your paper?

5. Analyze your *conclusion*:

Does the conclusion develop logically from what you have written? Do you think it gives the reader the feeling that you have said everything you intended to say about your subject?

If you are unsure of the answers to any of these questions, get the opinions of a reader or two. Ask them the specific questions you have doubts about.

Use the feedback you have received to help you decide what to revise in your draft. Then revise by adding, deleting, substituting, and/or moving ideas around.

When you have finished revising your draft, answer the following questions.

Self-Analysis

1. What were you unsatisfied with in the original draft?
2. How did you try to address the problems you noted?
3. What sections of the revision do you now feel satisfied with that you did not like in the original?
4. What sections of the revision do you still feel unsure of?
5. Is there anything else you might have considered doing to improve your original?
6. Are you generally satisfied with the revised version of your paper?

Revising can and should be fairly enjoyable. Sometimes, however, you may have completely lost interest in your original subject; sometimes, it may be that your first draft was just badly conceived. (For example, perhaps you chose a subject you really didn't know enough about.) If you can, abandon the project. It is difficult to write well on a subject you have begun to hate or grow tired of. If you do not have this option, consider the suggestions on page 56 to help you deal with this problem.

Before you revise any papers from now on, return at least briefly to this section to remind yourself of the questions to ask as you begin to revise.   ◄

➤ 9 ⤺

Polishing Revised Drafts

Later in this chapter, you will write a short autobiographical statement. To prepare for this assignment, you may want to write on one or more of the following journal suggestions.

Journal Suggestions

- Where are you in your life right now, and where do you want your life to go from here? What qualities in your personality will help you get there? What faults could hold you back?

- What would be a perfect job for you? Would you like to work with people, ideas, or machines? Do you want to be responsible for other people, or would you rather carry out orders? Could you work with a very flexible schedule, or do you need a regular routine and a clear framework in order to do your best work? Do you work well under pressure, or do you prefer to be able to take your time? Are you a perfectionist? When your work day is over, do you want to be able to forget it completely, or will your work be on your mind most of the time?

- Make a list of what you would like to accomplish or experience in your life.

- Make a list of some of the things you would do differently if you could live your life over. Or make a list of directions that you would like to have taken in your life. Do you wish you had learned to play music or to dance; do you wish you had studied other subjects or maybe become something completely different, for example, a professional athlete?

- Have you ever had a paying job? What did working at that job help you learn about work, about yourself, or about others?

You might also consider reading one or more of the following Reading Selections in the Appendix.

Readings
"Abraham Lincoln," page 358
Excerpt from *Two Years in the Melting Pot*, page 361

In some writing situations—for example, writing an essay exam or an informal letter—it may be impossible or unnecessary to take the time to polish your writing and find a better way to state your ideas. In other writing situations, however, expressing yourself carefully and correctly is extremely important. One instance of such a situation is writing an essay as part of an application form for a job or for admission to a school. Because you want to produce a favorable impression of yourself in this situation, you want to write as clearly and as correctly as possible. The following section will help you learn how to polish or perfect a piece of writing.

REPHRASING

Hint 10: Once your ideas are on paper, check the grammar, vocabulary, spelling, and punctuation to make the writing as correct as you can.

When you are revising, you reconsider large chunks of your essay. Your main concern is content—that is, *what* ideas you expressed and in what order. Once the revisions are finished and you are satisfied with the ideas you have expressed and the order in which you expressed them, it is time to concentrate on improving smaller sections of your paper. Your main concern will now be *how* you say something rather than what you say. Some of your sentences may need rephrasing and/or editing. Rephrasing has to do with making a sentence clearer and more to the point (that often means shorter). Editing means making a sentence grammatically and mechanically correct.

Alternative Sentences

Any idea can be expressed in a number of different ways. Look at the idea expressed in these sentences.

Because of its large population, China has begun a strict program to try to discourage couples from having more than one child.

Couples in China are being strongly encouraged to have only one child because the population there is already so large.

In order to decrease the number of people living in China, a new government program is urgently promoting the idea of one-child families.

> The population in China is too large. Therefore, the Chinese government is trying to convince couples to have only one child to try to reduce the size of the population.

As you can see, all these sentences give the same message, but they use different words. Read the following sentence.

> Some Chinese are reluctant to follow the government's program; nevertheless, they also realize that China has to reduce its rate of population growth.

On a separate sheet of paper, express the idea in that sentence in three different ways.

When you have finished, compare your sentences with those written by your classmates. Write a few of the different versions on the board.

The original sentence was perfectly acceptable. But as you saw, there are many ways to manipulate even a good sentence. The following example is not a good sentence. The ideas are loosely joined with *and* or *but*, which do not clearly show the relationship among the ideas. As a result, the writer had to repeat some words several times and had to use too many words for the ideas being expressed.

> If someone only has one child and then that child grows up, then there will only be that one child to take care of the parents because usually the child can share the responsibility with the brothers and sisters, but in this case there aren't any.

Be sure you understand the meaning of this sentence. Then write three alternative ways of expressing the same idea in one or two sentences. Try to clarify the relationships among the ideas and eliminate unnecessary repetition.

Write some of the alternatives suggested by the class on the board. In general, a good sentence in English is clear and direct and does not use extra, unnecessary words to express an idea. Are there any good alternatives on the board?

Now read the following paragraph. The second sentence is awkward and does not fit well between the first and third sentences. The language is more informal than that in the other sentences, and the relationship among the ideas in the sentence is not directly shown. Perhaps the writer did not know at the beginning of the sentence what the end would say. As a result, too many words were used to express the ideas in the sentence.

> A recent study on classroom behavior in elementary schools in the United States shows that teachers behave differently toward

boys and girls. There might be a boy in the class who, instead of raising his hand to get permission to answer a question, just shouts out the answer and the teacher accepts it even though he did not raise his hand first. But when a girl does the same thing, the teacher tells her that she should raise her hand and wait to be called on before giving an answer.

Now look at one way the middle sentence might be rephrased to make it fit better between the first and third sentences.

A recent study on classroom behavior in elementary schools in the United States shows that teachers behave differently toward boys and girls. When a boy shouts out an answer without raising his hand, the teacher accepts his comment. But when a girl does the same thing, the teacher tells her that she should raise her hand and wait to be called on before giving an answer.

EXERCISE 1: REPHRASING

In the following paragraph, the middle sentence is awkward for the same reasons as in the previous example. Rephrase that sentence and write it in the space provided.

In another study researchers found that when boys need help teachers tend to give boys instructions so that they can do things for themselves. But in the case of dealing with female students, the girls get much less chance to try to follow any kind of instructions because the teacher will just come over and do the things for the female students instead. This unconscious behavior on the part of the teacher encourages boys to be independent while it encourages girls to become dependent.

_____

_____

■

Again, write some of the alternative sentences from the class on the board and select the best ones.

Now look through a composition you have written for this class. Are you unhappy with any of the sentences? If you would like help rephrasing a sentence, share it with the class. Write the sentence on the board, along with the sentences that immediately precede and follow it. Each of your classmates will suggest an alternative way to say the same thing, and you can select the one you prefer.

If a reader ever says that a sentence you have written is awkward, wordy, or loose, or that you should rewrite or rephrase it, try the technique of writing three alternative sentences expressing the same idea.

Sentence Variety

Read the following excerpt from a short composition.

■ STUDENT WRITING

(1) Although women in both Iran and America are happy with their lives, what an Iranian woman does in a day is quite different from what an American woman does. (2) A housewife in Iran has no job, career, or social activity. (3) The housewife gets up earlier than anybody else in the house. (4) The housewife cooks the breakfast. (5) She wakes everybody up when the breakfast is ready. (6) She helps her husband and children get ready for work and school. (7) She starts cleaning the house and washing the clothes after everybody leaves home. (8) She goes grocery shopping for dinner around noon. (9) She stays busy until her lunch time. (10) She can have a little bit of free time after lunch, (11) but she can hardly even start on something before the kids get home from school. (12) The kids run all over the house. (13) They scream and cry and never listen to their mom until the husband comes back home and has dinner. (14) Everybody else is already in bed by the time she finishes. (15) She has to wash the dishes after dinner. (16) An American woman is very energetic compared to the Iranian woman. . . .

Adapted from Keihan Mani (Iran)   ■

This excerpt does not contain any errors in grammar, but the style is monotonous because nearly every sentence begins the same way: subject and verb. Here are some other possibilities to add more variety:

Prepositional phrase: (10) After lunch, she can have a little bit of free time.

Adverb clause: (7) After everybody leaves home, she starts cleaning the house and washing clothes.

Verbal phrase: (2) Being a housewife in Iran can mean no job, career, or social activity.

Adverb: (11) Unfortunately, before she can even start on something, the kids get home from school.

Combining sentences (12, 13) The kids run all over the house, screaming, crying, and never listening to their mom.

EXERCISE 2: VARIETY

Using these different methods, suggest ways to change the following sentences from the student's paper.

(3) _____

_____

(4) _____

_____

(5) _____

_____

(6) _____

_____

(8) _____

_____

(14) _____

_____

(15) _____

_____

(16) _____

_____
■

Now write out the entire paragraph and compare your version with that of at least one classmate. Did you make any other changes?

Showing the Relationship between Ideas

Read the following passage, which expresses one author's view on only children (that is, a child with no brothers or sisters):

Children who grow up without brothers and sisters may have a particularly difficult time adjusting to life. Many younger couples now want only one child. Only children get their parents' undivided attention and love. They may be extra generous with their own love. They may expect their spouses to give them undivided attention and love as their parents did. Their parents can afford to give them more materially. They have a hard time learning to share. Only children grow very attached to their parents. They must struggle to become independent. They learned how to play by themselves and to be alone. They may suffer less from loneliness.

Did you have trouble understanding this paragraph? Now read this version, in which sentences have been combined using adverbial subordinators (clause markers) and transitional expressions to show the relationships between sentences.

> **Although** the child who grows up without brothers and sisters may have a particularly difficult time adjusting to life, many younger couples now want only one child. **Because** only children get their parents' undivided attention and love, they may be extra generous with their own love. **On the other hand,** they may expect their spouses to give them undivided attention and love as their parents did. **Furthermore, although** their parents can afford to give them more materially, they have a hard time learning to share. **Another problem** they face is that **because** only children grow very attached to their parents, they must struggle to become independent. **On the other hand, since** they learned how to play by themselves and to be alone, they may suffer less from loneliness.

Was this version easier to understand? Logical connectors like transitional expressions and subordinators are guideposts for the reader. They tell the reader how the information in one sentence is related to the information in another sentence. Thus, the sentences are linked in some way that makes reading easier. (For other ways to link sentences, see Appendix C.) Look back at the second version of the passage and answer the following questions.

EXERCISE 3: RELATIONSHIP BETWEEN IDEAS

1. Which expressions in the text indicate that more information will be added? _____

2. Which expressions show that one sentence will follow the previous statement in sequence? _____

3. Which expressions indicate that the sentence will contradict something said earlier? _____

■

EXERCISE 4: RELATIONSHIP BETWEEN IDEAS

Now look at the following passage and try to make it easier to read by adding words to show the relationships between sentences more clearly.

Do you ever secretly feel that your academic success is the result of luck rather than the result of your own intelligence? If so, you may be suffering from the "impostor phenomenon." People suffering from this psychological condition do not believe that they are really intelligent despite their academic successes at school. _____ , these people feel guilty because they believe that they have deceived their teachers into thinking they are intelligent, while they themselves feel deep down that they are not.

The impostor phenomenon occurs mostly among young women, especially among beginning graduate students, women who are obviously intelligent. These women usually grew up in one of two types of families. In the first type of family, some other family member was designated the smart one in the family and the girl with the impostor feelings was designated as some thing else._____ , whenever that girl was successful academically she felt as though she were tricking people. She felt sure she wasn't the intelligent one in the family. After all, that's what her family had always told her.

_____ of family is the high achiever type that believes success or achievement comes easily and naturally for really superior people. As a result of this attitude in the family, the child may become afraid to admit that achievements have come from hard work. _____ , one young woman who suffered from impostor feelings never let her family see her studying _____ they had told her that really smart people don'tneed to study. _____ , she felt that if she studied and got good grades, she was tricking people into thinking she was intelligent. She knew she couldn't really be intelligent, because she had to study and she had been told that intelligent people don't have to study.

Even though their academic achievements prove their intelligence, these women cannot think of themselves as intelligent. _____ they think of themselves as cheaters, hiding from the world the truth that they are not as good as they seem, that they are only impostors. ∎

See Appendix C for possible answers.

Compare the logical connectors you used with those used by your classmates. Underline as many other transitional expressions and subordinators as you can find in the passage.

In using transitional expressions, you should be aware that even words with similar meanings (such as *however* and *never-*

theless) cannot be used interchangeably in all contexts. Furthermore, some connectors are more likely to be used in formal situations, others in informal situations:

> The families of these women did not trust them. Consequently, they do not trust themselves. (more formal)
> The families of these women didn't trust them. So, they don't trust themselves. (more informal)

Consult your teacher when you are not sure if a certain word may be used in a particular context.

Depending on where they appear in the sentence, logical connectors function differently in sentences, are punctuated differently, and change the emphasis in the sentence.

Logical Connectors: Type 1. Type 1 consists of adverbs, such as *however*:

> These women have impressive academic records. However, they refuse to believe in their own intelligence.

Note where these adverbs may appear in sentences and how they are punctuated.

1. _____ . However, _____ .
2. _____; however, _____ .
3. _____ . _____, however, _____ .
4. _____ . _____, however.

Logical Connectors: Type 2. Type 2 consists of prepositional phrases made up of prepositions (such as *despite*) and nouns or pronouns:

> Despite their academic achievements, these women refuse to believe in their own intelligence.

The preposition must be followed by a noun phrase, a noun clause, a gerund (verb ending with *-ing*), or a pronoun. Note where the prepositional phrases may appear in a sentence and how they are punctuated.

1. *Despite* + noun/gerund, _____ .
2. _____ *despite* + noun/gerund.

Remember that some prepositions consist of several words: *in addition to, in spite of, other than*, and so on.

Logical Connectors: Type 3. Type 3 consists of adverbial subordinators or clause markers (such as *although*) followed by clauses:

> Although they have impressive academic records, these women refuse to believe in their own intelligence.

Like all clause markers, these subordinators must be followed by a subject and a conjugated verb (subject: *they*; conjugated verb: *have*). Note where these words may appear in a sentence; remember that moving these clauses around may change the emphasis of the sentence.

1. *Although* + clause, ——————————————————————— .

2. ——————————————————————— *although* + clause.

Beginning the sentence with:

Although they have impressive academic records,

creates a stronger contrast with:

these women refuse to believe in their own intelligence.

The emphasis in a sentence also changes depending on which clause is subordinated. The idea within the subordinated clause sets the context or gives the background for the new information or idea in the main clause. The rest of the text is likely to follow logically from the idea expressed in the main clause, rather than from the background idea in the subordinate clause. Read the following two sentences:

1. Although her parents love her, they don't believe in her intelligence.
2. Although her parents don't believe in her intelligence, they love her.

In which one of these two situations are the parents more likely to be willing to pay for their daughter's college education? Predict what the next sentence is likely to be about for each of the sentences above.

Logical Connectors: Type 4. Type 4 consists of coordinators, such as *yet:*

> These women have impressive academic records, yet they refuse to believe in their own intelligence.

Coordinators join two complete sentences.

1. _____ , yet _____ .

2. _____ . Yet _____ .

The second pattern is seen more often with *yet* than with *and* or *but*.

Although transitional expressions, subordinators, and coordinators help the reader follow the logic of a text, it is not necessary to use an explicit logical connector in every sentence. In fact, overuse of these devices can be distracting and even confusing for the reader. No one can tell you how many logical connectors should appear in an essay. Instead, by using these types of transitional expressions and subordinators and by getting feedback, you will eventually develop a sense of when such expressions will clarify the relationships between sentences.

EXERCISE 5: RELATIONSHIP BETWEEN IDEAS

Practice using transitions by completing these unfinished sentences logically.

1. If you are thinking of buying a car, one of the most important factors to consider is your lifestyle. If you do a lot of city driving, making short trips to the grocery store or the bank, a big car would be more of a burden than a convenience. On the

other hand, _____

2. Although everyone knows that vitamins are important to good health, not everyone is ready to believe Dr. Linus Pauling's claim that massive doses of vitamin C can prevent colds. In fact,

_____

3. Although everyone knows that vitamins are important to good health, not everyone is ready to believe Dr. Linus Pauling's claim that massive doses of vitamin C can prevent

colds. Nevertheless, _____

4. Once again the Surgeon General has warned that smoking probably causes some form of cancer. A notice to this effect appears on every pack of cigarettes sold in this country.

   Despite _____

5. It seems obvious that the current trend in this country is toward the single life. Since 1970, both men and women have been waiting longer to get married. In 1970, the average age of people getting married was in the early twenties; by 1990, most people who got married were in their late twenties.

   Moreover, _____

   ∎

   Make an effort to experiment with different logical connectors. (See the list of transitional, subordinating, and coordinating expressions in Appendix C on page 416.) Look back at the passage on the impostor phenomenon (page 160). With your class, try different expressions you might have used and discuss what changes in meaning, if any, the different connectors create.

   During a revision, you will often eliminate sections of your text. When you do so, it is important to provide a smooth transition between the remaining parts. Look at the following paragraphs, which are part of a draft of a longer composition.

∎ **STUDENT WRITING**

   I became very interested in body language when my English grammar teacher told me where I came from by noticing a single gesture. First, he told me to count on my fingers from 1 to 6. He watched and then he told me I must be from Latin America. ~~Since that day, I became very interested in body language. In our conversation class, we used to talk about this topic. After every class I was more and more amazed because I learned new things about physical gestures, such as the fact that~~ in Japanese culture when your teacher or mother is talking to you, you have to lower your head to show that you respect her. But in my culture, if you put your head down while your teacher or mother was talking to you, she would think that you are not paying attention to her. ~~One day, I came across an interesting article about natural gestures. I was taught by the article that~~ you can easily tell whenever somebody is lying to you. ~~The article said that there are~~ some special gestures that people unconsciously make whenever they are lying to somebody. Some of such gestures are: scratching their nose or behind their ear, coughing a couple of times, or looking toward the floor as though they were trying to avoid looking in your eyes.

   Carlos Gun (Honduras)   ∎

EXERCISE 6: RELATIONSHIP BETWEEN IDEAS

The sections marked are the parts the student wanted to eliminate in the next revision. In the space provided, suggest ways to link the remaining sentences together smoothly.

. . . Latin America. _____

_____

_____ in Japanese . . .

. . . attention to her. _____

_____ you can easily tell . . .

. . . lying to you. _____

_____ some special gestures. . . .

∎

Using logical connectors is not the only way to link ideas in a composition. The flow of writing in English is often from given (already known or already introduced information) to new; in writing a new sentence, the writer nearly always refers back in some way to previously expressed ideas. By simply repeating key words or using pronouns or demonstratives (*this, these, that, those, such*) referring to those words, you can help the reader to see your text as a unified structure instead of as a series of unrelated sentences. Here is an example of the use of this technique.

■ STUDENT WRITING

Bangles, bracelets, and armbands are worn the world over as decoration, but because of their history, in Pakistan they are the symbol of men's oppression of women. It is said that in the old days, women were kept chained by their husbands and were treated as slaves. In fact, they were forced to wear handcuffs. With the coming of Islam, men became more civilized, but old traditions die hard. So bangles and bracelets took the place of chains and handcuffs and became the symbols of women's former bondage.

However, as time passed, yellow and red colors were added to the bangles and they became more ornamental and varied in design. Gradually, precious metals were used in making bangles, the more ornate and expensive the better. Since the bangles recalled the time when a woman belonged to her husband as his property, only married women wore them. A woman put them on when she married, and if by chance her husband died, she took the bangles off, never to touch them again. In this way bangles represented a more subtle symbol of women's servitude. The woman wearing beautifully designed and colored bangles became a walking show-case for her husband's wealth.

Altaf Amin (Pakistan) ■

Notice that in this paragraph, a transition word signals the beginning of the second part of the paper. Also notice that this writer used pronouns, demonstratives, key words, and synonyms to refer back to previous ideas. Repeating key words (*bangles*), synonyms (*oppression, bondage, servitude*), demonstratives, and pronouns to unify a text and using transitions to mark divisions are fairly typical practices in English writing. Look back at the passage on the impostor phenomenon and find examples of key words, synonyms, demonstratives, and pronouns that link the sentences together. Then look back at one of your own essays. In a different color ink, circle any repeated key words, synonyms, demonstratives, and pronouns you find in it.

EDITING

When to Edit

Evidence of careful editing is extremely important to some read-ers, who may form a negative impression of a writer because of the errors in a text. But even for readers who are much less con-cerned with grammatical and mechanical perfection, many er-rors in a final draft can be distracting. As a writer, you will need to evaluate your audience from several points of view, and one of them is whether and how much the members of your audience value correctness. Obviously, if your audience values correctness highly, you must do your best to produce a grammatically correct text. If your audience is more relaxed, you must decide for your-self how concerned you will be with eliminating all errors from your paper.

In any case, there is not much point in worrying about details of grammar and mechanical perfection until you are satisfied with the larger components of your text: the explana-tion of the ideas, their arrangement, the sentences, and so on. In other words, editing is one of the *last* tasks you do to finish a paper.

What to Edit

The causes of errors vary. Writers sometimes violate a rule because they do not know the rule exists. At other times, a writer may be aware of the rule but may not be sure exactly what it is or may have learned an incorrect version of the rule. Finally, a writer may know a rule perfectly well but may simply not notice an error.

Nearly every writer, native speaker or non-native speaker, makes errors in writing, but some errors are more "serious" than others either because:

> they make the sentence difficult to understand, or;
>
> they are, for one reason or another, especially jarring for most native speaker readers (for example, double negatives).

Less serious errors may simply be the result of inattention because of the writer's familiarity with the text. Nevertheless, whether your writing contains "serious" errors or less serious ones, you will need to edit carefully if you have decided to eliminate errors.

The following editing test will help you to determine which types of errors or mistakes in English are not obvious to you, either because you do not recognize them as errors or because you are not reading with enough attention to detail. The items in this test represent errors that non-native writers often make in their writing.

EXERCISE 7: EDITING TEST

This test is divided into two parts. In each part, you are to first read the entire composition through quickly to get an idea of the subject matter. Then go back to the beginning and mark and correct every error you find. If you are not sure how to correct an error, at least mark it. There are *22* errors in Part 1.

■ STUDENT WRITING

Part 1

When I left my home and parents to begin my studies abroad, I was told that going abroad was going to be the most thrill experience of my life. Studying in the foreign country was going to build my characteristics, enhance my sense of responsibility, and see new horizons to look forward to. I am living here only since September, but I see that what living abroad also does is to take away that period of carelessness, that spirit of freedom that is so special and still needs by teenagers.

Leaving home and parents for studying abroad was a striking experience. It was not only my family I was leaving but also my friends and the places I knew: whole part of my life. Once in United States, I had to face the problems of a new language, new friends, in short, a new way of life. Even a beginning is always difficult, all these changes are very enriching. I have been told many times that after overcome all these obstacles, people feel much better, much stronger than they did before they faced this difficulties. My answer to these claims are that as a result of my experiences here I will certainly have more confident. The problem is, however, that the timing had been wrong for me. I would have been better to wait until I'm older. Trying to make new friends, to speak a new language, and to face all the problem of a new culture when you have no one to confide in and when you have been taken out of the soil you knew makes you grow—not stronger—but older than you really are. You realize this when you talk to people are your own age, you see that their concerns are quite different from yours. What they have to worry about is what fraternity they will join or what will they do on Friday night. Similar interests are not enough between them and you. A gap has form between you and your own generation. ■

When you have finished, discuss your findings in class, compare your answers with those of your classmates, and refer to the corrected version on page 418 of Appendix C and to the explanations of these errors on pages 419–421. ■

EXERCISE 8: EDITING TEST
Now begin Part 2 and follow the same procedure. There are 18 errors in Part 2.

■ STUDENT WRITING

Part 2

Moreover, not only a new culture that you now have to face but also new responsibilities. It is no one but yourself to take care of you. *You* have to be sure that your phone bill is paid on time and that your money has spent conscientiously. You cannot bring your dirties clothes home during the weekend to the house of your mother and ask her to wash them for you because your studies are consuming the most your time or just because you are not feel like washing them yourself. Although you don't want to worry about all these details yourself, but you must. If you feel sick, you could not just call your mother and ask her what to do. You yourself will have to search for a doctor's phone number and call him. The success completion of all these duties is obviously requiring a great sense of responsibility. Someone would object that whether we take these responsibilities at this time or at other, this is how life is going to be anyway and that it is never too soon to start learning. But at 17, 18, or 19, you have still needed your foolishness in order to get to know yourself better and to expend that "youthful energy" which it is still boiling in you. Being very mature and very responsible forces you to hold back all this carelessness. To miss this freedom that you still need.

All people should be give the chance to live their own ages fully. Right now I would prefer been a teenager to being a mature adult. For a fruit ripened too quickly loses its flavor.

Adapted from Karen Moukheiber (Lebanon) ■

■

Once again, check your work against that of your classmates and then see page 418 of Appendix C for the corrected version and pages 421–422 for an explanation of these errors.

Look over the errors you were able to find and correct those you missed. Make a note for yourself of which kinds of editing errors you overlooked. When you are editing an essay, look particularly carefully for those kinds of errors.

In Appendix B, you will find a series of exercises on finding and correcting errors. Doing these exercises will help you sharpen your eye for editing.

How to Correct Errors in Your Own Writing

Correcting someone else's writing is not exactly the same as correcting your own. Often by the time you are ready to edit your own work, you have read the paper so many times that you may have trouble noticing errors. Here are some suggestions that may help you to edit better.

1. Try to let some time pass between working on the content of your paper and editing it. This distance in time may help you to focus more sharply on form.

2. Try to read your paper slowly, saying the sentences aloud or in your head.

3. Try to look for only one error at a time, for example, sentence boundaries, subject/verb agreements, verb tenses and forms, or *-s* errors.

4. Try reading your text one sentence at a time beginning at the end instead of at the beginning. By doing this, you will not be distracted by content and will be better able to concentrate on form.

5. Make marks in the margin where you are unsure of what you have written. Ask a native speaker, a classmate, or your teacher for the correct form. If you are unsure of a rule, ask your teacher or consult a grammar handbook. If you are unsure of spelling or word breaks, consult a dictionary.

6. Each time you edit, make a note of errors you want to be particularly careful to avoid next time you edit. To be sure you understand the grammar rule involved, write the rule in your own words and ask your teacher to check that you have written it correctly.

In addition to these suggestions, try the following activities before you begin a new editing task to help you ignore content and look only at language.

1. Reread the notes you made for suggestion 6 above.

2. Do one of the editing exercises in Appendix B. List the types of errors that you found and select three or four types to look for in the paper you are about to edit.

3. Look at the last essay in which someone (perhaps your teacher) pointed out your errors. List the types of errors you made and the number of times you made each one. Pick out the three most frequent types and focus on these three types of errors as you edit this paper.

➤ *Writing Assignment 9.1: Editing*

Writing
Assignment 9.1

Choose one of the papers you have already written and revised. Assume that you are now going to submit your work to a reader who will be very particular about clarity and correctness in writing.

1. Reread your draft, looking for sentences that seem either awkward or grammatically incorrect. Mark these sections.

2. Give your draft to a classmate and ask him or her to mark any sentences that seem either awkward or grammatically incorrect.

3. Using what you have learned in this section, work with a classmate to improve your style and correct any errors in your draft. Consult other classmates or your teacher if you have problems.   ◄

➤ *Writing Assignment 9.2: Autobiography*

Writing
Assignment 9.2

When students in the United States apply for admission to graduate school, for a scholarship, or for a job, the school or the company will often request a short autobiographical statement from the applicant. You too may someday be asked to write such a statement. In this assignment, you will prepare an autobiographical statement that you may actually be able to use in an application. Remember that writing an autobiographical statement to accompany an application is one of the writing situations in which usually it is quite important to pay attention to the clarity and correctness of your language. However, do not worry about editing until after you have written your statement and are satisfied with its content and organization.

From the following four possible situations, choose the one you think you are most likely to encounter.

1. You are applying for a scholarship that is available at your school for international students studying in the United States who have the following qualifications:
   a good academic record
   evidence of a promising academic future at the school
   interest in extracurricular activities
   leadership abilities
2. You are applying for admission to graduate school in your major.
3. You are applying for a part-time or full-time job to get some work experience in a field related to your major.
4. You are applying for a part-time job just to earn a little extra money while you go to school.

In this assignment, you will write a draft of an autobiographical sketch no longer than 300 words that will give the scholarship foundation, the graduate school, or the prospective employer an idea of your personality, your ability to express yourself, and your education and work experience.

If you have written a "time line" of your life (see the Journal Suggestions in Chapter 2), you may want to reread it now to prepare for this assignment. In addition, you may want to reread the readings suggested at the beginning of this chapter and also write on one or more of the suggested journal topics.

Once you have chosen a situation, write on a sheet of paper what you think the school official or employer wants to know about you and why this person needs this information.

Find someone else in your class who chose the same situation and discuss the following questions:

What kind of background would the best applicant for the graduate school, scholarship, or job probably have?

What kind of personality traits would the best candidate for the graduate school, scholarship, or job probably have?

What kind of interests would the graduate school, scholarship foundation, or employer want the applicant to have?

When you have finished discussing and thinking over these questions, write brief notes on what personality traits, interests, and experiences you want to mention in your autobiographical statement. Gather all your notes and write a first draft.

When you have finished your draft, answer the following questions.

Self-Analysis

1. What might your reader already know about you from your application form before even reading your autobiographical statement?

2. What might he or she probably still need to know?

3. What impression of your personality did you try to convey?

4. Which part of this autobiographical statement do you want the potential employer or school official to pay the most attention to?

5. If you had to shorten your statement, what would you leave out?

6. What part are you most satisfied with?

7. How could this autobiographical statement still be improved? What is the weakest part of it?   ◄

Writing Assignment 9.2 continues on page 178.

Because you are telling the story of your life, it might seem logical to start at the beginning and then describe significant events one at a time in chronological order. However, it is important to consider your audience and your purpose to help you decide which details to include and which details are irrelevant for this audience and purpose. Furthermore, to make reading as easy as possible for your reader, you must not only list the events in your life but also interpret their significance by grouping them logically and stating what the experiences you mention are intended to show about you.

Read your draft over once again with a pen in hand and make notes in the margin analyzing what you have written. Look at each fact you have written about yourself and note what that fact is meant to show about you—for example, that you work hard, that you are able to motivate yourself, that you have imagination, or whatever reason you have for mentioning that fact. When you have finished, look over your marginal notes.

> Could you improve your draft by rearranging information and grouping the facts of your life differently?
>
> Should you make more explicit your reasons for mentioning any of the facts of your life?
>
> Is there any other information you would like to add?

On the back of your draft or on another sheet, write down any changes you want to make in the draft, anything you want to keep in mind for your revision, or any additional information you want to consider adding when you revise. Then put the draft and your notes aside.

The following is a request for an autobiographical essay as part of an application for a teaching job outside the United States. The autobiographical statement that follows was written in response to this request.

Application Form

Please write an essay describing yourself that will help us get a better picture of the type of person you are. You might want to include your outside interests and activities, your past experiences and future aspirations, your strengths and weaknesses, or any other aspects of your life.

■ STUDENT WRITING

Applicant's autobiographical statement:

As an adolescent living next to Colombian and Cuban neighbors, I became extremely interested in studying Spanish. Thus, I decided to study Spanish in high school and later to pursue a Bachelor of Arts degree in Spanish literature. During my undergraduate years, I realized to become proficient in Spanish I would have to eventually go to a Spanish speaking country, so I planned my college career appropriately. My freshman year I was determined to save enough money to spend the summer in Guatemala City, Guatemala. After working all year at San Francisco State University's cafeteria, I was prepared to venture to Guatemala. Guatemala only aroused my curiosity more about the world and other cultures. My next goal I chose to conquer was acceptance to the university's Year Abroad Program in Spain. This again required careful planning. I not only had to earn money for the program, but I also had to maintain a good grade point average in order to be eligible.

Once I reached San Sebastian, I set my next goal: to learn to speak and understand Spanish very well and to become a part of the Spanish society. Since I knew Spanish people were not going to appear magically to practice conversing, I realized I had to be assertive and outgoing as well as not be dependent upon my American friends. The best way I knew to learn about the culture and people and to assimilate into society was to live with a Spanish family. Thus, I decided to live with a Spanish working-class family. My decision was one of the best I have ever made. I not only learned Spanish well and some Catalan, but I also acquired a second family. Living with my Spanish family educated me more than any university class I have ever taken. With an open mind and an open heart, I became a member of their family as well as developed an understanding for a different life-style and point of view.

At the same time as my year in Spain, I had the opportunity to meet many international students and to develop some very strong friendships. These friendships lured me to want to travel and learn about their cultures. During our semester breaks, I traveled throughout Europe.

After my junior year abroad, I returned to the university with a desire to see and learn as much about the world as possible. Once I graduated, I decided to return to Spain and find a job teaching English. Within a few weeks of my search, I was hired by Velasquez School where I spent the year teaching by the Direct Method. Even while teaching in Spain, I had my mind on another goal, pursuing a Master's degree in Teaching English as a Second Language. So I applied to a few universities and decided to attend Southern Illinois University, where I am currently completing my degree.

With the M.A. degree in TESL, I would like to teach overseas for several years. Eventually, I would like to pursue a career as a Language Teaching Specialist in the Foreign Service or possibly direct international educational exchanges with universities in the United States and abroad. ■

EXERCISE 9: AUTOBIOGRAPHY

1. What is your impression of this writer? _____

_____

_____

2. What personality traits do you think this writer was trying to emphasize? _____

_____

_____

3. What aspects of his education, work experience, and interests did he try to emphasize? _____

_____

_____

_____

4. How would these traits and experiences help him to get hired? _____

_____

_____

_____

5. For each fact about his life that the writer mentioned, try to figure out what that fact was meant to show.

6. Analyze the organization the writer used by labeling each paragraph to indicate what it discusses. What is each paragraph about?

1. _____

2. _____

3. _____

4. _____

5. _____

Does this order seem effective, or can you suggest some other order? _____

_____

7. Now analyze each paragraph individually. Do all the sentences in the paragraph relate to the main idea (the label you wrote) of that paragraph? Mark any sentences that seem out of place. If you can find a more appropriate place to include that information, use arrows to indicate where you might move the sentence.

8. Look at how the sentences follow one another. Each sentence should be clearly related to the next one and should flow smoothly into it. Use arrows to suggest any changes that might make the sentences flow better. ∎

EXERCISE 10: AUTOBIOGRAPHY

This draft is about 550 words long. Since the application requested a 300-word essay, the draft must be shortened considerably. Keeping in mind that this is an application for a teaching job outside the United States, shorten the essay to fewer than 300 words by deleting any irrelevant information and combining information from several sentences into one sentence. The first few sentences have been done for you. As you shorten this essay, keep in mind the qualities of personality, education, and experience that this writer probably wanted to project to his potential employers.

As an adolescent living next to Colombian and Cuban neighbors, I became extremely interested in studying Spanish. Thus, ~~I decided~~ *after* ~~to study~~ *studying* Spanish in high school, ~~and later~~ *I decided* to pursue a Bachelor of Arts degree in Spanish literature. ~~During my undergraduate years, I realized to become proficient in Spanish I would have to eventually go to a Spanish speaking country, so I planned my college career appropriately. My freshman year I was~~ determined *to go to a Spanish-speaking country,* to save enough money to spend the summer in Guatemala City, Guatemala. ~~After~~ working all year at San Francisco State University~~'s cafeteria, I was prepared to venture to Guatemala.~~ Guatemala only aroused my curiosity more about the world and other cultures. My next goal I chose to conquer was acceptance to the university's Year Abroad Program in Spain. This again required careful planning. I not only had to earn money for the program, but I also had to maintain a good grade point average in order to be eligible.

Once I reached San Sebastian, I set my next goal: to learn to speak and understand Spanish very well and to become a part of the Spanish society. Since I knew Spanish people were not going to appear magically to practice conversing, I realized I had to be assertive and outgoing as well as not be dependent upon my American friends. The best way I knew to learn about the culture and people and to assimilate into society was to live with a Spanish family. Thus, I decided to live with a Spanish working-class family. My decision was one of the best I have ever made. I not only learned Spanish well and some Catalan, but I also acquired a second family. Living with my Spanish family educated me more than any university class I have ever taken. With an open mind and an open heart, I became a member of their family as well as developed an understanding for a different life-style and point of view.

At the same time as my year in Spain, I had the opportunity to meet many international students and to develop some very strong friendships. These friendships lured me to want to travel and learn about their cultures. During our semester breaks, I traveled throughout Europe.

After my junior year abroad, I returned to the university with a desire to see and learn as much about the world as possible. Once I graduated, I decided to return to Spain and find a job teaching English. Within a few weeks of my search, I was hired by Velasquez School where I spent the year teaching by the Direct Method. Even while teaching in Spain, I had my mind on another goal, pursuing a Master's degree in Teaching English as a Second Language. So I applied to a few universities and decided to attend Southern Illinois University, where I am currently completing my degree.

With the M.A. degree in TESL, I would like to teach overseas for several years. Eventually, I would like to pursue a career as a Language Teaching Specialist in the Foreign Service or possibly direct international educational exchanges with universities in the United States and abroad.   ■

                                                                                                                                                       ■

Peer Response

Continuation of
Writing
Assignment 9.2

Take the autobiographical statement you have written and exchange papers with at least one other student. Use the following questions to guide your response to your classmates' papers.

1. What general impression did you get of the writer's personality from this autobiographical statement?
2. What section of the statement was most impressive?
3. What part was most interesting?
4. What part seemed irrelevant, if any?
5. Look at how this draft is organized. How many major sections are there? Label each section to indicate what it discusses. Now look at the labels you wrote. Does the order

in which the material was presented seem effective, or can you suggest some other order?

6. Do the sentences in each paragraph flow smoothly from one to the next, or do any of the sentences seem out of place? If any sections seem out of place, can you suggest somewhere else to include that information?

7. As you consider each fact the writer mentioned, can you see clearly what that fact was intended to show about the writer? Mark any sections whose purpose is not clear to you.

8. What further suggestions could you make to improve this autobiographical statement and make it more effective?

Revision

Using your classmates' analyses of your autobiography, revise what you have written.

Finally, when you are satisfied with the content and organization of your autobiographical sketch, look carefully at the language you used and edit for clarity, conciseness, and grammatical correctness.   ◄

> PART THREE

Applying Writing Processes for Academic Purposes: Analyzing, Evaluating, Arguing

➤ *UNIT FOUR*

Using Published Sources

≻ 10 ≺

Summarizing, Paraphrasing, and Quoting Sources

To prepare for the work in this chapter, write on one of the following journal suggestions.

Journal Suggestions

- Summarize a movie you have recently seen or a novel or story you have read. Write as much as you can in 10 minutes. Then spend 10 more minutes explaining how this book or movie was important to you personally, to society, or in the world of art.
- Summarize a class lecture that you found particularly interesting. Write as much as you can remember of the lecture in 10 minutes. Then spend 10 more minutes explaining what made this lecture so interesting to you.

Now read either "Who Are Smarter—Boys or Girls?" or "Are Men Born with Power?" in the Appendix.

Readings
"Who Are Smarter—Boys or Girls?" page 367
"Are Men Born with Power?" page 371

Then take notes on a separate piece of paper as though you were going to give a report on the article to your classmates.

Now look at the notes you took. You probably used one of three methods to take your notes: summary, paraphrase, or quotation. In this chapter, you will learn how to use all three of these very important ways of referring to published information.

WRITING SUMMARIES

Writing good summaries requires accurate reading and the ability to find the main idea and most important supporting evidence in a piece of writing. Summaries are always quite a bit shorter than the original texts, perhaps 75 percent shorter. Sometimes, particularly for a book, the summary is much shorter than the original, perhaps 99 percent shorter. When you write a summary, you give your readers an idea of the content of an article or book and save them the time and trouble of reading the entire original.

To write a good summary, keep the following in mind:

1. Read the original carefully.

2. Mention the source and the author at the beginning of the summary.

3. State the author's main idea without distorting those ideas or adding your own.

4. State the author's most important supporting evidence or subpoints without distorting them. Do not include details.

5. Use your own wording. Occasionally, however, a phrase in the original may be especially striking, interesting, or controversial. In that case, you may use the author's exact words if you put quotation marks around them.

6. Don't include your own ideas or comments. The summary should include only the author's ideas.

7. Periodically remind the reader that you are summarizing someone else's idea.

The following selection discusses the problems of staying up all night to study for exams. Before you read, answer these questions:

1. What do you think of the idea of staying up all night to study for an exam?

2. What do you think of using stimulants to help stay alert?

3. Do you think students usually recover well from staying up all night?

4. Have you ever stayed up all night studying for an exam?

> How did you feel during the exam? How did you feel the rest of the day? How well did you do on the exam?

Now read the selection quickly to get the main idea.

■ PROFESSIONAL WRITING

The Dangers of Cramming

Midnight, and the spiral notebook is barely half full. The rest of its pages, scribbled with organic chemistry equations, litter the dorm-room floor. Every few minutes the figure hunched over the desk tears away another page, having memorized as much as he can, and passes it on to his friend. And thus the two roommates continue all night, dropping the pages to the carpet after each has absorbed his fill.

Welcome to the all-night cramming session, which most students resort to at some desperate point in their college careers. Armed with the energy of youth, they simply ignore their bodies' cries for sleep, trying to fend off fatigue with doses of coffee or, occasionally, drugs. Teachers and parents have long argued that cramming does more harm than good—and the latest research into sleep needs and patterns suggests that they are right.

For some people, disruptions in the regular sleep cycle can cause temporary intellectual lapses—and stimulants can set off severe side effects. Thus, for every student who manages to memorize the chemical synthesis of bona-S-rubber at 5 A.M. and then triumphantly finds that precise question on his test at 9, there are more than a few who lament the "obvious" answers they blew on a multiple-choice exam because they "just couldn't focus."

The outcome of all-nighters is unpredictable because the impact of sleep loss varies so widely. "Some people are markedly impaired by even a small decrease in sleep time," says David Buchholtz, a neurologist and sleep therapist at The Johns Hopkins Hospital in Baltimore, "while others can go without sleep for a few nights without any demonstrable loss of performance." People also have vastly different minimum requirements: a full night's rest can range from 4 to 10 hours. It is critical, experts stress, for each person to know how much sleep he needs.

Heavy use of stimulants can compound the problem. Many students assume that large quantities of coffee or a few amphetamines will increase alertness; they don't. In fact, stimulants merely disguise—briefly—a reduced capacity to grasp, retain, and retrieve information. "Caffeine does not correct the cognitive impairment caused by lost sleep," Buchholtz says. "A person may be awake, but he'll have to deal with an intellectual deficit, and his concentration won't be there. He can actually have 'microsleeps' and stare at the same word for five minutes."

Nor are unpredictable naps the only penalty of substance abuse. Coffee drinkers should watch out for Caffeine Intoxication Syndrome, an onset of anxiety, panic, headaches and a frustrating inability to sleep. Most people would have to drink about 10 cups to fall into this condition, but some are so sensitive that it can hit them after only 2 to 3 cups. Speed [an amphetamine] is far more hazardous. Overdoses can lead to auditory hallucinations and paranoia. In addition, according to Larry Alessi, assistant professor of psychiatry at The Johns Hopkins Medical School, "if someone uses speed for many weeks and then stops, he may 'crash' into severe depression."

Unless a person abuses his body with stimulants, he should be able to snap back fairly quickly from an all-nighter. One full night of rest will usually produce complete recovery from up to 48 hours of sleep deprivation; normal, healthy people have been known to stay awake for as long as a week without lasting ill effects. On the second night, there is usually an increase in REM (rapid eye movement) sleep, the phase in which dreaming occurs. Normally, REM sleep is beneficial, but some people report particularly graphic and disturbing nightmares associated with a sudden increase in REM.

Then there are the problems of students who want to get a good night's sleep before an exam but just can't. Stress often promotes insomnia. It may cause the reticular activating system, the structure in the brain that is responsible for alertness, to stay on too long; this prevents sleep-inducing mechanisms from doing their job. What do experts advise a student who finds himself tossing and turning for a half hour or so on the eve of a test? He should get up and try an ordinarily relaxing activity, like snacking or watching television, until he is tired. Some people find that making notes about what's worrying them can exorcise those concerns until the morning.

Sleeping too *much*, authorities agree, should not worry most people. Even after an extended night of "rebound" sleep, the brain arouses itself when its needs have been fulfilled. Clinically depressed people do often retreat into slumber to avoid the waking hours, but true clinical depression is accompanied by other noticeable symptoms such as loss of appetite, decreased self-esteem and even thoughts of suicide.

In the end, the best formula to follow when finals arrive is one that students have been taught for years—moderation. There will surely be times when excelling, or perhaps just passing, requires pushing bedtime back, but any major changes in sleep patterns should be made cautiously. As Buchholtz suggests, "The key is keeping perspective and not ever overdoing it."

(Keith Ablow, *Newsweek on Campus*
May 1985, p.9)   ■

EXERCISE 1: SUMMARY

Now read the selection again and summarize it in one sentence of not more than 25 words. As with most summaries, use the present tense. (You needn't mention the name of the author or the title of the article yet.)

_____

_____

_____

Write several of the one-sentence summaries from the class on the board. Choose the best ones. Here is one possibility:

Staying up all night to study, especially with the help of stimulants, does not help you learn and can have negative side effects.

Next, label each paragraph with a subheading indicating the subject discussed in that paragraph. The first three paragraphs have been done for you.

1 introduction—description of a cramming session

2 cramming, more harm than good

3 temporary mental lapses

4 _____

5 _____

6 _____

7 _____

8 _____

9 _____

10 _____

When you have finished, compare your subheadings with those of your classmates. If the headings for any paragraph are quite different from one another, reread that paragraph and select the heading that best states the subject of the paragraph.

Which paragraph seems to state the main point the author wants to make in this article? Paragraph _____

Write that main point or thesis here. _____

_____

Now look at your list of subheadings and group together headings that deal with similar subjects. Give each grouping a name.

How many paragraphs seem to make up the introduction? _____

What are the other groupings you formed?

_____

_____

_____

_____

_____

∎

Now write a short summary (100 to 150 words) of this arti-cle. Remember that the summary should be in the present tense. Begin by mentioning the original source. Here are possible ways to include the source.

In his article entitled "The Dangers of Cramming," Keith Ablow $\left\{ \begin{array}{l} \text{informs us} \\ \text{states} \\ \text{claims} \\ \text{shows us} \end{array} \right\}$ that . . .

Or:

In "The Dangers of Cramming," Keith Ablow $\left\{ \begin{array}{l} \text{indicates} \\ \text{discusses} \\ \text{explores} \end{array} \right\}$ the problems . . .

Or:

The article "The Dangers of Cramming" by Keith Ablow exam-ines the negative effects . . .

Or:

Cramming, according to Keith Ablow in his article "The Dangers of Cramming," can do more harm than good.

(Note the correct punctuation and capitalization of the citation.)
Continue the summary, using your list of subheadings and your groupings as a guide to help you remember the main points covered in the article. At least once in your summary, remind your readers that you are summarizing by using a phrase like the following:

The author goes on to say . . .

Or:

Ablow also reports that . . .

Or:

The article further states that . . .

EXERCISE 2: SUMMARY

Now read the following summaries of this article. Each summary has good features, and each also has some weaknesses. Look back to the beginning of this section to review the points to keep in mind when writing a summary. After you have finished reading each summary, list its strong and weak features. Use the following checklist.
A good summary should do the following:

- Include a mention of the source.
- Correctly interpret the original.
- Include no editorial comments.
- Include only the most important points, without details.
- Use the summarizer's own words, not those of the original author (unless in quotation marks).

Summary 1

In "The Dangers of Cramming," Keith Ablow explains that students who try to stay up all night studying for exams are probably doing themselves more harm than good. Most of these students did not bother to study hard enough during the term and when exams come they feel they have to try to catch up and learn everything all at once. The problem with disrupting normal sleep patterns in this way is that the students may fall into a temporary intellectual lapse, and after the exam the next day they lament the obvious answers they blew because they just couldn't focus. Ablow points out that using stimulants to stay awake can be dangerous because they can cause unexpected side effects. On the other hand, most young people can recover from an "all-nighter" with one good night's sleep. Some students suffer from not being able to fall asleep when they are nervous and others may worry about sleeping too much, but the author advises moderation and regular sleeping habits as the best formula.

Summary 2

Contrary to what many students think, staying up all night to study for an exam is not very efficient. Such a disruption in sleeping habits can actually make the student less mentally alert the next day and cause "microsleeps," in which the student cannot concentrate. Taking drugs to help stay awake can cause "Caffeine Intoxication Syndrome" with accompanying headaches and feelings of anxiety, according to neurologist and sleep therapist David Buchholtz of The Johns Hopkins Hospital in Baltimore. Although for most people it would probably take at least 10 cups of coffee to produce this syndrome, some people are so sensitive that they can develop unpleasant side effects with only 2 or 3 cups of coffee. In most young people other kinds of sleep disorders are rare or temporary and one good night's sleep can get them back to normal. As with many other things, the best advice is to not make major and drastic changes in sleeping habits and always think in terms of moderation.

Summary 3

According to Keith Ablow in "The Dangers of Cramming," if you stay up all night trying to study for an exam, you may find yourself the next morning actually less prepared for the exam than if you had just gone to bed, gotten a good night's sleep, and taken your chances with the exam. The reason is that major disruptions in sleep patterns can cause a lack of mental alertness, so that even if you studied for the exam you may not be able to remember much the next day. Furthermore, no matter what people say about not needing much sleep, scientists know that everyone needs a good night's sleep before a big day, usually 7–9 hours. Stimulants used to help students stay up all night may trick the students into feeling awake even when their minds are going to sleep on them and they stare vacantly for minutes at a time. In addition, even mild stimulants such as caffeine can cause unpleasant side effects if taken in too great a quantity. Moderation is the watch word. Study during the whole term, not just before the exam; you are sure to do better in school if you don't overdo it.

Summary 1

Strong features	**Weak features**

Summary 2

Strong features	**Weak features**

Summary 3

Strong features	**Weak features**

Now look at your own summary again. List its strong and weak features just as you did for the sample summaries.

Strong features	**Weak features**

■

➤ *Writing Assignment 10.1: Summary of "Who Are Smarter—Boys or Girls?" or "Are Men Born with Power?"*

Writing
Assignment 10.1

In academic courses, teachers often ask students to read material and then to summarize what they have read. What do you

imagine is the purpose of such an assignment? _____

_____

_____

Use the summarizing procedure outlined in this section to write a summary of either "Who Are Smarter—Boys or Girls?" (page 367) or "Are Men Born with Power?" (page 371). Remember that the first step in writing a summary is reading the original carefully until you feel you understand it. You may also want to refer to the notes you took earlier on this selection (page 185). Your summary should be about 100 to 150 words long and should show that you understood the argument in the selection.

When you have finished, exchange summaries with a classmate. Evaluate each other's summaries, using the following questions as a guide.

Peer Response

1. Is the source given correctly at the beginning of the summary?
2. Do you agree with your classmate's notion of the main idea of the selection?
3. How did your classmate express the main idea?
4. How did you express it?
5. Are the main supporting subtopics included in your classmate's summary?
6. What are they?
7. Are there details that can be eliminated? If so, mark those sections on your classmate's paper.
8. Do you have the impression that your classmate understood the selection? If not, indicate the sections that you feel show misinterpretations.

Summary Revision

When you have finished answering the peer response questions, rewrite the summary your classmate wrote. In your revision, make any corrections you feel are necessary. Give the revised version to your classmate, who will rewrite the summary, taking into account your comments and your revised version.   ◄

➤ *Writing Assignment 10.2: Summary of Classmate's Writing*

Writing
Assignment 10.2

Take an essay written by one of your classmates. Following the same procedure, summarize the essay in 100 to 150 words. Then give the summary to the classmate who wrote the essay. He or she will read your summary and answer the following questions.

Original Author's Response

1. Did your classmate cite your name and the name of your essay correctly? If not, make the necessary corrections.
2. Did your classmate accurately state your main points? If not, correct any misinterpretations you found.
3. Are there details in the summary that could be eliminated?
4. Is the summary between 100 and 150 words long?   ◄

WRITING PARAPHRASES

Often in doing academic work, you will find yourself needing information from material in the library to use in some form in a paper or report you are writing. Paraphrasing is using your own words to report someone else's material or ideas. A paraphrase allows you to use another writer's material to support a point you are making in your own work without using the other writer's exact wording. You will probably use paraphrasing when you want to change the style or the language used in the original, either to make it easier to understand or to make it fit better into your own piece of writing. Unlike a summary, a paraphrase is usually about the same length as the original, but both the words and the sentence structure of the original must be changed in a paraphrase.

Here is part of a paper on the problems of getting rid of toxic waste. In this section of the paper, the writer is trying to show that burning waste has negative effects on the environment.

. . . While it is obvious that poisonous materials which may be the by-products of manufacturing must be destroyed somehow, we must be very careful of how we destroy them. Otherwise, we might produce disastrous effects on the environment. We cannot simply burn waste and let the smoke pollute the air.

At this point, the writer needs specific facts to support her claims. She wants to use information from an article entitled "Storing up Trouble: Hazardous Waste" in *National Geographic* in March 1985. The article includes a report on the efforts of a woman named Verna Courtemanche to close down a hazardous waste incinerator near her town. The plant, which was operated by a man named Charles Berlin, was badly polluting the atmosphere. This is the section that the writer wants to use in her paper.

> "In 1972 Berlin and a partner opened a hazardous waste incinerator. Often it was overloaded, smothering the countryside in acrid smoke so dark and dense that firemen on the horizon would take it for blazing houses and race over."

In order to incorporate this information from the article in her paper, the writer first has to change what she has written so that the new information will fit smoothly.

> . . . While it is obvious that poisonous materials which may be the by-products of manufacturing must be destroyed somehow, we must be very careful of how we destroy them. Otherwise, we may find ourselves in a situation like that of a small town in New England in 1972, when . . .

Complete this sentence by paraphrasing just the first simple sentence from the article. Be sure to change both the words and

the structure of the original sentence. _____

_____

You may have written something like this:

> . . . when a plant, owned and operated by Charles Berlin and another man, was built to burn hazardous waste.

Notice that *hazardous waste* does not have to be changed because this is a technical expression. Although you must normally change the original wording, you may use a technical term from the original if there is no word to substitute for it.

EXERCISE 3: PARAPHRASING
The second sentence from the article is more complicated:

> "Often it was overloaded, smothering the countryside in acrid smoke so dark and dense that firemen on the horizon would take it for blazing houses and race over."

To paraphrase this sentence, you can try one of two methods.

1. Read the sentence several times carefully to make sure you understand the meaning. Then cover up the sentence and try writing down the substance of the sentence from memory in your own words.

   _____

   _____

   Now check the original. Did you leave anything important

   out? If so, add it. _____

   _____

   Did you use exactly the same words as the original? If so,

   change them. _____

   _____

   If this method works for you, use it. If not, try the following method.

2. Begin the sentence differently and change all the nouns, verbs, adjectives, and adverbs you can as you complete the sentence. You can also break one long sentence into shorter ones or combine ideas in short sentences into one longer one. Complete the following sentence beginnings by paraphrasing the original in four different ways.

   1. Sometimes firemen _____

      _____

   2. Because Berlin put too much waste in his incinerator,

      _____

   3. The incinerator often _____

      _____

4. The country surrounding the factory _____

_____

∎

Now complete the paragraph by adding your paraphrases of the information from the *National Geographic* article.

. . . While it is obvious that poisonous materials which may be the by-products of manufacturing must be destroyed somehow, we must be very careful of how we destroy them. Otherwise, we may find ourselves in a situation like that of a small town in New England in 1972, when . . .

Compare your solutions with those of your classmates.

For practice using the paraphrasing methods described above, paraphrase the following six sentences so that they form a paragraph or two. All of these sentences come from the article describing Charles Berlin's hazardous waste incinerator and Verna Courtemanche's fight to force the government to close the plant. Some of the vocabulary is quite difficult. Be sure you understand the meaning of the original sentences before you try to paraphrase them. Begin your paragraph with this sentence:

Living in the vicinity of Berlin's dump site soon became intolerable.

Continue by altering the words and sentence structures of the original to form a coherent paragraph:

1. The corrosive fumes turned convertible car tops into rags, reddened children's faces with rash, and swelled their eyes shut.
2. Citizens living near the incinerator and its foul lagoons saw the value of their homes crash and believe that their health is threatened.
3. Verna Courtemanche . . . led a decade-long fight to get federal and state government to intervene and begin a cleanup.
4. Verna and friends harried state officials by phone, rally, and letter for four years before Berlin's noxious dump site was permanently closed.
5. The owner of the facility, when faced with legal action, abandoned the site and declared bankruptcy.
6. Illegally buried containers unearthed by cleanup crews

near the incinerator held a witches' brew of cyanide, pesticides, acids, and PCBs.

Sometimes the original may contain a nontechnical expression that you find particularly striking. In that case, you do not need to change that special expression, but put quotation marks around it to show that you are using exactly the same words as the original. In the preceding exercise, for example, what words did you use to express the idea of "a witches' brew"

in sentence 6? _____

_____

If you found the expression striking, you might leave it as it is. In that case, paraphrase the rest of the sentence and put quotation marks around the expression you are retaining from the original.

EXERCISE 4: PARAPHRASING
Rewrite sentence 6 here, retaining the expression "a witches' brew."

6. _____

_____

Do not quote excessively because more than one or two quotations like this become distracting for the reader.

USING QUOTATIONS

In summarizing and paraphrasing, you use your own words to explain or report someone else's ideas. In quoting, you use not only another author's ideas or material but also that author's exact words. Writers quote sources rather than paraphrase them when the original wording is particularly striking or interesting or when they want the reader to know exactly what another writer has written.

Quoting a source is somewhat complicated because of all the conventions that must be followed. In the simplest form, when you use someone else's exact words, you put quotation marks (two, not one) on either side of the quoted material. In the preceding exercise, you paraphrased sentences from an original source. You might also have quoted the original instead of paraphrasing. Here is an example of how to punctuate a quotation.

> Living in the vicinity of Berlin's dump site soon became intolerable. According to a National Geographic report, "The corrosive fumes turned convertible car tops into rags, reddened children's faces with rash, and swelled their eyes shut. Citizens living near the incinerator and its foul lagoons saw the value of their homes crash and believe that their health is threatened."

Notice that the quotation marks are placed around the entire quotation, not around individual sentences. Also, the quotation marks are placed *after* the final period.

Quotation marks always appear immediately before and after the quoted words. They can never stand alone at the beginning of a line, like this:

> "Citizens living near the incinerator and its foul lagoons saw the value of their homes crash and believe that their health is threatened.
> "

Sometimes when you are quoting a source, you may find that you don't need all the words the original used. When this is the case, you may skip a few words in a sentence or even a few sentences in a paragraph. To show where you left material out, use three dots, or ellipsis points.

> Living in the vicinity of Berlin's dump site soon became intolerable. According to a National Geographic report, "The corrosive fumes turned convertible car tops into rags, reddened children's faces with rash, and swelled their eyes shut. Citizens . . . saw the value of their homes crash. . . ."

If you want to quote several sentences from a paragraph but not all of them, use ellipsis points between the sentences you quote to show where other sentences have not been included. Ellipsis points tell the reader that material is missing.

Sometimes when material is left out, the remaining words do not fit smoothly into your own text. In order to create a smooth fit, you will need to manipulate your own text and/or eliminate words from the quotation. How might you manipulate the paragraph above, for example, if you wanted to add the following information:

> "Verna and friends harried state officials by phone, rally, and letter for four years before Berlin's noxious dump site was permanently closed."

Here is one possibility:

> Living in the vicinity of Berlin's dump site soon became intolerable. According to a National Geographic report, "The corrosive

fumes turned convertible car tops into rags, reddened children's faces with rash, and swelled their eyes shut. Citizens living near the incinerator and its foul lagoons saw the value of their homes crash and believe that their health is threatened." In an effort to close the plant, townspeople "harried state officials by phone, rally, and letter. . . ."

When only a few words of the original are particularly striking, you may quote just those words and paraphrase the rest of the sentence.

When work crews finally arrived to clean up the dump site, they found metal cans buried underground filled with "a witches' brew" of deadly chemicals.

Occasionally, it may be necessary to insert a word or two into the quoted material in order to clarify the quotation for the reader. This happens rarely, but it may be done by putting brackets around the one or two added words.

In an effort to close the plant, "Verna [Courtemanche] and friends harried state officials by phone, rally, and letter for four years. . . ."

The brackets indicate that you, the writer of the article, have added your own words to a quotation taken from another source.

Finally, if you are quoting more than about 50 words or three lines, separate the quoted lines from your own text by indenting the entire quote, as in the following example. Notice that when the quotation is set off in this way, quotation marks are not used.

The corrosive fumes turned convertible car tops into rags, reddened children's faces with rash, and swelled their eyes shut. Citizens living near the incinerator and its foul lagoons saw the value of their homes crash and believe that their health is threatened. Outdoor activity eventually became restricted to walking between house and car, so repulsive and potentially dangerous was the air.

In typewritten compositions, the entire quotation is indented five spaces on both the left and the right side and centered on the page. The quotation is often single-spaced to set it off even more from the rest of the text.

It is important to follow the formal conventions for quoting and paraphrasing, but it is even more important to develop a sense of when to summarize, paraphrase, or quote material from a printed source. What you do will depend mainly on your assignment. If you are asked, for example, to report on a particular article or book, you will probably summarize most of it, paraphrase especially important points, and quote sections that not only are important but that have been written in an especially striking way.

On the other hand, when you are asked to develop your own ideas, you may use another writer's material to support your ideas. Apply the same criteria you use when you are selecting supporting material from your own experience and observations. But remember that it is still your paper. It should not become simply a collection of ideas and quotations from other sources. Use paraphrases and quotations to support your points, not to substitute for them.

Be sure you understand your assignment. You may want to consult with your professor about whether you are expected merely to report someone else's ideas or to develop your own, supporting them with outside sources, or perhaps to combine a report with your own evaluation.

Even when you are merely reporting on someone else's material, use quotations sparingly—only when the exact wording of the original is particularly striking or important. Otherwise, paraphrase the ideas in your own words.

SEQUENCED WRITING PROJECT: SUMMARIES

Sequenced Writing Project

If you are doing the Sequenced Writing Project, in this assignment you will look for three pieces of publicly available published material to summarize. The published material may be articles in journals, newspapers, or pamphlets, or even visual material, such as videos. Locate three publications you think will give you information that will be helpful in your final project report. You may have to locate more than three and select the best ones.

This assignment has two main parts:

1. a straightforward summary of the three documents, and
2. a framework for the summaries. The framework is a normal introductory paragraph and a concluding paragraph in which you briefly discuss the three documents together, perhaps linking the most important or interesting information you obtained from your three sources.

Follow the directions in this chapter on writing summaries, paraphrasing, and quoting; the directions in Chapter 7 on writing introductions and conclusions; and the directions in Chapter 9 on showing the relationship between ideas to create a coherent whole. You should, for example, decide which document you will summarize first, second, and third and provide some logical link between the summaries—for example, mentioning that the next summary contains a different type of information from the last, or elaborates on the information from the last, or approaches the topic from a different perspective. Remember to include a thesis statement in the introduction that will make it clear what the point of this paper is with its three summaries. This may prove to be quite a challenge, and you may wish to get extra help from your classmates or professor.

When you finish your paper, ask a classmate to read it.

Peer Response

1. Was the writer successful in linking the three document summaries together in one paper with a clear main point? If not, where do you see problems?
2. Are the three sources given correctly in each summary?
3. Did the information from the sources seem important, interesting, or useful? If not, where do you see problems?
4. Does it seem that paraphrases and quotations were used well? If not, where do you see possible problems?

This assignment in the Sequenced Writing Project continues at the end of Chapter 11, where you are directed to create a bibliography for your sources.

> 11 <

Documenting Sources

When you use material from an outside source in your writing, you must cite the source. In this chapter, you will learn the basics of how to document published sources in your own work.

HOW NOT TO PLAGIARIZE

You should first understand something about using published sources. What authors write, their ideas and their words, are considered to be their property, in a sense, just like a coat or a car. If you want to use someone else's property, you must ask to borrow it. If you want to use someone else's ideas or words, it is considered extremely important in English writing to "give credit," that is, to say exactly who wrote these words or ideas, and when and where they were written. If you do not follow the conventions of quoting and giving credit, you are considered to be stealing, or *plagiarizing*, someone else's ideas or words. Plagiarism is considered quite a serious offense; in some cases, plagiarism is actually a crime.

Students sometimes say that they use an author's words because the author writes better than the students feel they can. You may use another author's words as long as you make it clear that these words were first used by that author. Remember, however, that quotations should always be used sparingly.

This section will demonstrate how to use and cite another author's material. First look at the following paragraph from an article by David P. Barash called "What to Tell Children About Nuclear War." The article appeared on page 85 of *Science Digest* in July 1986.

■ PROFESSIONAL WRITING

A study by psychiatrists William Beardslee and John Mack has shown that American children become aware of nuclear war before age 12. Among older children, one half say this awareness affects their plans for marriage and the future. The Beardslee and Mack study, based on questionnaires given to hundreds of school-age children, shows that in the group examined, a significant number were "deeply disturbed" about the nuclear threat, profoundly pessimistic, and often just plain scared.   ■

Here are some correct and incorrect examples of using and documenting this original source.

Version 1
The Beardslee and Mack study, based on questionnaires given to hundreds of school-age children, shows that in the group examined, a significant number were "deeply disturbed" about the nuclear threat, profoundly pessimistic, and often just plain scared.

This version uses the exact wording from the original without quotation marks around the sentence, and there is no citation to show where this statement comes from. This is the most obvious form of plagiarism.

Version 2
The Beardslee and Mack study, based on questionnaires given to hundreds of school-age children, shows that in the group examined, a significant number were "deeply disturbed" about the nuclear threat, profoundly pessimistic, and often just plain scared (Barash 85).

In this version, the student added a citation. But the citation alone is not enough since the student still used the exact words of the original. Both the quotation marks and the citation are necessary.

Version 3
Hundreds of school-age children were given questionnaires. The results showed that a significant number were profoundly pessimistic and often just plain scared (Barash 85).

Although there is a citation and some of the wording has been changed, this version still plagiarizes the original. There are whole phrases that are written in the original form, not in the student's own words.

Version 4
"Hundreds of school-age children were given questionnaires. The results showed that a significant number were profoundly pessimistic and often just plain scared" (Barash 85).

This version is not plagiarism, but it is incorrect. Quotation marks must not be used unless all the words within the quotation marks are exactly the same as the original. In this version, some of the wording is different and therefore should not be enclosed in quotation marks.

Version 5
"The Beardslee and Mack study, based on questionnaires given to hundreds of school-age children, shows that in the group examined, a significant number were 'deeply disturbed' about the nuclear threat, profoundly pessimistic, and often just plain scared" (Barash 85).

This version is formally correct. The quotation marks are used to show that the original material was quoted exactly, and the citation indicates the source of the original material. Notice that the words "deeply disturbed" are set off with single quotation marks to show that they appeared within quotes in the original text. Although this version is formally correct, however, the words and phrases in this quotation are not so striking that the whole passage is worth quoting exactly.

Version 6
According to research by Beardslee and Mack many young children in this country are quite frightened about the real possibility of a nuclear war. This fear has made many of these children pessimistic about the future (Barash 85).

This version is correct, and it is preferable to the previous version. Here the student used her own words to paraphrase the wording in the original article, and she also cited her source so that anyone who wants to can look up the original and read the complete article.

Version 7
As a result of their study of hundreds of children, researchers Beardslee and Mack have come to the conclusion that "in the group examined, a significant number were 'deeply disturbed' about the nuclear threat, profoundly pessimistic, and often just plain scared" (Barash 85).

This version is also correct. Here the student combined her own paraphrasing with a quotation of the most striking part of the original text. She made certain her words and those taken directly from the source fit together; she quoted accurately and cited her source.

HOW TO USE CITATIONS

If you paraphrase an idea, summarize an article or even a paragraph, or quote a fact, statistic, example, anecdote, or anything else someone else said or wrote, you must give that person credit. There are several systems currently used in academic and nonacademic writing to document a source; before you write a paper for a course, you should find out what conventions are used by that academic discipline. The system shown here, the style of the Modern Language Association (MLA), is fairly common and simple. (Another widely used system is that of the American Psychological Association, or APA. Consult your professor to find out whether the MLA system is acceptable or whether you must use APA or some other system.) The MLA system of documentation consists of two parts:

1. Within your paper, you must cite or indicate very briefly the original source for the information by putting the author's last name and the page on which this material appeared in parentheses after your paraphrase, summary, or quotation. Note the citation for the following paraphrase of another's idea.

> American children even under the age of 12 know about and are afraid of nuclear war (Barash 85).
>
> LAST NAME   PAGE NUMBER

Here is an example of a quotation and its citation.

> "Among older children, one half say this awareness affects their plans for marriage and the future" (Barash 85).
>
> LAST NAME   PAGE NUMBER

Note that the period goes after the citation, while the quotation marks go after the last word quoted.

If there is no author, use a shortened form of the title of the article in the citation. For example, the citation for an unsigned article entitled "Faking the Red Menace," which appears on page 1 of a journal called *Nation*, would look like this:

> (Faking 1)

If your school has a student paper, get a copy for each person in class and together decide how different articles from that paper would be cited.

2. At the end of your paper, you must include a bibliography listing all the original sources you paraphrased, summarized, quoted, and in some instances merely consulted in your paper. There are two basic formats for the bibliography entries.

For an article appearing in a periodical or journal:

Shawcross, William. "Playing by the Hama Rules."

LAST NAME, FIRST NAME.   "NAME OF ARTICLE."

<u>Rolling Stone</u> 6 Dec. 1984: 33–36, 64–69.

NAME OF MAGAZINE DATE: PAGE NUMBERS.

For a book:

Roszak, Theodore. <u>The Making of a Counter Culture.</u>

LAST NAME, FIRST NAME. *TITLE OF BOOK.*

Garden City, New York: Anchor Books, 1969.

CITY OF
PUBLICATION   PUBLISHER, DATE.
(AND STATE IF THE   (SHORTEST
CITY IS NOT WELL KNOWN): RECOGNIZABLE NAME)

Here are two examples of the use of published material, one a paraphrase and the other a quotation. Note how the original sources are cited.

Original from a periodical (i.e., a magazine, journal, or newspaper article):

> "The claim by conservatives that media coverage is skewed to the left has been aired repeatedly by the very networks and newspapers that are the targets of the charge."

Paraphrase and citation:

> Conservatives complain that media are too liberal, and yet the same news organizations that are being criticized are the ones who are broadcasting the attacks (Reynolds 6).

Original from a book:

"Technology will help us manage the information society only to the extent that its members are skilled in utilizing it."

Quotation and citation:

"Technology will help us manage the information society only to the extent that its members are skilled in utilizing it" (Naisbitt 26).

Bibliography entries for these two sources would look like this:

Bibliography

Naisbitt, John. <u>Megatrends</u>. New York: Warner Books, 1984.
Reynolds, Richard. "Not Ready for Prime Time." <u>Mother Jones</u>
　　　Aug./Sep. 1985: 6-8.

The bibliography appears at the end of the paper, on a separate sheet. The entries are listed in alphabetical order by author's last name, which is flush with the left margin. If the entry is more than one line long, all the lines after the first one are indented five spaces.

Here are examples of how to document other kinds of material in your bibliography. Skim this section to familiarize yourself with the kinds of examples included, and return to this section when you cannot remember the detailed conventions for documenting sources.

For a source with no author:

"Taking Shots at the Shoot-Out: World Cup." <u>Newsweek</u> 7 July
　　　1986: 14-15.

(When no author is given, the article is listed in the bibliography in alphabetical order according to the first letter of the title.)

For a source with two authors:

Aronowitz, Stanley, and Henry Giroux. <u>Education Under Siege</u>.
　　　South Hadley, Mass.: Bergin and Garvey, 1985.

(Note that only the first author's name is listed last name first.)

For a source with three authors:

Ellis, Mark, Nina O'Driscoll, and Adrian Pilbeam. <u>Professional
　　　English</u>. London: Longman, 1984.

For a source with more than three authors:

Hughey, Jane B., et al. <u>Teaching ESL Composition</u>. Rowley, Mass.: Newbury House, 1983.

(Note: *et al.* means "and others.")

For a text appearing in an anthology:

Olsen, Tillie. "Tell Me A Riddle." <u>The Experience of the American Woman</u>. Ed. Barbara H. Solomon. New York: Mentor, 1978. 313-47.

For an article in an encyclopedia:

"Quantum theory." <u>New Columbia Encyclopedia</u>. 1975 ed.

(Note that page numbers are not necessary since articles in encyclopedias appear in alphabetical order.)

For a newspaper article:

Roth, Norm. "Tale of Two Cities--Two Strikes." <u>Labor Today</u> [Chicago] Oct./Nov. 1986, sec. A: 10-11.

(Note that the name of the city is included in brackets if it does not appear in the title of the newspaper.)

For editions after the first:

Charters, Ann. <u>The Story and Its Writer</u>. 2nd ed. New York: St. Martin's, 1986.

For reprints:

Sheehy, Gail. <u>Passages</u>. 1976. New York: Bantam, 1977.

(This book was originally published by one publisher in hardback in 1976, and then reprinted by another publisher in 1977. Note that only the date of the first publication is necessary, not the name of the original publisher.)

For an unpublished manuscript:

Wang, Wanling. "Differences Between Chinese and American Shoppers." Unpublished manuscript, 1993.

For more information on documentation formats, see handbooks for your particular academic field or ask instructors in your major.

Following are descriptions of a variety of sources. Prepare a bibliography using whatever information from the descriptions you need to write a correct entry for each source. All the titles appear in capital letters; indicate each title correctly in your entry, capitalizing and using italics or quotation marks as necessary. Begin your bibliography on a separate sheet labeled "Bibliography" at the top.

1. This article was entitled *The Negotiation Waltz.* It was written by John Greenward and appeared in *Time* magazine on pages 41–42 in the August 1, 1983, issue of volume 122, number 5.

2. This unsigned article appeared in *The Daily Beacon*, published at the University of Tennessee in Knoxville, Tennessee, on Monday, February 6, 1984. It was entitled *Crime Bills up for Debate* and was on page 2, columns 6 and 7.

3. This book was written by Ken Kesey and copyrighted in 1962. It was entitled *One Flew Over the Cuckoo's Nest* and was published by Signet Publishing Company in New York, New York. It was 272 pages long.

4. This story entitled *The Secret Sharer* was written by Joseph Conrad, and it appeared in the third edition of a book edited by Lynn Altenbernd and Leslie L. Lewis entitled *Introduction to Literature: Stories*. The book was published in 1980 in New York by Macmillan Publishing Co., Inc. The story appeared on pages 97–126.

EXERCISE 1: CITATION
Now prepare a citation for each source for the page or section indicated.

1. page 42 _____

2. column 7 _____

3. page 131 _____

4. page 115 _____

Check your answers against the answers to these exercises in Appendix C. ∎

EXERCISE 2: CITATION
In the next exercise you will practice quoting, paraphrasing, summarizing, and citing. The following is an excerpt from pages 1–2 of a book by Michael Harrington called *The Other America*, in which Harrington discusses poverty in the United States. The book was first published in 1962 by the Macmillan Company;

this excerpt is taken from the edition published by Pelican Books in New York in 1971. First read the excerpt quickly to get the main idea of each paragraph.

■ PROFESSIONAL WRITING

(page 1)

There is a familiar America. It is celebrated in speeches and advertised on television and in the magazines. It has the highest mass standard of living the world has ever known.

In the 1950's this America worried about itself, yet even its anxi-
5   eties were products of abundance. The title of a brilliant book [*The Affluent Society*, by John Kenneth Galbraith] was widely misinterpreted, and the familiar America began to call itself "the affluent society." There was introspection about Madison Avenue and tail fins; there was discussion of the emotional suffering taking place in the
10 suburbs. In all this, there was an implicit assumption that the basic grinding economic problems had been solved in the United States. In this theory the nation's problems were no longer a matter of basic human needs, of food, shelter, and clothing. Now they were seen as qualitative, a question of learning to live decently amid luxury. While
15 this discussion was carried on, there existed another America. In it dwelt somewhere between 40,000,000 and 50,000,000 citizens of this land. They were poor. They still are.

To be sure, the other America is not impoverished in the same sense as those poor nations where millions cling to hunger as a de-
20 fense against starvation. This country has escaped such extremes.

(page 2)

That does not change the fact that tens of millions of Americans are, at this very moment, maimed in body and spirit, existing at levels beneath those necessary for human decency. If these people are not starving, they are hungry, and sometimes fat with hunger, for that is
25 what cheap foods do. They are without adequate housing and education and medical care.

The Government has documented what this means to the bodies of the poor, and the figures will be cited throughout this book. But even more basic, this poverty twists and deforms the spirit. The
30 American poor are pessimistic and defeated, and they are victimized by mental suffering to a degree unknown in Suburbia.   ■

1. Quote the sentence beginning on line 28 and cite it correctly.
2. Paraphrase the sentence beginning on line 18 and cite it.
3. Use a combination of direct quotation and paraphrase of the sentence beginning on line 21 and cite it.
4. Prepare a bibliography entry for this book.
5. Summarize this text in 50 to 75 words.   ■

When you use information from published material be sure to cite and document whatever you use carefully and accurately.

SEQUENCED WRITING PROJECT: BIBLIOGRAPHY (Continued from Chapter 10)

Sequenced Writing
Project

Following directions in this chapter, write a bibliography for the three sources you summarized in Chapter 10. Be sure to begin your bibliography on a separate page.

➤ *UNIT FIVE*

Academic Writing Tasks

$\succ 12 \prec$

Analyzing Issues

In several of the assignments in this chapter you will be asked to write about education. To prepare for these assignments, consider writing on one or more of the following suggestions.

Journal Suggestions

- Stephen Hawking, a brilliant scientist, has said this about his experience at the university:

  > The prevailing attitude at Oxford at that time was very anti-work. You were supposed to be brilliant without effort, or to accept your limitations and get a fourth class degree. To work hard to get a better class of degree was regarded as the mark of a gray man—the worst epithet in the Oxford vocabulary.
  >
  > (*Black Holes and Baby Universes*, 1993, p. 14) ■

  What do you suppose is meant by a gray man? Have you had experiences similar to the one Hawking describes? Do you know students who are proud of *not* working to succeed in school, or are students you know proud of working hard to succeed? What do you think of the attitude Hawking describes?

- In the quotation above, Hawking seems to be saying something about peer pressure, that is, the feeling that a person must behave the way all his or her friends or peers behave. Have you ever felt pressure from your friends or peers to do something you would prefer not to do or vice versa? How did you react? Are you now pleased with your reaction?

- What courses should (or should not) be required in high school? In college? Of foreign students? Why? Should physical education be a requirement? Should students get credit for courses like bowling, ping-pong, driver's education, tennis, dancing, gymnastics? Poker? Why or why not? How much time is reasonable to have a young child, an adolescent, a college student spend in class per week? How much time is reasonable for homework? Should foreign languages be required? For everyone? Why or why not? Should literature be required for engineers? Math for literature majors? Why or why not?

- What is a seven-year-old child's school day like in your country? Should children be pushed to learn a great deal when they are very young and don't yet know enough to rebel, when they are best at learning some things (languages, for example)? What other things are important for a child to get from school? Moral training, religious instruction, sex education, a sense of patriotism, community spirit, competitiveness? What else do schools teach in addition to academic subjects? Respect for authority? Is that a good thing or not?

A series of writing tasks in this chapter will ask you to analyze and present arguments in ways similar to those involved in academic writing assignments. (For a longer discussion of the characteristics of an academic argument, see Chapter 14, pages 253–264.) Your objectives will be to develop the following skills:

> Writing in an objective tone
> Analyzing logically and systematically, point by point
> Using various outside sources to support your position
> Considering the audience for your argument

To see some examples of formal and informal analyses related to education, you might want to read the following articles in Appendix A:

Readings
Excerpt 2 from *Savage Inequalities*, page 374
"Is There a Doctor in the Classroom?" page 378
"Voices from the College Front," page 382

ANALYZING BOTH SIDES

One characteristic of academic writing is often an objective or neutral tone. That means the writer tries to sound calm and almost uninvolved, even if he or she actually feels very strongly about the issues discussed. To help you develop an objective tone in your writing and practice logical point-by-point analysis, your first task will be to examine two sides of an issue.

Read the following article from a newspaper.

■ **PROFESSIONAL WRITING**

School System a Key to Japan's Success

TOKYO—"I have a son," said a taxi driver I met the other day in the old city of Nara. "He is a student at Tokyo University. I plan to visit him this weekend." It was a Japanese father's subtle way of telling a visitor: "My son is doing very well. His future is assured. We are proud of him." And why not? Tokyo University is, by reputation, the best of the 95 national universities in Japan. Yet here is a taxi driver's son rubbing elbows in the classroom with the children of business executives and public officials.

Japan, perhaps more than the United States, is an educational meritocracy in which a student who does well on entrance examinations, regardless of family wealth or social connections, can expect to attend the best schools and compete for the best jobs in government and corporate life. And therein lies one of the keys of Japan's industrial success.

Japanese schools are difficult, competitive, and traditionally strong in mathematics and science. One student in five is an engineering major (compared with fewer than one in 10 in the United States).

There is almost no illiteracy in Japan. Summer vacations last only about six weeks and some students continue to take classes during the summer break. Saturday morning classes are standard procedure.

Unlike their American counterparts, Japanese teen-agers must learn a second language. High school students take English classes up to seven times a week. I spent a day at Hibiya High School, the oldest in Tokyo, and found the English class looking at films on Abraham Lincoln and Johnny Appleseed.

Some experts say there is nothing in Japan comparable to the best American high schools—the schools where bright students are challenged to do better and slow students are given remedial help. That may be true. But the overall level of achievement in Japanese high schools tends to be much higher than in the United States.

Still, there are dissatisfactions in Japanese education. Classes are so large that teachers have little time for individual tutoring. The typical class at Hibiya High has 47 students. Critics of Japanese schooling say a student who can't keep up sometimes becomes frustrated or angry. This may help to explain the high suicide rate among students and the sharp increase in violence against teachers.

Then there is the problem of course rigidity. Aki Hito, a Hibiya junior who spent last year as an exchange student in Kalamazoo, Mich., said he liked the more flexible curriculum in American schools. "If I wanted to study French, I could take four years of French," he said. . . .

But the most common complaint about Japanese schooling is that students are engulfed and often terrified by the importance of doing well on tests as a matter of family honor. This leads to an unhealthy emphasis on memorization and an openly expressed feeling in Japan that neither the young people nor their parents are as creative as they should be. Hibiya's principal, Shinichiro Ohno, frankly agrees with critics that the Japanese school system is "overheated," that students take too many *juku* (cram) courses so they can score well on tests and get into the more prestigious high schools and colleges.

Thousands of students cram for years to win entrance to the "right" college. In effect, they become *ronin*, or warriors without a master, trying to avoid the disgrace of attending an inferior college or no college at all. In a typical year, 360,000 students take the entrance exam for 100,000 freshman slots at the selective national universities. Of those, 240,000 take the individual exams required by each school. Some parents, to bypass this trauma, enroll their children in private elementary and secondary schools so they can be assured of acceptance at a prestigious private college.

Unfortunately, this obsession with credentials is well-founded. Being admitted to a good college is considered a ticket to future security in Japan, where rank and status are extremely important.

Strangely enough, for most Japanese students getting into college is much more difficult than getting through. The national tendency is to treat college as a kind of four-year happy time before going off to work. "Your [America's] students are behind when they leave high school," a Japanese friend told me. "They catch up when they go to college."

The cost of college in Japan appears modest by American standards, averaging about $1,000 a year in tuition at national universities and $2,000 or more at private colleges. In addition, freshmen make a one-time, lump-sum payment ranging from $500 to $1,000. The good news, from a parent's viewpoint, is that a student pays the same tuition in his senior year as he did as a freshman. There are no unpleasant surprises along the way.

(Adapted from Kenneth Eskey, "School System
a Key to Japan's Success," Scripps Howard
News Service)   ∎

EXERCISE 1: ANALYZING AN ISSUE

Now answer these questions:

1. Is this article complimentary or critical of the Japanese school system? How do you know? _____

_____

2. The article has two main sections. Where does the second section begin? _____

3. Write a subheading for each of the two sections:

    a. _____

    b. _____

4. What transition does the author use to signal the beginning of the second section? _____

5. Write down five other ways he might have made the same transition.

    a. _____

    b. _____

    c. _____

    d. _____

    e. _____

6. List some of the good aspects of the Japanese school system discussed in the article. _____

_____

_____

_____

7. List some of the negative features of the Japanese school system the article mentions. _____

_____

_____

_____

■

➤ *Writing Assignment 12.1: Education*

Your purpose in this assignment is to inform by examining an issue objectively, analyzing both its strengths and weaknesses or
its advantages and disadvantages. You may choose to write on
the pros and cons of the school system in your home country or
some aspect of the school you are attending now, or you may
write on any subject with two clearly opposing sets of features.

Invention

To prepare for this assignment, you may want to make two lists
side by side. On one side, list positive features of your topic; on
the other side, list negative features. Write down as many pros
and cons as you can think of. Or you might write an internal dialogue in which one voice presents the virtues of your topic and
the other voice insists on its vices.

After you have examined your subject through one of these
invention activities, share the results with your classmates and
see if they can add to your list of pros and cons or if they can add
arguments to your internal dialogue.

When you write your draft, keep in mind the needs of your
audience.

Who will your audience be for this discussion?

Will these people already know something about the subject
or not?

Will these people be more interested in the strengths or
weaknesses of your subject? Why?

Does your audience have any responsibility for the subject as
it is? Or has your audience perhaps had first-hand experience with the subject?

What information will your audience need in order to understand and even agree with your analysis?

If you are discussing the strengths and weaknesses of the educational system in your own country, remember that unless you
are writing only for your compatriots, you must explain any aspects of that system your audience may not be familiar with.

Be clear in your own mind and in your essay about your
topic. If you are discussing an educational system, make sure
that you indicate whether your comments refer to elementary

school, junior high school, high school, technical school, college, or university.

The ability to analyze critically and objectively is an important skill to develop both for your school career and for your real life. Remember that an analysis is not simply a listing of good and bad features. What are some possible ways to analyze a topic? Consider how you might analyze each of your points about your subject. Look through your invention writing and add comments on each feature you mention. Ask yourself questions like these:

> What caused this strength or weakness? What are the reasons this feature is an advantage or a disadvantage?
>
> What are the consequences of this feature?
>
> What is the history of this feature? Did good intentions end in bad results?
>
> What anecdotes, incidents, or personal experiences might show this feature in action or show why or in what way this feature is good or bad?
>
> How can this feature of the system be compared with those in similar systems?

Development and Organization

When you have made comments on each of your points, consider again your audience and purpose and select the points you will include in your analysis. Remember that your supporting points must be appropriate and sufficient in number for your audience to understand and perhaps agree with your analysis. (See the following sections of Chapter 6, "Selecting Supporting Material" and "Arranging Supporting Material." You have several options for organizing your points on this subject:

Chapter 6 will help you select and arrange your supporting material.

> Discuss all the strengths and then all the weaknesses, or vice versa.
>
> Arrange your points in order of importance, from most important to least important or vice versa.
>
> Discuss a single feature at a time, mentioning both the positive and the negative aspects of that feature before discussing the next one.

Perhaps your material will suggest another, more appropriate arrangement. In deciding how to organize your information, keep your audience and purpose in mind. Remember also that you will need to include an introduction and a conclusion.

Finally, as you write, try to make sure that your tone is objective. This does not necessarily mean that you must not favor one side over the other but that even if you state that you prefer one side, your description of both sides is fair and neutrally written. The following list should help you establish an objective tone.

1. Use a formal style in your writing. For example, write out contractions.
2. Because generalizations are usually more subjective than is supporting evidence, be sure that for every generalization you have clear evidence to support your point.
3. Refer to specific incidents and facts as much as possible. This will help your tone to remain objective.
4. Avoid stating that what you have written is your opinion.
5. Avoid appeals to emotion. Instead, try to make your discussion logical.

When you have finished your first draft, answer these questions.

Self-Analysis

1. Are you satisfied overall with the essay you wrote?
2. What parts do you think are most successful?
3. Do you feel that you have maintained an objective tone in the essay?
4. What parts do you feel unsure about or dissatisfied with?
5. How would you improve the essay if you had more time?
6. Did you find this topic interesting to write about? Why or why not?

Now give your essay to a classmate to comment on. If you wrote about your educational system, find a classmate who is unlikely to be familiar with it.

Peer Response

1. What kind of hook did the introduction use to get your attention?
2. What is the main point of each paragraph?

3. How is the discussion organized?

4. What parts of this essay require more explanation for the intended audience? Are there any sections that are difficult to understand because they refer to aspects of the topic with which you are unfamiliar?

5. Are there any sections that simply list facts instead of analyzing them?

6. Are there any sections that do not sound neutral and objective?

7. Is the analysis balanced? That is, are both the positive and negative features of the topic discussed?

8. What is the best part of this discussion? Why do you think so?

9. Do you have any further comments or suggestions?

Revision

Try to get responses from at least two classmates. You may find it useful to write brief responses to their comments or short notes about what you want to consider for your next draft. Then gather your invention writing, your first draft, your classmates' responses, and your self-analysis and revise your essay. ◄

EXPLAINING A PROBLEM

In the next assignment, you will be explaining a problem. To get you thinking about problems, consider writing on one or more of the following suggestions.

Journal Suggestions

• What is culture shock? Have you ever experienced it? Can you remember when it began, how you felt, and how you began to recover from it? Do you have advice or suggestions for other people who are suffering from culture shock right now?

• What are the major social problems in your country right now? Crime? Racism? Divorce? Overpopulation? Explain as much as you can about the problem(s).

• Do you learn languages easily? Why are some people better

at learning languages than others? What is it that makes language learning so difficult? What can people do to improve their ability in a second language? What helped you the most when you were learning English?

➤ *Writing Assignment 12.2: Problem on Campus*

Writing Assignment 12.2

Use the insights you developed in the previous assignment to help you analyze and discuss a problem objectively. Think of things you have objected to since you began studying here. You may want to look through old journal entries for ideas. Are there policies in this school, for example, that have seemed unfair or senseless to you?

You may also want to think about the different kinds of problems discussed in the following reading selections in the Appendix.

Readings
"Voices from the College Front," page 382
Excerpt from *Two Years in the Melting Pot*, page 361

Invention

Begin thinking about this subject by first making a list of these policies. Try to think of policies that other people may not realize cause problems for someone like you. For example, some schools close their dormitories during Thanksgiving or Christmas, and this policy can cause problems for international students who have no place to stay during these holidays. Then select two or three of the policies that annoy you the most. Write each of these policies at the top of a page and list under each one exactly what your objections are. Then choose one of them to develop into an essay. Continue inventing by creating an internal dialogue in which one voice complains about the policy and the other voice answers the complaints. (Or use some other invention technique, if you prefer.)

Keep these points in mind:

Choose a policy that could reasonably be changed.

Avoid subjects that people always complain about, like the lack of parking spaces or the boring food at the cafeteria, unless you feel that you can explain some aspect of the problem others are unaware of.

You will not be offering solutions in this assignment. Instead, your purpose is to inform by stating the problem and clarifying each aspect you object to. Concentrate on explaining as clearly as possible exactly what the problem is.

Development and Organization

As you prepare to write your first draft, ask yourself these questions:

Why is this problem worth discussing publicly? Why should your audience be aware of this problem? Even though you are not going to propose a solution, is this a problem that can in fact be solved?

What are the causes of this problem? Will your audience sympathize more with your position if you show that you understand how the problem came about? What are the immediate causes of the problem? Are there more remote, less obvious causes worth pointing out to help the reader understand either your position or the background of the situation you are discussing?

What are the consequences of the problem you are discussing? For whom specifically is this a problem? Are there several categories of people who suffer because of this situation? Are the consequences only short-term, or are there also some less obvious long-term consequences you can point out?

Why should your audience be concerned about the problem? How does this problem relate to them personally? How might the problem affect them? How might the problem affect other people's opinion of them?

As you consider how to organize your material, examine your invention writing to see whether you can categorize causes, results, or people affected by the problem. Before deciding on the most effective arrangement, consider these possible ways to organize your material:

From least important to most important (or the reverse)

From distant causes or consequences to immediate ones (or the reverse)

From most general to most specific (or the reverse)

From most obvious or well known to least obvious or well known (or the reverse)

Now write your essay in the form of an editorial or letter to the editor of your school paper stating your objections to a policy at your institution. Include an introduction and a conclusion. Your audience is anyone who reads your school paper: the rest of the student body—international students and native students—professors, and administrators. Your purpose is to present your perspective on a policy that you find unfair, senseless, or otherwise objectionable and that you assume your audience members will also object to once they have heard your views. Watch your tone. You do not want to sound hysterical or like a chronic complainer; you want to project an image of yourself as calm and logical. Keep your audience clearly in mind; avoid insulting other students, faculty, or administrators. You want them to share your point of view.

Make it as easy as possible for your audience to follow your analysis. Look again at the list of ways to organize your information. Which type of organization would be most effective given your audience, your purpose, and the seriousness of your topic or complaint? For example, if you are revealing a problem you assume the audience knows nothing about, you may need to give some background before you describe the specifics of the problem. If, on the other hand, your audience knows about the problem but perhaps does not consider it very serious, you may want to begin with shocking specific results of the problem and then move to more general implications. Whichever form of organization you choose will depend on your subject, your audience, and your purpose.

When you have written a first draft, answer these questions:

Self-Analysis

1. Why did you choose this subject?
2. Did you state the problem fairly and completely?
3. What did you assume your audience already knew about this problem?
4. In the assignment, you were asked not to propose solutions. If you were going to propose a solution, however, what would it be?
5. How did you organize your information?
6. Why did you choose this organization?
7. What is the strongest part of your paper?
8. What is the weakest part?

Now analyze the paper of at least one classmate by answering these questions.

Peer Response

1. How familiar were you with this problem before reading this paper?
2. What does the writer want the reader to think or do as a result of reading the paper?
3. What did you learn from this paper that you had not really considered before?
4. What is the best feature of this discussion from your point of view?
5. Is the problem clearly explained?
6. Did the writer convince you that this problem is serious and worth discussing?
7. What aspects of the problem did the writer concentrate on?
8. What does each paragraph discuss?
9. How would you describe the tone of the writing? Does the writer sound like a reasonable and responsible student with a legitimate concern?
10. If you were the person responsible for the problem discussed, how would you react if you had read this article in the school paper?
11. If you had written this essay, would you send it to the paper? Why or why not?
12. Do you have further comments or suggestions to improve this draft?

Revision

Get responses to your draft from several classmates and discuss sending it to your school paper. Then revise your draft and decide whether or not to send it. ◄

➤ *Writing Assignment 12.3: Solution to Problem on Campus*

Writing
Assignment 12.3

In this assignment, you will take the discussion of a problem one step further. Rather than focusing on the problem, your main focus will be considering solutions, using the description of the problem as background. You may use the same subject you chose for the previous assignment or you may suggest solutions to a different problem.

Invention

Before you offer solutions, it is important first to make sure that the problem is clear in your mind. To help you do so, begin by analyzing the problem according to the suggestions in the previous assignment.

Next, think over possible solutions to the problem. You may want to list solutions, explaining each one briefly and then noting the pros and cons of each proposed solution. Or you may want to use the internal dialogue technique, with one voice proposing solutions and the other voice criticizing each one.

Development and Organization

One way to organize your material is first to discuss the problem in as much detail as is necessary for the reader to understand the solutions you will propose. Discuss each aspect of the problem that you think is significant. Then begin proposing solutions. Keep in mind the audience that will be reading your solutions.

How likely are the audience members to agree with your solution?

How likely are they to have thought of this solution already and rejected it? What will you have to do to convince them to reconsider your solution?

Is your audience in a position to implement your solution? If so, do you need to describe your solution in detail, or can you simply suggest a direction to consider in trying to deal with the problem?

Your discussion will be more convincing if you show that you have considered several alternative solutions to the problem. You may decide to favor one of these solutions, or you may decide simply to discuss several possible solutions without selecting one you prefer. If you think one solution is clearly the best one, you may want to leave the discussion of that solution for last. As you discuss each solution, show how it addresses each of the issues you raised in your statement of the problem. Include, if you can, both immediate results of your solution and long-term results. When you discuss your preferred solution, be sure you explain why you feel that that solution is the best one.

Self-Analysis

When you have finished a draft of your paper, answer these questions:

1. What is the problem, and for whom is it a problem?
2. How has this problem affected you personally?
3. How did you come up with this solution to the problem?
4. Is your solution realistic? Could it actually be adopted to solve this problem?
5. What are the main objections to the solution you propose?
6. Can you think of any negative results that might occur if your solution were adopted?
7. Can you think of anyone who might be adversely affected by the solution you propose?
8. Has anyone thought of this solution before as far as you know?
9. Why has this problem not been solved before?

Peer Response

Now exchange papers with at least one classmate and answer these questions.

1. How familiar were you with this problem before you read the paper?
2. From reading only about the problem, what solution could you have proposed?
3. Is the problem discussed clearly enough so that you can understand the solutions proposed?
4. How many solutions are proposed?
5. In discussing the best solution, did the writer show how it addresses each issue raised in the statement of the problem?
6. To what extent do you think that the best solution proposed is a reasonable response to the problem?
7. Can you think of any negative consequences that might result if the proposed solution were adopted?
8. What comments do you have on the tone of this paper?
9. What is the best feature of this paper?
10. Do you have any other comments to improve this draft?

Revision

When you have considered your classmates' responses, reread your draft, your invention writing, and your self-analysis. Then revise your paper.   ◄

SEQUENCED WRITING PROJECT FINAL REPORT: ANALYSIS OPTION

Sequenced Writing
Project

As your final report in the Sequenced Writing Project, you may choose to analyze and report on your findings here or you may choose to make an argument based on the material you have gathered. If you choose to develop an argument, see Chapter 14 and Writing Assignment 14.2 for help and directions.

You have now explored your topic by writing about its importance to others and to yourself, doing a survey, interviewing an expert, and summarizing documents on your topic. You now know a great deal about your topic. In this final report, you will draw on all your previous explorations.

First reread all the papers you have written so far for this project. Also look again at your notes for these assignments. Because some time has passed since you made those notes, you may have a new perspective and you may now decide to include material that you had previously skipped. You may also want to push your ideas on this topic further through some of the invention strategies you have learned or developed.

Analyze all the material you have gathered and reread it. Refer to the questions on pages 221 and 222 for help. Choose a main theme or thesis that you want as the core of your final report and several points you would like to make about your topic based on everything you have learned or written. Include only the most interesting, informative, or convincing material you have gathered. As you decide how to organize your information, refer to the questions and suggestions on page 226. As usual, consider whom you intend as the audience for this report and what you consider its purpose to be: that is, what are you trying to accomplish with this report?

As you write this report you will probably find yourself citing information or perhaps wanting to quote either from your own previous papers written for this project or from your published sources. Be sure to follow the conventions you learned in Chapter 10 and 11. Don't forget to include a bibliography. To cite your own unpublished manuscript in your bibliography, see page 210.

When you have finished a draft of this report, answer these questions.

Self-Analysis

1. Why should your audience be interested in reading this report?
2. What are you satisfied with in this project?
3. What are you still dissatisfied with?
4. If you had this project to do over again, what would you do differently?

Give your report to at least one classmate for comments.

Peer Response

1. How important or interesting do you find this report?
2. How easily can you follow the writer's ideas?
3. How well has the writer used his or her data to explain or illustrate points made in the report?
4. What is the best feature of this report?
5. What is its weakest part?
6. What can you suggest to the writer to strengthen any weak parts?
7. What other suggestions do you have to improve this report?

Revision

Read your classmates' comments and reconsider all your own writings on this topic. Now revise your paper.

An alternative approach to this Sequenced Writing Project Final Report, the Argument Option, appears in Chapter 14.

➤13➤

Responding to Written Arguments

In this chapter you will be writing about education. To get ready for the Writing Assignment, consider writing on one or more of the following suggestions.

Journal Suggestions

- Read the following quotation and comment on it in your journal.

  > . . . the school [is], . . . at least in part, an institution that adapts ideology to changing economic and social conditions, and produces a new version of ideology for each generation.
  >
  > Schools not only teach academic knowledge; they teach work according to schedule, acceptance of authority, and competition among individuals and between groups. They also help provide a justification for the hierarchies of society, so that, for instance, people accept that manual labor should pay less than mental labor.
  >
  > (Greg Myers, "Reality, Consensus, and Reform in the Rhetoric of Composition Teaching," *College English* Feb. 1986) ■

  Do you agree with this point of view? Why or why not?
- What do you think of the idea of teaching children at home instead of in schools? What advantages do you think there might be if the parents handled the child's education? What disadvantages?

ANALYZING WRITTEN ARGUMENTS

Besides presenting an objective discussion of an issue, academic writing often requires responding to someone else's writing. The following two articles discuss the question of whether or not "gifted" children should be separated from regular classes and receive more accelerated instruction than average children do. Kenneth Mott, a well-known educator, believes that separating gifted children is better for both the gifted children and the average children; Bruno Bettelheim, a famous child psychologist, opposes special classes for gifted children.

Before reading these essays, discuss the following questions in class.

1. Should the best students in grammar school and high school attend special classes separated from the average students?

2. Do such classes exist in your country? Are they successful?

3. Have you ever been put into a special accelerated class? If so, how did you feel about this at the time? How do you feel about it now?

4. If not, how did you feel about the fact that other students were being given special classes?

Before reading each essay in its entirety, read just the first paragraph, the last paragraph, and the first sentence in each of the remaining paragraphs to get an overview of the essay. Then read the essay through quickly. Finally, read the essay again more carefully, this time marking sections you find particularly interesting, convincing, or unconvincing. Write your comments in the margins, especially if you have an example to contribute.

■ PROFESSIONAL WRITING

Grouping the Gifted: Pro

I regard gifted children as those who possess some quality or innate ability which has been recognized and identified by any number of testing and observation devices and who manifest interest and success in either physical, intellectual, or artistic pursuits.

These might be children who are gifted athletes but who have real trouble mastering academic subject matter, or students who are poor athletes but are highly intellectual "quiz kids" who knock the top off all measuring devices. "Gifted" may describe pupils of average intelligence who have exceptional ability in art or music, or it may refer to the child with an IQ of 135 who excels in everything.

How can we deal with these gifted? I firmly believe that we should group them as nearly as possible according to interest and ability (giftedness) and challenge them with a type of program that will help them to grow to the fullest extent of their abilities and capacities.

This grouping could take the form of special subject arrangements in the elementary grades, a situation in which a class is heterogeneously grouped most of the day but is divided at times into special interest or ability class groups for special instruction. In high school, it may take the form of grouping students in regular classes according to any number of criteria but basically those of interest and proficiency (or lack of proficiency) in various subject areas.

One of the basic arguments against grouping the gifted is the fear of creating a caste of intellectual snobs. Similarly, some educators fear that the average and slow students would come to regard themselves as inferior.

If my definition of the gifted is accepted, then these fears are groundless. After all, the schools have grouped gifted athletes for years. Yet how many athletes regard themselves as part of an elite? Do varsity athletes look down upon other pupils as inferior? The vast majority of them apparently do not.

Consider also the amount of "gifted grouping" in speech, music, art, and journalism. Schools have readily grouped the gifted in these areas without any apparent ill effect. To the extent of my observation, encouraging gifted debaters, musicians, artists, and writers to develop their special talents does not create envy or feelings of inferiority among less talented students.

If educators sincerely desire to promote individual growth and self-respect, they have no grounds, as far as I can see, to fear any kind of grouping. The teacher, not the manner in which a class is organized, determines students' attitudes toward individual differences. Before he can hope to instill the proper attitude, however, the teacher needs to make a critical analysis of his own attitudes toward differences.

If a group of gifted or non-gifted students forms the wrong concept about themselves, the fault probably lies with the teachers, parents, or administrators. I have confidence that if teachers accept and respect individual worth, that if they challenge and spark interests in young people, the individual student will mature and grow successfully along the lines of his interests and abilities. I say, let those with similar "gifts" associate, plan, and enjoy being together.

Many educators disagree with the idea of gifted grouping because they believe that it does not affect achievement significantly. They cite pilot studies which indicate that no significant change in achievement results when children are separated into slow and accelerated classes.

The fact is, however, that in a vast majority of pilot studies the children have been grouped only according to IQ scores, which are far from reliable, and the conclusions have been based on achievement scores which measure only mastery of factual detail.

Unfortunately, there are no reliable devices for measuring growth in such areas as creativity, attitudes, personal adjustment, latent interest and talent, and innate capability.

My opinion, which is based on more than a decade in the classroom, is that learning skyrockets when individuals are grouped according to interest and ability and are motivated, challenged, and inspired by a type of school work that will yield some measure of success to them.

Heterogeneous classrooms frequently produce frustration in children who are persistently unable to do the same work that most of the other children do. Frustration is also produced when bright children are not properly challenged by their school work, as is too often the case in heterogeneous classrooms.

I have little fear of gifted students' being pushed beyond their endurance, for I have faith in the ability of most teachers to recognize the limits to which any student should be pushed. On the other hand, I don't believe giftedness should be wasted away simply because a bright or talented student is content to proceed at what is — for him — a snail's pace or to stand at the top of a class of students with less ability.

Several schools with which I am familiar have experimented with grouping the gifted in a reading program. (Their regular procedure had been to have three or four reading groups in one classroom under one teacher. The teacher's time was divided among several small groups.)

The experiment involved putting slow readers from different classrooms in one classroom, average readers from different classrooms in another class, and fast readers in still another class. Each classroom still had one teacher, but he no longer had to divide his time among several different groups. The control group consisted of a class organized and taught under the regular procedure mentioned above.

After two years, the researchers found greater overall progress at all reading levels in the experimental group. In fact, some slow readers joined the average ones and some average ones moved up to the fast group. In this case, special ability grouping paid dividends all around.

I believe the same results could have been achieved in science, social studies, mathematics, or English. By decreasing the range of interest and/or ability levels, the teacher is able to do more toward helping individual growth.

While I do not believe that children should be regarded as resources to be molded to the needs of society, I do believe that as individuals they are endowed with certain characteristics and attributes—"gifts" of nature—which represent their potential success in life. Where children have certain "gifts" in common, they should be allowed to work and study together.

(Kenneth Mott)   ■

■ PROFESSIONAL WRITING

Grouping the Gifted: Con

An argument often advanced on behalf of special classes for gifted children is that in regular classrooms these children are held back and possibly thwarted in their intellectual growth by learning situations that are designed for the average child. There can be little doubt that special classes for the gifted can help them to graduate earlier and take their place in life sooner. On the other hand, to take these students out of the regular classroom may create serious problems for them and for society.

For example, in regular classrooms, we are told, the gifted child becomes bored and loses interest in learning. This complaint, incidentally, is heard more often from adults, parents, or educators than from students. Nevertheless, on the strength of these complaints, some parents and educators conclude that special classes should be set up for the gifted.

Although some children at the top of their class do complain of being bored in school, the issue of why they are bored goes far beyond the work they have in school. If the findings of psychoanalytic investigation of feelings have any validity, feelings of boredom arise as a defense against deep feelings of anxiety. To be bored is to be anxious.

The student who is bored by his studies is the student who can take few constructive measures of his own to manage his anxieties. Consequently, he represses or denies them; he must ask others, specifically his teachers, to keep him frantically busy, studying and competing intellectually so that he will not feel anxiety.

The gifted child who is bored is an anxious child. To feed his neurotic defense mechanisms may serve some needs of society, but to nourish his neurosis certainly does not help him as a human being.

Psychology, like nature, does not permit a vacuum. If study material does not hold the student's attention because of his easy mastery of it, the result is not necessarily boredom. Other intellectual interests can fill the unscheduled time. Is it reasonable to assume that gifted children learn only when pressed by the curriculum?

Several years ago I observed what happened to a number of gifted children who were taken out of a highly accelerated, highly competitive, private school and placed in a public high school of good academic standing where, by comparison, the work was so easy as to be "boring."

Close inspection revealed an interesting and worthwhile development in most of the transplanted youngsters. In the special school for the gifted, these children had shown little ability to use their own critical judgment. Instead, they had relied heavily on their teachers' direction. In the slower-paced school, no longer having to worry about keeping up, these students began to reflect spontaneously on many problems, some of which were not in the school program.

The students acquired on their own a much deeper appreciation of life, art, literature, and other human beings. No longer exhausted by meeting assigned learning tasks, these youngsters had energy to branch out, broaden their interests, and understand far more deeply.

Prolonged, rarely assailed security may be the best preparation for tackling difficult intellectual problems. Because the gifted child learns easily, he acquires a feeling of security in a regular class. On the other hand, if such a child is put into a special class where learning is not easy for him, where he is only average among a group of extremely gifted youngsters, he may, as often happens, come to feel that he has only average abilities which are not up to coping with difficult challenges.

Another argument advanced for special classes for the gifted is that removing highly capable students from the regular classroom lessens anxiety among the slower learners. Possibly so. But how do anxieties become manageable except through a friendly working relationship with someone felt to be superior—in this case, the faster learners in the classroom?

In many of our big cities today, the students left behind in the non-collegiate programs are marked as a lower breed. Indeed, most of them come from poor, lower-class homes. Surrounded by students who have little interest in acquiring an education, lacking companionship with students who want to learn, and receiving no encouragement at home, these children apply themselves even less than they would if there were good students in class with whom to identify.

In order to achieve educationally, many children from economically impoverished homes need to be challenged and motivated by example. Grouping deprives these children of such stimulation. They are left behind as second-class students, a situation which is more likely to create hopelessness than to lessen anxiety. Should some of them display outstanding leadership or ability, they are sent away to join their intellectual peers, leaving the non-gifted group even more impoverished.

Grouping children intellectually has much in common with mountain climbing. In mountain climbing, the guides usually distribute themselves ahead of and behind beginners or less skilled climbers. Placed in the center of the group with people who have learned both the skill and teamwork required in mountain climbing, the beginner is likely to learn quickly and well.

If, however, all of the good climbers are put into one party, and all of the poor ones in another, the second group is likely to fail miserably or perish altogether.

When the debate over what is the "best" education for the child reaches an impasse, the argument is frequently switched to what is best for society. Today we are told that we need more scientists and more engineers to "survive." Therefore, we must speed the growth of young people who have the necessary talent.

Does anyone really know what the needs of society will be thirty years hence? Can science guarantee survival? Might society not have a greater need for fresh, imaginative ideas on how to organize a worldwide society? Might we not have a greater need for [women and] men of broad social vision than for scientists? And since ideas mature slowly, maybe what we need is not a speeding up but a slowing down of our all-too-fast pace.

I am not suggesting that we dismiss our concern for the gifted, that we leave well enough alone. On the contrary, our schools can and must be improved. I am simply saying that arguments for the special education of gifted children do not yet rest on scientifically solid ground. What we need now is not quick remedies but carefully balanced and controlled experiments, based on hard thinking and planning.

(Bruno Bettelheim)   ■

Before you can respond to another's position, you must be sure you understand it and the arguments with which the writer supports that position. When making an argument, writers use some or all of the following techniques:

Giving examples

Using analogies (comparing this situation to another situation)

Mentioning and responding to opposing views

Appealing to authority (citing experts in this area who agree with the position)

Pointing out consequences or implications of both pro and con positions

EXERCISE 1: ANALYZING ARGUMENTS

Which of the following techniques did Mott and Bettelheim use? Put a check mark in the spaces below for each technique use.

Technique	Mott	Bettelheim
Examples	_____	_____
Analogies	_____	_____
Opposing views	_____	_____
Authorities	_____	_____
Consequences	_____	_____

1. What examples did Mott use, and what were they supposed to prove? _____

_____

2. What examples did Bettelheim use, and what were they supposed to prove? _____

_____

3. What analogies did Mott use, and were they convincing?

_____

4. What analogies did Bettelheim use, and were they convincing? _____

5. Where did Mott show that he was taking into account the objections of the other side? _____

6. Where did Bettelheim show that he was taking into account the objections of the other side? _____

7. How did Mott show that the objections to his opinion were not valid or significant? _____

_____

8. How did Bettelheim show that the objections to his opinion were not valid or significant? _____

_____

9. Analyze Mott's argument. Separating gifted children will have the following benefits:

to the gifted children _____

_____

to the average children _____

_____

to society _____

_____

Keeping all children, gifted and average, together will have the following disadvantages:

to the gifted children _____

_____

to the average children _____

_____

to society _____

_____

10. Analyze Bettelheim's argument. Keeping all children, gifted and average, together will have the following benefits:

to the gifted children _____

_____

to the average children _____

_____

to society _____

_____

Separating gifted children from average children will have the following disadvantages:

to the gifted children _____

_____

to the average children _____

_____

to society _____

_____

■

➤ *Writing Assignment 13.1: Education for Gifted Children*

You have summarized the arguments and analyzed the techniques each writer used to defend his position. These activities
were meant to help you understand both sides of this issue. Now
think over your own reactions to the two arguments. In this assignment you will respond to one of these essays. You may agree
or disagree with the basic position, or you may agree or disagree
with specific points from the argument. Although you may eventually change your mind, decide, before you begin to write, on
your own position on this issue and analyze it by asking yourself
what you have read, heard, seen, or experienced that makes you
feel as you do. Why do you agree or disagree with these writers?
Begin by indicating which arguments seem most and least convincing to you and why.

Mott's Arguments

Most convincing _____   **Why?** _____

_____   _____

_____   _____

_____   _____

Least convincing _____   **Why?** _____

_____   _____

_____   _____

_____   _____

Bettelheim's Arguments

Most convincing _____   **Why?** _____

_____   _____

_____   _____

_____   _____

Least convincing _____   **Why?** _____

_____   _____

_____   _____

_____   _____

_____   _____

Now that you have analyzed the strengths and weaknesses of both arguments, what is your own position? Did either writer change your thinking about whether gifted children should be educated separately?

Now begin to construct your response. You do not need to respond to every point made. Instead, pick two to four especially interesting or convincing or unconvincing points that you would like to comment on, either to agree or to disagree. Choose points from each author or from just one. State those points here.

1. _____

2. _____

3. _____

4. _____

Invention

Explore your ideas by discussing your subject with classmates and other friends. They may give you some ideas you had not thought of before. Before you begin your first draft, do some kind of written invention activity. Try looking at each point you listed above and writing down whatever ideas come to your mind either in agreement or disagreement. If you *disagree* with an idea, answer or object to the point by offering contradictory

    facts
    statistics
    observations
    experiences
    causes
    effects

either from your own experience or reading or from the two essays. If you *agree* with an idea, give additional examples

insights

explanations

information

that the writer did not consider, know about, or include. In addition, you may want to list, brainstorm, outline, loop, or cube to explore your ideas.

Your audience is your classmates, who have also read both essays. Your purpose is a combination of informing and convincing in order to provide your classmates with new perspectives on or insights into the ideas discussed on this subject.

Development and Organization

When you are given an assignment like this one, your professor may suggest how he or she would like you to organize your discussion. If you do not get such directions, here is one way to approach a writing assignment in which you must respond to written material. Set up your paper by using the material to which you are responding as the reference point for organizing your own comments. Once you have selected the points you wish to address, arrange your essay so that you discuss each point in a separate paragraph. You might use the following overall structure for your discussion.

Introduction: Brief summary of writer's basic position
Transition to
Statement of your own agreement or
disagreement

Discussion: Point 1: Remind the reader of what the writer said
Make your comment or give your evidence
Point 2: Follow the same procedure as in point 1
Point 3: Follow the same procedure as in point 1
and so on

Conclusion: Briefly summarize your own conclusions.

Begin your first draft with a very brief summary of the essay in order to refresh the reader's memory. Then state your basic position—agreement or disagreement. This agreement or disagreement should be expressed in your thesis. (Avoid writing, "I basically agree/disagree . . .")

Remember to give proper credit when you quote, para-

See Chapters 10 and 11 for help with summarizing, paraphrasing, quoting, and citing sources.

phrase, or summarize from the original. At the end of the paper, on a separate sheet, include a bibliography.

In academic writing, your tone should remain calm and logical. If you attack another piece of writing too viciously or if you attack another writer personally, you will discredit your own writing and lose the support of most members of an academic audience. Keep in mind that a convincing argument also displays the writer's ability to understand the other side of an argument and to concede or admit the persuasiveness of any opposing points that are valid.

When you have finished your first draft, answer the following questions.

Self-Analysis

1. Did you enjoy reading the essays?
2. Did you enjoy writing a response?
3. What was the easiest part of this paper to write?
4. What was the hardest part of this paper to write?
5. Are you satisfied with your discussion?
6. What is the best argument you made in your paper?
7. Are you still unsure of or dissatisfied with any part of your paper?
8. If you had more time, what changes would you make?

Exchange papers with at least one other classmate and answer the following questions about your classmate's paper.

Peer Response

1. Is the summary of the essay accurate?
2. What points did your classmate make that you had not thought of before?
3. Comment on the tone of this paper.
4. What are the best parts of this paper? The most original? The most clearly expressed? The most logically argued? What is the most striking example?

      5. Were any sections unclear, hard to follow, or not convincing?

      6. Do you have any further comments?

Revision

After you have received feedback from your classmates, use their comments and your own self-analysis to help you revise your draft. ◄

$\succ 14 \prec$

Arguing from Written Material

One of the most common academic writing assignments involves using published material in your own work. In this chapter you will practice synthesizing information from different sources to construct your own argument.

USING PUBLISHED MATERIAL IN AN ARGUMENT

In this chapter, you will be dealing with issues related to men and women workers. To get you thinking in this direction, consider writing on one or more of the following suggestions.

Journal Suggestions

- What assumptions do people in your country make about a young couple who has just gotten married? What do their parents and society expect of them? What do they expect of each other?

- Are girls brought up differently from boys in your culture? At what age do people seem to start treating them differently? What differences are there in their behavior? At what age can you see these differences? Think back to your experiences in elementary school, for example. How do the differences in upbringing become apparent in the adult male and the adult female?

- When did you first consciously realize that you were a boy or a girl? Is there an incident connected with that realization? How did life change for you after that point? How did your attitudes about yourself and others change? Have you ever wanted to be the other sex? Why or why not?

- How does your culture view men and women who never get married? Who never have children? Is there much pressure

247

on people to get married? Is there much pressure on married couples to have children? Does your society view unmarried women differently from unmarried men?

To do the Writing Assignment in this chapter you will need to read or reread selections in Appendix A. But before you do so, answer the following questions:

1. Is work in the house considered "women's work" in your culture? Why or why not?
2. Who usually takes care of young children in your culture—the mother, the father, grandparents, social agencies like day-care centers? Why do you think this arrangement has evolved?
3. What kind of work is considered strictly "men's work"?
4. Do many women in your culture work outside the home? Is this a good arrangement?
5. If men and women do different work in your culture, why do you think this is so? Do you think this is a good arrangement?

Now read or reread the following articles.

Readings
"Who Are Smarter—Boys or Girls?" page 367
"Primate Studies and Sex Differences," page 353
"Are Men Born with Power?" page 371
"A View from Other Cultures: Must Men Fear 'Women's Work'?" page 389

When you finish reading, spend 10 minutes freewriting about your general reaction to what you have just read. This freewriting will help you put together the next Writing Assignment.

EXERCISE 1: ANALYZING ARGUMENTS
When you have finished writing your first reaction to the articles, analyze each one objectively. Each essay makes an argument. Summarize Linton's argument (in "Primate Studies and Sex Differences," page 353) in one sentence.

Linton argues that _____

_____

Compare your sentence with those of your classmates and try to come to an agreement on her basic argument. Now list at least two main ideas she uses to support her argument; next to each one write your reaction:

Linton's points   **Your reaction**
_____   _____

1. _____   _____

2. _____   _____

Next look again at the essay by Fisher, "Are Men Born with Power?" (page 371). How do you think the writer wants the reader to answer that question?

Men are/aren't born with more power than women.

Now list at least two points used to support the writer's position; next to each one write your reaction:

Fisher's points   **Your reaction**
_____   _____

1. _____   _____

2. _____   _____

Next look at the article on education, "Who Are Smarter— Boys or Girls?" (page 367). What is the main argument in this article?

This article argues that _____

_____

Compare your sentence with those of your classmates and try to come to an agreement. Now list important supporting points and your reactions.

Supporting points   **Your reaction**
_____   _____

1. _____   _____

2. _____   _____

3. _____   _____

Finally, what is the main point of the Van Leeuwen article ("A View from Other Cultures: Must Men Fear 'Women's Work'?" page 389)? The article summarizes three explanations for the differences between men's and women's work. Write down the main idea of each explanation and your reaction:

Explanation	Your reaction
1. Nature vs. culture	
2. Domestic vs. public	
3. Object relations and family life	

∎

➤ *Writing Assignment 14.1: Dividing Up Men's and Women's Work*

Writing
Assignment 14.1

Now that you have analyzed the position taken in each of the articles, use this information to help you formulate an argument on the subject of how and why work is divided between men and women. What are your own beliefs on this subject? Decide what your basic position will be in your discussion:

- You might argue that men and women should be expected by societies to do the same work and explain why you think so.
- You might argue that men and women should do different kinds of work and explain which type of work each one should do and why this seems like a reasonable or fair arrangement to you.
- You might describe the system of dividing labor in your own culture and argue that this system is fair or that this system is unfair.
- You might explain and argue for the fairness of any of your own beliefs about the division of labor and use information from the four articles you have just analyzed to support or to disconfirm your own information and arguments.

You might find an entirely different kind of argument to make using information from these articles. Take a position and defend it by referring to the logic, statistics, or facts in the selections and by adding information from your own experience or reading.

Your audience is your classmates, some of whom are certain to have had a different reaction from yours. Remember that you want to adopt the tone of an academic argument. Yet you may have strong feelings about the subject. If you do feel strongly about your position, spend 10 to 15 minutes writing your emotional reaction to these issues without making any particular argument at all. Call your opponents names; make illogical, unsupported generalizations; let your writing scream if you need to. Getting the emotion out of your system in this way should make it easier to adopt the objective, logical tone needed for your paper.

See Chapters 10 and 11 for help with using and citing published materials.

If you quote or use material from any of the selections, be sure to give proper credit and to include a bibliography on a separate sheet of paper at the end of your paper. Refer to these selections as though you had found them *not* in this book but in their original sources.

When you have finished a draft, answer these questions.

Self-Analysis

1. Are you satisfied with this paper?
2. What do you feel is your strongest argument?
3. Which argument still seems weak or unconvincing to you?
4. If you had more time, what else would you do to this paper?

Now give your paper to at least one classmate for feedback.

Peer Response

1. What is the position your classmate argued?
2. What is the main supporting evidence used to defend this position?
3. Write a response disagreeing with your classmate's paper. Even if you agree with your classmate, find every argument you can to rebut or argue against the position taken in the paper.

Revision

After your classmate has responded to your argument, review your classmate's rebuttal, the four selections, your invention writing, and your self-analysis. Then revise your paper, taking into account the objections raised by your classmate.   ◄

CONSTRUCTING YOUR OWN ARGUMENT

We formulate and express opinions constantly based on what we see, hear, or read. In writing an argument in an academic context, you must be particularly careful to be clear and logical. To get you thinking about the positions you take on various issues, consider writing on the following suggestions.

Journal Suggestions

- What kinds of changes have you seen occurring in your country in your lifetime? What caused these changes? What has been the result? Are these changes for the better? Why or why not?

- What are the important disputes in your major field right now? Make a list of these questions or issues. Is there anything in your field that the experts are trying to convince nonexperts of? List these issues. Give the arguments the experts use and compare these arguments with what the general public believes.

- Read the following statements. If you agree with the statement, write *yes* in the space provided. If you do not agree, write *no*. Comment in your journal on any statements that provoke your interest.

_____ 1. Intelligent couples have a duty to have children even if they don't want any.

_____ 2. If you are living in a foreign country, you should do what the people there do, even if you disagree with what they do.

_____ 3. Students should leave their parents' home and begin to live independently at about the age of 18 or 20.

_____ 4. It is better to have only one child because you can give that child all your attention.

_____ 5. It is easier to be a man than a woman in this world.

_____ 6. Grades are bad because students work only for good grades instead of really trying to learn.

_____ 7. Even if a couple is very unhappy in their marriage, the couple should stay together at least until their children leave home.

_____   **8.** International students should not have to take English classes unless they themselves feel the need to do so.

_____   **9.** It is best to be exposed fairly early to the difficulties and misery in life because you will then be prepared to face hardships when you are older.

An academic argument is not like an argument or disagreement over an issue like abortion or capital punishment. In those cases, our positions are often based on personal moral codes; these codes themselves, we believe, are enough to prove or justify our positions. A change in opinion would occur only after deep rethinking of the moral code. An academic argument, on the other hand, is characterized, for the most part, by its lack of emotional appeals. Instead, an academic argument appeals to logic. It is more like a marshaling of evidence in support of an intellectual position. Academic arguments tend to surround intellectual issues and to appeal to facts and logic for support rather than to emotions or to ethics. Although it may seem strange to you, a professor reading your paper may be less interested in what position you take than in how you argue for your position, what evidence you have to support it, and what logic you use to defend it.

Controversial issues, like abortion, capital punishment, or questions of religion or politics, are difficult subjects for academic argument because people often have very deeply held convictions on these subjects. Therefore, you are unlikely to persuade anyone of your opinion in a short essay, or perhaps even in a long book. Furthermore, unless you are an expert on these subjects, you will not have anything new to say that might change someone's mind or add to the discussion.

Write down two convictions you hold very deeply and are unlikely to change your mind about.

1. I strongly believe that _____

_____

2. I strongly believe that _____

_____

There are many other issues on which reasonable people can disagree and hold opposing points of view. Write down two beliefs you hold less deeply and could be persuaded to change your mind about.

1. _____

2. _____

➤ *Writing Assignment 14.2: Controversial Issue*

Writing
Assignment 14.2

In this assignment, you will choose a controversial issue and write an essay stating your point of view. Here are some examples of general topics that students have chosen in the past.

> What rights do animals have relative to those of humans?
>
> Should life be sustained artificially?
>
> Are food additives really bad?
>
> Should children with AIDS be allowed in classrooms?
>
> Should employees be tested for drug use or for genetic abnormalities?
>
> Why don't women hold more managerial positions?
>
> Is surrogate mothering moral?
>
> Should developing countries build nuclear power plants?
>
> Should rock-and-roll lyrics be censored?
>
> Do arranged marriages have any place in the modern world?

You may also want to review articles you have already read in Appendix A of this book to see what kinds of controversial issues other people have discussed. For example, you may want to read the articles on the media and violence listed below. This may help you decide on a topic to write on, and you may want to use information from these articles to support your points.

Writing
Assignment 14.2
continues on page
262

Readings
"On Kids and Slasher Movies," page 394
"Public Enemy Number One?" page 397   ◄

The Audience

In persuasive writing, or in writing in which you are trying to demonstrate the validity of a position, the question of audience is even more important than usual. When you write privately in your journal or in your invention writing, your primary focus is on yourself, your feelings, your ideas. When you write publicly, your focus shifts away from you and toward your subject and the audience for your writing. In analyzing an object, an event, or an idea, your focus is on that object, event, or idea, and you must concentrate on communicating information. As you move from analysis or exposition toward argumentation, your focus shifts again, this time in the direction of your audience. Information on your subject is still important, of course, but in persuasive writing the importance of the relationship between writer and reader increases.

1. private writing   focus: writer
2. public writing
   a. exposition   focus: subject
   b. persuasion or argumentation   focus: audience

You have been considering your audience in all the writing you have been doing, but in writing to influence the audience's opinions on a subject, it is particularly important to know who that audience is. To judge your audience, answer the following questions.

How much does your audience already know about this subject? How much does your audience care about this subject one way or the other?

Does the audience probably agree with you on this subject? If so, why are you writing about it? To give additional information or support the audience had perhaps not thought of before?

Does the audience probably disagree with you on this subject? If so, what are the chances of getting them to agree with you? How can you get this audience to change?

How strongly do your audience members hold their beliefs on this subject?

If you expect to change your audience's mind, how much of a change can you reasonably expect? For example, if you are writing about Islam for Christian audience members, you are unlikely to get them to change religions. On the other hand, it might be possible to get them to understand better and therefore respect Islam more. ◄

THE WRITER'S CREDIBILITY

In the previous chapter, Bruno Bettelheim made the statement that a bored child is an anxious child. Did you believe or agree with that statement when you read it? When you were a child, were you ever bored? Do you think your boredom was only a symptom of anxiety? If your personal experience contradicts Bettelheim's statement, you probably did not believe him. Why is Bettelheim's statement at least worth considering? For many readers, the mere fact that this statement appears in print is not enough to convince them, especially if their personal experience contradicts it. On the other hand, Bettelheim is a well-known child psychologist who has studied and written on child psychology for many years. Because of this fact, most readers would not immediately dismiss his statement, even if they were quite surprised by it. Bettelheim has credibility because of his education and professional experience. In persuasive writing, it is particularly important to establish your credibility, that is, to convince your reader that you know what you are talking about. You can establish your credibility by showing that your knowledge of the subject is based on:

Education, training, or both

Extensive personal experience or observation

Reading or other contact with authorities on the subject

Because writer credibility is so important, ask yourself as you write or prepare to write what makes you enough of an authority on the subject to convince an audience to believe you. What in your experience or education makes you an expert on this subject?

If your expertise comes from reading, you must consider the source of your information. Who can be considered an authority on a given issue? A legitimate authority has education, training, or experience in the subject. Also, a legitimate authority's point of view is objective, not biased by self-interest. For example, if a fast-food restaurant claims to serve the best hamburgers in town, self-interest in promoting its hamburgers makes this claim biased and not objective. Therefore, the restaurant is not a good source of information. Finally, a legitimate authority must be reliable, not known to distort the truth.

EXERCISE 2: CONTROVERSIAL ISSUES
What kind of person would you consider an authority on the following subjects?

1. animal rights _____

2. sustaining life _____

3. food additives _____

4. AIDS _____

5. drug/genetic abnormality testing _____

6. women in managerial positions _____

7. surrogate mothering _____

8. nuclear power plants _____

9. censorship _____

10. arranged marriages _____

■

Your credibility as a writer on any subject is strengthened if you show that you are familiar with and have seriously considered opinions that do not agree with your own.

Tone

Academic arguments are characterized more by logical appeal than emotional or ethical appeals. Students sometimes become very involved with their subjects and make the mistake of using too many emotional or ethical appeals. As a result, their writing sounds more like political speechmaking than academic arguments. Be especially cautious about using rhetorical questions in argumentation. This is the type of question to which the person asking believes there is only one reasonable answer; politicians regularly use such questions in speeches.

> Is this the kind of attitude we want to develop in our children?
>
> What kind of a society is this that allows . . . ?
>
> Will we never understand that . . . ?

These kinds of questions can be very effective because they appeal to emotions and ethics. Before you ask such a question, however, you must be very sure that your audience already agrees with you about the answer. In general, these questions are more appropriate in impassioned speeches than in academic essays. Concentrate on keeping your tone objective.

DANGERS IN DEVELOPING YOUR ARGUMENT

As you read earlier, some of your professors may be more interested in how you develop your argument than in what position you take, but both are important. In order to construct a strong and logical argument, avoid these common flaws.

Exaggeration and unsubstantiated generalizations
Oversimplification of your argument or of the opposing argument
Logical flaws
Appeals to inappropriate authorities
Emotionally charged words
Out-of-date facts

Exaggeration and Unsubstantiated Generalizations

The ability to generalize from facts or examples is important in academic writing and particularly important in argumentation. If you use a generalization to support a position or an opinion, it must be a valid generalization, not a sweeping, unsubstantiated generalization. In other words, you must be careful not to exaggerate the meaning of a fact or an example. For example, if you observe middle-class North American families and compare them with middle-class families in Latin America, you may come to the conclusion that Latin Americans spend more time with members of their extended families than North Americans do. This is probably a valid generalization; it can be directly supported with statistics showing the amounts of time each group spends. If you use that information to generalize that North American family members do not love one another, you are making a sweeping, unsubstantiated generalization or jumping to an unwarranted conclusion. These kinds of generalizations weaken your argument. You can correct the problem by substantiating or by limiting or qualifying the generalization.

> **Sweeping generalization:** International students study all the time; Americans go out and have fun.
> **Substantiation:** Of the students at the library on Saturday night, 60 percent are international students even though they make up only 1 percent of the student population.
> **Qualification/limitation:** Many international students study very hard. International students *seem* to study harder than Americans do.

Oversimplification

Be careful not to oversimplify your own position or the opposing position.

> **Oversimplification:** The reason so many people receive welfare is that they would rather not have to work for a living.

There are many reasons why people need public assistance. A statement such as this reveals ignorance of the subject and makes the writer seem incapable of dealing with complex causes and results.

False Dilemma. A false dilemma is a form of oversimplification. The writer seems to claim that there are only a limited number of ways of looking at a situation.

> The United States will have to choose between increased military spending or the very real possibility of foreign invasion.

With this kind of reasoning, the writer seems to be trying to trick the reader into believing that these two possibilities are the only ones that exist. An intelligent discussion would attempt to explore other options. While predicting the consequences of an action is a good technique for supporting your position, do not exaggerate the consequences.

False Analogy. In a false analogy, the writer compares two situations and insists that they are alike or that what happened in one case will happen in the other.

> Being a surrogate mother is like being a prostitute; you let another person use your body for money.

When you use an analogy, be careful that the two cases really are similar. In fact, analogies do not prove anything; rather they are mainly useful in helping the reader to understand your explanation or position.

Logical Fallacy/Flaw: Arguing in a Circle

Be careful not to use what you are trying to prove as your evidence.

> Using drugs like marijuana or cocaine weakens your willpower. People who use these drugs do so because they are weak and need help from artificial sources to survive.

In trying to prove that drugs weaken willpower, the writer states that people who use drugs are weak. It is impossible to tell which is the cause (people take drugs because they are weak) and which is the effect (drugs make people weak) the writer is trying to establish.

Logical Fallacy/Flaw: Irrelevancies

The evidence you use to support your position must be clearly related to that position.

> Women say they want economic equality, but they still want men to carry packages for them and give up their seats to let a woman sit down. This shows that women do not really want equality with men. They want the benefits of equality but not the disadvantages.

In this case, the writer is discussing economic equality. Carrying packages and giving up seats are social issues and have nothing to do with economic equality. Therefore, it is illogical to use these examples to argue about economic equality.

Logical Fallacy/Flaw: Non sequitur

A non sequitur is a conclusion that does not logically follow the evidence.

> International students criticize United States foreign policy and the ignorance of the American public about world issues. It is obvious from their behavior that these students are not grateful for the education they are receiving here.

There is no logical connection between these two sentences. Opinions that international students may have about the United States or about Americans have nothing to do with their gratitude one way or the other.

Logical Fallacy/Flaw: After, therefore, because

Be careful not to say that one event caused another merely because it happened before the other.

Several years ago school systems in this country began offering sex education classes. We now see the results. What these children learned in sex education classes they put into practice, and we find ourselves in a true crisis: a tremendous rise in the number of teenage pregnancies. This tragic increase in the number of teenage pregnancies is the result of the sex education classes these children had in school.

The fact that sex education classes were instituted at some time before the increase in teenage pregnancies does not mean these classes caused or even contributed to the increase. This kind of reasoning is superficial and illogical.

Inappropriate Authorities

When you refer to an authority, make sure that it is a legitimate authority (see page 256). Also, determine whether your audience is likely to accept the authority you mention. A valid academic argument about the secular world would not use the Bible, for example, or the Qur'an as an authority. Celebrities are also not good authorities unless they are known to be knowledgeable or experienced in the area you are discussing.

Bandwagon

Occasionally, writers urge readers to believe something or do something because others believe it or do it. The simple fact that others do something is not sufficient support for an argument, although this approach is widely used in advertising.

Drink New York Seltzer. Everyone else does.

Charged Words

Certain words produce irrational emotional reactions in readers, and in an academic argument you do not want to arouse emotional reactions but to appeal to logic. Therefore, avoid depending on positively or negatively charged words to support or make your argument for you. Here are some typical examples of words that are charged for many people in this country.

Positively charged words	**Negatively charged words**
motherly love	communism
patriotic	drugs

Out-of-Date Facts

If you are citing an outside source of information to defend a position you have taken, be sure that you use current facts.

ORGANIZING YOUR ARGUMENT: INDUCTIVE/DEDUCTIVE

Continuation of Writing Assignment 14.2

You can arrange your argument in several ways. One way is to state your opinion and then explain your defense of that point of view step by step. That is a deductive approach. You might also use an inductive arrangement, in which you review the reasons step by step that lead to a conclusion. You present the conclusion after giving the reasons that led you to it.

General organization of a deductive argument:
I feel this because of this, this, this.

General organization of an inductive argument:
Because of this, this, this, I feel this.

In the deductive approach, you begin with your generalization and continue with your supporting evidence. In the inductive approach, you begin with your evidence and lead up to your generalization. In addition, in an inductive argument the evidence usually is arranged so that the most convincing evidence comes toward the end, somewhere near the generalization.

Addressing the Opposition

A good argument considers and evaluates opposing points of view. Set aside at least one section of your paper to honestly discuss arguments against your position. As you consider opposing points of view, you may either:

admit the strength of a particular point the opposition makes

and/or:

rebut or argue against the opposition.

Using both techniques strengthens your argument because it suggests that you have weighed all the evidence on both sides of an issue. A typical pattern is to concede (admit the strength of) one counterargument—

> While it is true that . . .
> Although there is no question that . . .
> Despite the fact that . . .

—and then to rebut (argue against) a more important counterargument by showing that it is weak, superficial, incomplete, or unproven.

Keep your tone controlled and reasonable. Try to sound as though you have carefully considered all sides and have formed an opinion on the issue but are open to change if the other side can produce better arguments.

Finally, make copies of the pages of any publications you use to support your position. Underline the sections of those pages that you quoted or paraphrased.

When you have finished a draft of your paper, answer these questions.

Self-Analysis

1. Why did you choose this topic?
2. What is the main point you are trying to make?
3. What is the main idea of each development paragraph?
4. Are you satisfied with what you wrote?
5. What are you most satisfied with?
6. What are you least satisfied with?
7. What else would you like to do with this paper?

Now have at least one classmate answer the following questions about your paper.

Peer Response

1. What is the main point of the paper?
2. What is the main idea of each development paragraph?
3. How much did you know about this subject before reading this paper?
   a great deal   1   2   3   4   5   nothing
4. How much did you learn from reading this paper?
   a great deal   1   2   3   4   5   nothing

5. Are you convinced by your classmate's argument?

   completely   1   2   3   4   5   not at all
   convinced   convinced

6. What parts of the argument convince you the most?
7. What parts of the argument do you find unconvincing?
8. Can you locate any logical flaws (errors) in this essay?
9. If your classmate cited any published material or any authority, how convincing do you find that support?
10. Is there any evidence that your classmate considered opposing points of view?
11. Do you have any further comments?

Revision

Use the feedback you get from your classmates to revise your paper.   ◄

SEQUENCED WRITING PROJECT FINAL REPORT: ARGUMENT OPTION

Sequenced Writing Project

Perhaps as you were gathering and analyzing material for your Sequenced Writing Project, you developed strong opinions about the topic. If you choose to, you can use the material you gathered to make an academic argument. Follow the same instructions as given in this chapter for writing on a controversial issue, beginning on page 254.

➤ *UNIT SIX*

Essay Exams: Some Strategies

PART 3

APPLYING WRITING PROCESSES FOR ACADEMIC PURPOSES: ANALYZING, EVALUATING, ARGUING

15

Preparing for an Essay Exam

Writing an essay for an exam is a little different from writing a regular essay, composition, or article. You can probably guess most of those differences yourself.

EXERCISE 1: EXAMS

Audience

1. Who is your audience for an essay exam? _____

   _____

2. What does this audience already know about the subject of

   your essay? _____

   _____

3. Why is this reader reading this essay? _____

   _____

Purpose

1. Why are you writing about this subject? _____

   _____

2. What are you trying to show or prove? _____

   _____

3. What do you want the reader to know after reading your

   essay exam answer? _____

   ■

In some ways, writing an essay exam is easier than writing a regular essay because you do not have to decide on your audience or purpose. The professor already knows the answer to the essay exam question and wants to find out if you know it well enough to discuss the subject clearly. You will not need to worry about writing a striking introduction or conclusion; these sections are less important in essay exams and in fact may not be present at all. On the other hand, you rarely have enough time on an essay exam to revise what you write. Furthermore, because you will not be writing a first draft and a revision, you cannot use your first draft as a discovery draft. In an exam situation, you need to know the material quite well before you write. Finally, because of the lack of time to rewrite, planning and preparing quickly what you want to include in your answer become more important than usual. This chapter will help you develop strategies for taking essay exams.

EXAMINING THE EXAM QUESTIONS

When you receive an exam, first look it over to determine whether you are being asked to write an essay or simply a short answer of a sentence or two. A short-answer exam usually tests knowledge of facts. An essay exam tests your ability to relate facts or show the significance of facts. In an essay exam, you are expected to select and organize information. The wording of the exam will indicate if you need to answer in a few sentences or in an essay.

> Is the question complicated? If so, you are probably expected to write an essay to answer the question.
>
> Is the answer complicated? If so, you probably need to write a long answer.
>
> Does the question suggest a brief or a long response? If the question says *discuss, explain, define,* you probably will be writing an essay. If the question says *list* or *briefly identify,* you probably need to write only a sentence or two.
>
> How much time have you been given? If you have 50 minutes to answer two questions, you are probably expected to write essay answers. If you have 50 minutes to answer 25 questions, you obviously cannot write much on each one.

If you cannot decide how detailed your answer is supposed to be, ask your professor. An answer that is adequate for a short-answer test is not adequate for an essay exam.

For an essay exam, the first step is to be sure that you understand exactly what the question is asking by looking at the way your professor has worded the question. The question will tell you *what* the professor expects and may suggest *how* to arrange your material. Look for words like *discuss, explain,* and any of the following:

> Give examples to show that . . .
> Illustrate . . .

(Here the professor wants you to prove or support a point by giving examples of specific instances in which a generalization proves to be true.)

> Compare . . . to . . .
> Contrast . . . with . . .
> What are the major differences between . . . and . . .
> Discuss the advantages of . . . over . . .

(Here you are being asked to show how two or more concepts, objects, events, or procedures are alike or different.)

> What are/were the causes of . . .
> What are/were the results/effects of . . .
> Why . . .
> What factors contributed to . . .
> What is the effect of . . .
> What has been the result of . . .
> Discuss the reasons for . . .

(These questions are asking about the relationship between events or situations, either what led to the event or situation or what resulted from the event or situation.)

> What types of/kinds of . . .
> Classify . . .
> Discuss the most important features of . . .

(This kind of question is asking you to consider a number of items and to arrange them in categories or to analyze what something is made up of.)

> Define . . .
> What does . . . mean

What is meant by . . .
How does . . . define . . .

(Here you are being asked to give a definition.)

How does . . . work
Explain the process by which . . .
Trace the development of . . .

(Here you are to describe a process step by step or explain how something functions or develops chronologically.)

Sometimes students do not do well on essay exams because they misread the question. If the question asks for a definition of management in business and you write about the effects of good management on profits, you will not get credit even though you may have known the answer.

EXERCISE 2: EXAMS

Look at the following sample exam questions and circle the key words, the ones that indicate what type of answer the professor is asking for. How would you go about answering each question?

1. We have discussed several types of astronomical phenomena this term. Write a short essay in which you describe the distinguishing characteristics of a supernova.

2. Discuss the formation of hail.

3. The five major world religions have many features in common but also differ from one another in significant ways. What basic differences distinguish Islam from Christianity?

4. What is meant by constitutional monarchy? In your answer, give examples in the world today and discuss how each example matches or varies from the classical definition of constitutional monarchy.

5. Classify the forms of nonverbal communication used by human beings.

6. Current popular music has its roots in a number of musical forms. Illustrate the influence of soul and blues music on current popular music.

7. What were the major factors contributing to the social un-
rest in the United States in the 1960s?   ■

EXERCISE 3: EXAMS

One excellent way to prepare for an essay exam is to try to guess
what kinds of questions the professor may ask. To practice this,
list every class you are now taking in addition to your English
classes. If you are taking only English classes, think of the last
term in which you had different types of classes. List them all
here.

1. _____

2. _____

3. _____

4. _____

Check with your classmates to see if anyone else is taking
any of the same courses. If they are, work together. Now pick the
course in which you are most likely to have an essay exam and
think of the types of knowledge you have gained from this
course. Together with any classmates who are taking the same
course, draw up a list of possible essay exam questions. Write
as many as you can. Use the sample key words and phrases
on pages 268–269 to help you think of different types of questions.

1. _____

2. _____

3. _____

4. _____

5. _____

6. _____

7. _____

8. _____

9. _____

10. _____

                                                                 ■

INVENTION

☆   Once you have read an exam question carefully and know what it is asking for, try to retrieve from your memory as much as possible on the subject as quickly as possible. One good way to do that is to use one of the invention techniques you have learned. Because you are not trying to explore your thoughts but rather to remember everything you can, listing is probably the fastest, most efficient technique to use. Make the list in the margin of the exam paper. That way, even if you cannot cover everything on your list in the amount of time you have, at least the professor will see what you intended to include in your answer. You may even get some credit for the ideas in your list that were not included in the essay answer. Jot down everything you can think of related to the exam question. Don't worry yet about whether or not everything will be useful. Make the list as long as you can.

WRITING AN ANSWER

Next, you need to consider how to organize your information. Your professor will find your thoughts easier to read and understand if you present them in an organized way. If you have all the facts but write about them randomly, your professor may become confused and perhaps even be unable to recognize that all the facts are there. You can begin to organize the list by grouping similar items, writing *1* next to all the items of one type, *2* next to items in a second category, and so on.

To focus on the exact answer to the question, write a thesis statement at the beginning of your answer. Very often the wording of this thesis will be quite similar to the question itself.

Question: **How did Freud divide the human psyche?**
Beginning of answer: **Freud divided the human psyche into three parts: the id, the ego, and the superego.**

What do you think the student would write next? _____

_____

EXERCISE 4: EXAMS
How would you begin the first sentence of an essay to answer each question on page 269–270?

1. _____
2. _____
3. _____
4. _____
5. _____
6. _____
7. _____

■

As you write, check the wording of the question several times to make sure that you have not accidentally drifted away from the subject.

When you are writing an essay exam, look carefully at the prompt, or the question you are to answer, to see if your professor is calling for specific examples or instances of general ideas. In an essay, these specifics allow the professor to see that you have not simply memorized some general ideas on a subject. Instead, you have comprehended the general idea fully enough so that you can apply it and show how the idea works in a particular instance. In most situations in which you are writing an essay exam at all, less value is placed on the ability to memorize material than on the ability to apply and/or evaluate that material. Thus, read the prompt carefully; if it calls for examples, be sure to include them.

Most essay exams are written under the pressure of a time limit, and such a limit sometimes makes students nervous. If you feel nervous about an exam, read through the entire exam before you begin to write and answer the question you feel most secure about first. Starting from strength may help you to calm down by the time you get to the next question. Write as much information as you can, but be sure to pace yourself. That is, keep an eye on the clock so that you do not spend too much time on any one question.

Finally, although most teachers understand that time pressure may cause you to make errors you would be able to catch if you had more time, try to save a few minutes at the end of the exam to read over what you have written. If you have the opportunity to read your answer several times, read first for your ideas and then for grammatical and mechanical correctness. Furthermore, although you will be trying to write fast, be careful not to write so quickly that your writing becomes illegible. Your professor may not be able to understand what you have written and may even become irritated at having to struggle to figure out your words.

>16<

Practicing Taking Essay Exams

In this chapter, you will practice writing essay answers to the different types of questions. Note that some questions will require you to use a combination of strategies to answer the question completely. To imitate the exam situation, your answers should be written in class with a fixed time limit.

ORGANIZING AN ESSAY EXAM: DIVISION AND CLASSIFICATION

Classifying items into categories is a way human beings deal with the profusion of separate items surrounding us; it is a way of organizing and making sense of the world. We try to organize the world by dividing the huge whole into parts and/or classifying the many parts into types. Then we can look at each division or classification in a more organized way, one at a time. To help you think in terms of divisions or classifications, consider writing on one or more of these suggestions.

Journal Suggestions

- What types of problems is your country facing right now? Social, political, economic? Can any of these categories of problems be subdivided? Which are the most difficult to solve? Why?
- In your field of study, how is knowledge divided? That is, what types of experts are there in your field? (For example, among engineers, there are mechanical engineers, civil engineers, nuclear engineers, and so on.) What are the characteristics of each division or type?

When you are writing about a complicated subject, one approach to organizing your discussion is either to divide the subject or to classify the many parts into categories. After the initial division or classification, you may discuss each division or category by describing its features and how those features distinguish this division or category from the others.

➤ *Writing Assignment 16.1: Practice Essay Exam*

Writing
Assignment 16.1

Read the selection "History Proves It: Other Systems of Naming Work" in Appendix A (page 337). Then write two or three questions on this selection that a professor might ask on an essay exam.

1. _____

2. _____

3. _____

Now look at the following question. Did you ask this one?

1. What types of systems have people used for naming themselves?

Before answering this question, do some invention writing to get your ideas down on paper. This type of question suggests an organizational pattern in which you classify or divide up a subject. Begin by determining which categories you will deal with in your answer (types of systems for naming). Then develop your answer by examining each category and describing the characteristics of each type. In other words, first divide up your subject and then discuss each category.

On another sheet of paper, answer the question as though it were part of an essay exam. Do not look back to the selection. Write your essay in class in 20 minutes. Be sure to leave time to reread and edit your answer.

When you have finished, analyze your answer.

Self-Analysis

1. Did you have enough time to include all the ideas you intended to include?
2. Did you have any time left to edit?

3. How many divisions or categories are there in your paper?
4. Do any sections seem too short to you? If so, what did you leave out?

Now ask a classmate to analyze your answer.

Peer Response

1. Did your classmate include all the important divisions or categories? If not, what is missing?
2. Is each category or division explained enough? If not, what is missing?
3. Compare the statement of the main idea of the answer with the wording of the question. Is it clear from the statement of the main idea that the essay will address the question directly?
4. Are there any grammatical or mechanical errors?

Revision

Now look back at the selection. Are there any important points you forgot to mention? Decide where you would put them, and mark your paper with asterisks at those points.

Revise your answer, including any additional points at the asterisks and correcting any errors your classmates noticed.   ◄

ORGANIZING AN ESSAY EXAM: CAUSE AND EFFECT

The ability to determine accurately the causes of a given situation or the effects of another is an important intellectual ability to develop. Causes and effects are often complex; writing about them helps us to examine them more carefully. To help you think in terms of causes and effects, consider writing on one or more of the following suggestions.

Journal Suggestions

- If you have siblings, where do you come in the family—oldest, youngest, or somewhere in the middle? What are the effects of being the oldest, youngest, middle, or only child?

Which position would you rather have? Can you see certain personality similarities among all the oldest children you know? The youngest? Only children? How are the children in these categories similar? Why do you think they have developed the particular traits you identified?

• Should children receive a well-rounded education, studying even things they don't want to study? Has this ever happened to you? Were you later grateful for that education, or was it wasted on you? Should children be allowed to study what they want, going with their inclinations and talents, or even against their talents? Few reasonable people would argue for either extreme, but where should we draw the line and why? What are the effects of allowing children to choose what they want to study? What are the effects of forcing children to study something they are not interested in?

When discussing cause and effect, be sure to think in terms of both immediate and long-term causes and effects. Also keep in mind that the fact that one event occurs before another does not necessarily mean that the first event caused the second. Finally, in an essay exam you will probably have to do more than simply list causes and effects. Try to make the logical connection between a cause and an effect explicit. That is, explain why or how a given cause produces a particular effect.

➤ *Writing Assignment 16.2: Practice Essay Exam*

Writing
Assignment 16.2

Read one of the following selections in Appendix A: "Who Are Smarter—Boys or Girls?" (page 367) or "Are Men Born with Power?" (page 371). After you have read the selection, write two or three questions on the reading that a professor might ask on an essay exam.

1. _____

2. _____

3. _____

Now look at the following questions. Did you ask one of these questions?

1. Some men seem unwilling to do what they consider women's work. Explain possible reasons for this unwillingness.

2. According to the selection, the fact that girls are physically more developed than boys when they start school gives girls an advantage in the early grades. Explain both the immediate and long-term effects of that initial advantage.

Choose one of these questions to answer in a short essay. First do some invention writing to get your ideas down on paper.

On another sheet of paper, answer the question as though it were part of an essay exam. Do not look back to the selection. Write your essay in class in 20 minutes. Be sure to leave time to reread and edit your answer.

When you have finished, analyze your answer.

Self-Analysis

1. Did you have enough time to include all the ideas you intended to include?
2. Did you have any time left to edit?
3. How many causes or effects does your paper discuss?
4. Do any sections seem too short to you? If so, what did you leave out?

Now ask a classmate to analyze your answer.

Peer Response

1. Did your classmate include all the important causes or effects? If not, what is missing?
2. Is each cause or effect explained enough? If not, what is missing?
3. Compare the statement of the main idea of the answer with the wording of the question. Is it clear from the statement of the main idea that the essay will address the question directly?
4. Are there any grammatical or mechanical errors?

Revision

Now look back at the selection. Are there any important points you forgot to mention? Decide where you would put them, and mark your paper with asterisks at those points.

Revise your answer, including any additional points at the asterisks and correcting any errors your classmates noticed. ◀

ORGANIZING AN ESSAY EXAM: DEFINITION

In nearly every course you take in school you will need to learn definitions of new words and new meanings for common words. To help you think about definitions, consider writing on one or more of the following suggestions.

Journal Suggestions

- Think of terms describing items or ideas particular to your culture that your classmates are unlikely to know unless they have visited your country. These might include articles of clothing, types of dwelling, special food or drink, concepts, or special kinds of jobs or roles in society. Define each term in a sentence or two. Then select one or two of the more interesting or unusual ones and describe them in more detail.
- Make a list of terms from your field that you think would be useful for the general public to understand. Define each one in a sentence. Select one or two to define more fully.

Most written definitions do one of two things. A definition may explain an unfamiliar term like *pterodactyl, miscegenation, quark,* or *electron,* or it may give a special meaning to a familiar term like *family* or *injustice.* When you write a definition, it is often useful to relate the new term or the special meaning of the familiar term to concepts or items that readers already know. In an essay exam, this will let your teacher know that you have not simply memorized a meaning but have understood and internalized it. Traditionally, a definition first places the item or concept to be defined into a broad category or class and then specifies the special features that distinguish that item from other members of the same class.

A termite is an antlike social insect that feeds on wood.

The definition may continue with a physical description of the termite, a chronology of its life cycle, and/or an analysis of the division of labor in a termite colony or of the types of termites. A definition may proceed by negation. Thus, a comparison with the more familiar ant may help explain what a termite is *not*.

Special definitions of familiar terms fall into two categories: (1) a technical definition of a commonly used term that has a special meaning in a particular field, like the special meaning of the word *space* in architecture; or (2) a personal definition that seeks to give special insight to a commonly used term, like a personal definition of what *injustice* really means. In such definitions, the writer may use an example or recount an incident to lead the reader to think about the familiar concept in a new way.

Whichever type of definition you are writing, begin by referring to what the reader already knows.

Either:

> **Generally situate the term in a category:** A termite is an antlike social insect. . . .

Or:

> **Establish a common ground of agreement on the term:** The family is the most basic unit of human social organization.

Then show how this term is different from others in the same category by the following means:

- Describe it.
- Compare it to something the reader is likely to know already.
- Illustrate what it is by recounting an anecdote or giving examples.
- Analyze it by dividing it into its components.
- Explain how it is used or how it functions.

For some examples of definitions, see these Reading Selections: the excerpt from *Black Holes and Baby Universes* (page 318), in which Stephen Hawking explains what a scientific theory really is, and "Darwin Revisited" (page 315), which provides a new meaning for Darwin's term "survival of the fittest."

➤ *Writing Assignment 16.3: Practice Essay Exam*

Writing
Assignment 16.3

Read the following selection in Appendix A: "Nonverbal Communication" (page 344). After you have read the selection, write two or three questions on the reading that a professor might ask on an essay exam.

1. _____

2. _____

3. _____

Now look at the following question. Did you ask this one?

1. What is meant by the term *nonverbal communication*? Give some examples of different types of nonverbal communication.

Before answering this question, do some invention writing to get your ideas down on paper.

On another sheet of paper, answer the question as though it were part of an essay exam. Do not look back to the selection. Write your essay in class in 20 minutes. Be sure to leave time to reread and edit your answer.

When you have finished, analyze your answer.

Self-Analysis

1. Did you have enough time to include all the ideas you intended to include?
2. Did you have any time left to edit?
3. Did you begin your definition by placing what you were going to define in a category?
4. Did you use any negative definitions?
5. Do any sections seem too short to you? If so, what did you leave out?

Now ask a classmate to analyze your answer.

Peer Response

1. Did your classmate's definition place the term in a category and show what distinguished this item from others in the same category? If not, what is missing?
2. Compare the statement of the main idea in the answer with the wording of the question. Is it clear from the statement of the main idea that the essay will address the question directly?
3. Are there any grammatical or mechanical errors?

Revision

Now look back at the selection. Are there any important points you forgot to mention? Decide where you would put them, and mark your paper with asterisks at those points.

Revise your answer, including any additional points at the asterisks and correcting any errors your classmates noticed.   ◄

ORGANIZING AN ESSAY EXAM: COMPARISON/CONTRAST

In an essay exam, a question that requires a comparison is meant to determine whether you have understood the features of the items to be compared well enough to discuss them together. Your professor may or may not ask you to evaluate which of the items compared is better, but he or she will be looking for a discussion of the most important features of the items.

To help you think about comparisons, write on one or more of the following suggestions.

Journal Suggestions

- What changes have occurred in your country in your lifetime? Compare what life was like before with what life is like now.

- What changes have occurred recently in your field of study? Have there been major breakthroughs in the past several years? What differences are there between the way experts regard your field now and the way they did in the past?

- Can you think of two or more political points of view, or political parties, that are important in your country at the moment? What are the differences between these points of view?

- Think of an ethnic, religious, or political minority in your country. Compare that group with the dominant culture from as many points of view as you can.

There are two traditional ways to present comparisons. You can discuss item A in the first part of your paper, use a transition to move to the next section, and then discuss item B in the second half of the paper. Or you can alternate between item A and item B, discussing the first feature of A then the first feature of B, then discussing the second feature of A then B, then the third feature, and so on. If you have many details to include, this arrangement may help your reader follow your discussion better. Either:

Main Idea. Item A1. Item A2. Item A3. Item A4. Transition. Item B1. Item B2. Item B3. Item B4. Conclusion.

Or:

Main Idea. Item A1. Item B1. Item A2. Item B2. Item A3. Item B3. Item A4. Item B4. Conclusion.

Thinking in terms of these patterns when you are writing an answer of comparison will help you to remember points you might otherwise have forgotten. In other words, you may remember to make point 3 about item A but forget to mention that point about item B. This framework will help you remember. You may decide that point 3 about item B is insignificant and does not need to be mentioned. But at least you will not have failed to mention it just because you forgot.

➤ *Writing Assignment 16.4: Practice Essay Exam*

Writing Assignment 16.4

Read the following selection in Appendix A: "Who Are Smarter — Boys or Girls?" (page 367). After you have read the selection, write two or three questions on the reading that a professor might ask on an essay exam.

1. _____

2. _____

3. _____

Now look at the following question. Did you ask this one?

1. According to the selection, mothers treat their boy and girl babies differently. Explain what the differences are and compare the results of these different ways of treating young children.

Before you answer the question, do some invention writing to get your ideas down on paper.

On another sheet of paper, answer the question as though it

were part of an essay exam. Do not look back to the selection. Write your essay in class in 20 minutes. Be sure to leave time to reread and edit your answer.

When you have finished, analyze your answer.

Self-Analysis

1. Did you have enough time to include all the ideas you intended to include?
2. Did you have any time left to edit?
3. Which pattern of organization did you use?

Now ask a classmate to analyze your answer.

Peer Response

1. Did your classmate include all the important points to be compared? If not, what is missing?
2. Is there a clear statement of the main idea at the beginning of the answer?
3. Compare the statement of the main idea of the answer with the wording of the question. Is it clear from the statement of the main idea that the essay will address the question directly?
4. Which pattern of organization did your classmate use?
5. Are there any grammatical or mechanical errors?

Revision

Now look back at the selection. Are there any important points you forgot to mention? Decide where you would put them, and mark your paper with asterisks at those points.

Revise your answer, including any additional points at the asterisks and correcting any errors your classmates noticed.   ◄

Postscript

Now that you have completed the tasks assigned to you in this book, you should feel confident that you have come a long way toward successfully approaching and completing any writing task you encounter in your other academic work. One last word of advice:

> If you have problems with or questions about any writing assignment you get, even if you are writing an exam or writing outside an academic context, don't hesitate to ask for help. Ask the professor who made the assignment, your classmates, your former professors, or anyone else you think might help. Sometimes just asking the questions will give you different ideas about how to solve the problem.

Also, return to this book if necessary for guidance or to remind yourself of how you did a task assigned here. The advice in this book applies not just to this course but to many other types of writing as well.

May all the writing you do come easily and turn out successfully.

APPENDIXES

➤ *APPENDIX A*

Readings

SUGGESTED READINGS

The following readings are loosely linked to the Writing Assignments you will be doing. Although the readings may not directly address the subjects you will write on, they bring up issues related to the assignments. They are meant to focus you in the general direction of the assignment. They are also meant to be interesting. Therefore, you do not have to read the selections closely. Whenever you can, use context to guess the probable meanings of words you do not know. Don't worry if you do not understand every word. Read for interest and general information.

Excerpt from *Bury My Heart at Wounded Knee* by Dee Brown

"Discovering the Truth about Columbus" by Charles Sugnet and Joanna O'Connell

"Do Not Disturb"

"Sacred Places" by Dan Baum

"Auto-cracy Is Being Exported to Third World" by Mary Morse

"The Japanese Funeral Ceremony and the Spiritual World after Death" by Masako Imamiya

"Japanese *Miai*" by Taisuke Akasaka

"Taking the Bungee Plunge" by Ginia Bellafante

"Darwin Revisited" by James Marti

Excerpt from *Black Holes and Baby Universes* by Stephen Hawking

"The Quality of Mercy" by Rita Williams

Excerpt from *Eight Little Piggies* by Stephen Jay Gould

Excerpt 1 from *Savage Inequalities* by Jonathan Kozol

"History Proves It: Other Systems of Naming Work" by Sharon Lebell

From "The First Four Minutes" by Leonard Zunin

"Nonverbal Communication" by Deena R. Levine and Mara B. Adelman

"How to Spot a Liar" by Benedict Carey

"Primate Studies and Sex Differences" by Sally Linton

"Abraham Lincoln" by Abraham Lincoln

Excerpt from *Two Years in the Melting Pot* by Liu Zongren

"Who Are Smarter—Boys or Girls?"

"Are Men Born with Power?" by Helen Fisher

Excerpt 2 from *Savage Inequalities* by Jonathan Kozol

"Is There a Doctor in the Classroom?" by Laurie Ouellette

"Voices from the College Front" by Natasha Tarpley

"A View from Other Cultures: Must Men Fear Women's Work?" by Mary Stewart Van Leeuwen

"On Kids and Slasher Movies" by Michael Ventura

"Public Enemy Number One?" by Mike Males

From *Bury My Heart at Wounded Knee*

Chapter 1: Their Manners are Decorous and Praiseworthy

Before you read, consider these questions:

1. What images of American Indians or Native Americans do you have now or did you have as a child?
2. What images do you associate with Native Americans? Bows and arrows? Buffalo? Where did you learn about Native Americans?
3. What do you know about the history of the arrival of Europeans on the American continent?

The following text is the beginning of the first chapter of a book called Bury My Heart at Wounded Knee. *Wounded Knee is the site of a massacre of 150 to 350 American Indian men, women, and children by American soldiers in 1890. This book presents the history of the American continent from the point of view of the millions of people already living here before the Europeans arrived. It is a bloody and horrifying history, one that is not usually taught in schools. Instead, most children learn about the bravery of the Europeans who left their homes in Europe to take over this new land. In fact, because they didn't know how to survive in this new land, many of these European invaders would have died without the help they received from the native peoples, who took pity on them. But in many instances, once the Europeans had established themselves, they often repaid the kindness of the native peoples with horrors: The native people were lied to, tricked, made into slaves, and forced to accept and adopt the white man's way of life. If they did not accept the white man's ways, or if they resisted, they were destroyed. The Europeans called them savages and blamed the Indians themselves for the white man's massacre of the men, women, and children of these Indian tribes. It is a history to be ashamed of.*

> *Where today are the Pequot? Where are the Narragansett, the Mohican, the Pokanoket, and many other once powerful tribes of our people? They have vanished before the avarice and the oppression of the White Man, as snow before a summer sun.*
>
> *Will we let ourselves be destroyed in our turn without a struggle, give up our homes, our country bequeathed to us by the Great Spirit, the graves of our dead and everything that*

*is dear and sacred to us? I know you will cry with me,
"Never! Never!"*

—TECUMSEH OF THE SHAWNEES

It began with Christopher Columbus, who gave the people the
name *Indios.* Those Europeans, the white men, spoke in different dialects, and some pronounced the word *Indien,* or *Indianer,*
or Indian. *Peaux-rouges,* or redskins, came later. As was the custom of the people when receiving strangers, the Tainos on the island of San Salvador generously presented Columbus and his
men with gifts and treated them with honor.

"So tractable, so peaceable, are these people," Columbus
wrote to the King and Queen of Spain, "that I swear to your
Majesties there is not in the world a better nation. They love
their neighbors as themselves, and their discourse is ever sweet
and gentle, and accompanied with a smile; and though it is true
that they are naked, yet their manners are decorous and praiseworthy."

All this, of course, was taken as a sign of weakness, if not
heathenism, and Columbus being a righteous European was convinced the people should be "made to work, sow and do all that
is necessary and to *adopt our ways.*" Over the next four centuries (1492–1890) several million Europeans and their descendants undertook to enforce their ways upon the people of the
New World.

Columbus kidnapped ten of his friendly Taino hosts and carried them off to Spain, where they could be introduced to the
white man's ways. One of them died soon after arriving there,
but not before he was baptized a Christian. The Spaniards were
so pleased that they had made it possible for the first Indian to
enter heaven that they hastened to spread the good news
throughout the West Indies.

The Tainos and other Arawak people did not resist conver-
sion to the Europeans' religion, but they did resist strongly when
hordes of these bearded strangers began scouring their islands
in search of gold and precious stones. The Spaniards looted and
burned villages; they kidnapped hundreds of men, women, and
children and shipped them to Europe to be sold as slaves.
Arawak resistance brought on the use of guns and sabers, and
whole tribes were destroyed, hundreds of thousands of people in
less than a decade after Columbus set foot on the beach of San
Salvador, October 12, 1492.

Communications between the tribes of the New World were
slow, and news of the Europeans' barbarities rarely overtook the

rapid spread of new conquests and settlements. Long before the English-speaking white men arrived in Virginia in 1607, however, the Powhatans had heard rumors about the civilizing techniques of the Spaniards. The Englishmen used subtler methods. To ensure peace long enough to establish a settlement at Jamestown, they put a golden crown upon the head of Wahunsonacook, dubbed him King Powhatan, and convinced him that he should put his people to work supplying the white settlers with food. Wahunsonacook vacillated between loyalty to his rebellious subjects and to the English, but after John Rolfe married his daughter, Pocahontas, he apparently decided that he was more English than Indian. After Wahunsonacook died, the Powhatans rose up in revenge to drive the Englishmen back into the sea from which they had come, but the Indians underestimated the power of English weapons. In a short time the eight thousand Powhatans were reduced to less than a thousand.

In Massachusetts the story began somewhat differently but ended virtually the same as in Virginia. After the Englishmen landed at Plymouth in 1620, most of them probably would have starved to death but for aid received from friendly natives of the New World. . . . [They] regarded the Plymouth colonists as helpless children; they shared corn with them from the tribal stores, showed them where and how to catch fish, and got them through the first winter. When spring came they gave the white men some seed corn and showed them how to plant and cultivate it.

For several years these Englishmen and their Indian neighbors lived in peace, but many more shiploads of white people continued coming ashore. The ring of axes and the crash of falling trees echoed up and down the coasts of the land which the white men now called New England. Settlements began crowding in upon each other. In 1625 some of the colonists asked Samoset [one of the native people] to give them 12,000 additional acres of Pemaquid land. Samoset knew that land came from the Great Spirit, was as endless as the sky, and belonged to no man. To humor these strangers in their strange ways, however, he went through a ceremony of transferring the land and made his mark on a paper for them. It was the first deed of Indian land to English colonists.

Most of the other settlers, coming in by thousands now, did not bother to go through such a ceremony. . . .

In 1675, after a series of arrogant actions by the colonists, King Philip [as the English called Metacom, another native person] led his Indian confederacy into a war meant to save the tribes from extinction. The Indians attacked fifty-two settlements, completely destroying twelve of them, but after months of fighting, the firepower of the colonists virtually exterminated the Wampanoags and Narragansetts. King Philip was killed and his head publicly exhibited at Plymouth for twenty years. Along with other captured Indian women and children, his wife and young son were sold into slavery in the West Indies.

When the Dutch came to Manhattan Island, Peter Minuit purchased it for sixty guilders in fishhooks and glass beads, but encouraged the Indians to remain and continue exchanging their valuable peltries for such trinkets. In 1641, Willem Kieft levied tribute upon the Mahicans and sent soldiers to Staten Island to punish the Raritans for offenses which had been committed not by them but by white settlers. The Raritans resisted arrest, and the soldiers killed four of them. When the Indians retaliated by killing four Dutchmen, Kieft ordered the massacre of two entire villages while the inhabitants slept. The Dutch soldiers ran their bayonets through men, women, and children, hacked their bodies to pieces, and then leveled the villages with fire.

For two more centuries these events were repeated again and again as the European colonists moved inland through the passes of the Alleghenies and down the westward-flowing rivers to the Great Waters (the Mississippi) and then up the Great Muddy (the Missouri). . . .

[By the 1800s] more than three centuries had . . . passed since Christopher Columbus landed on San Salvador, more than two centuries since the English colonists came to Virginia and New England. In that time the friendly Tainos who welcomed Columbus ashore had been utterly obliterated. Long before the last of the Tainos died, their simple agricultural and handicraft culture was destroyed and replaced by cotton plantations worked by slaves. The white colonists chopped down the tropical forests to enlarge their fields; the cotton plants exhausted the soil; winds unbroken by a forest shield covered the fields with sand. When Columbus first saw the island he described it as "very big and very level and the trees very green . . . the whole of it so green that it is a pleasure to gaze upon." The Europeans who followed him there destroyed its vegetation and its inhabitants—human, animal, bird, and fish—and after turning it into a wasteland, they abandoned it.

On the mainland of America, the Wampanoags of Massasoit and King Philip had vanished, along with the Chesapeakes, the Chickahominys, and the Potomacs of the great Powhatan confederacy. . . . Their musical names remained forever fixed on the American land, but their bones were forgotten in a thousand burned villages or lost in forests fast disappearing before the axes of twenty million invaders. Already the once sweet-watered streams, most of which bore Indian names, were clouded with silt and the wastes of man; the very earth was being ravaged and squandered. To the Indians it seemed that these Europeans hated everything in nature—the living forests and their birds and beasts, the grassy glades, the water, the soil, and the air itself.

Dee Brown

1. This text discusses actions taken against the American native peoples by three of the several groups of Europeans who settled here. Which groups are discussed?
2. How was their behavior similar?
3. How would you describe the behavior of the native peoples, according to this text?
4. From reading this excerpt what would you say is the author's purpose in writing this book?

Journal Suggestions

- What is your reaction to this brief summary of what happened to the American native peoples? Write a journal entry recording your reactions. Make comments or note anything you found interesting.
- When people face change, two common reactions are to resist the change or to adapt to the change. But some changes are so much detested that people would rather die than accept the change. Is this ever a reasonable reaction? Some people might argue that it is never reasonable to give up one's life to resistance. It is better to adapt to change. Do you agree?

Discovering the Truth about Columbus

500th Anniversary Celebrations Stir Grass-Roots Groups to Tell the Other Side of the Story

Before you read, consider these questions:

1. Have you heard the name Christopher Columbus? What do you know about this person?
2. Do you know of historical figures who are honored by one group of people and hated by another group? What created the feelings on each side?

Columbus was the Italian ship captain who has traditionally received credit for "discovering America." He has long been considered a hero because history books have usually described him as a brave adventurer who sailed around the world when many Europeans were afraid to go too far out on the sea because they thought the earth was flat and they might fall off the edge. Some accounts credit Columbus with the idea that it would be possible to reach the East by sailing west because the world was in fact round and not flat. Columbus Day is a holiday in the United States (although some groups refuse to participate), which commemorates the arrival of Columbus in the "New World," and in 1992, the United States and other countries celebrated the 500th anniversary of Columbus' landing. But recently people have looked again at Columbus' behavior once he landed in the Western hemisphere and have discovered a different, more sinister, and ugly picture.

Remember the U.S. bicentennial, when it seemed like all the oil companies simultaneously tried to change their names to "America" or "Spirit of '76"? Well, if you thought that was bad, get ready for the 500th anniversary of Columbus' so-called discovery of America.

·················

And what are they in such a hurry to commemorate? Howard Zinn opens his book *People's History of the United States* (Perennial Library, 1980) by quoting Columbus' log entry on his first encounter with the Arawak people of the Caribbean. Columbus observed that "they would make fine servants," and that "With 50 men we could subjugate them all and make them do whatever we want." He and his successors went at the "Indians" with genocidal ferocity; probably three million died from war, slavery, and labor in the mines on the island of Hispaniola (now Haiti and the Dominican Republic) in the first

15 years after 1492. The entire population of nine million was virtually wiped out within 40 years.

••••••••••••••••

Contrary to grade-school mythology, Columbus did not undertake his voyages out of curiosity or to prove the world was round; rather, he had promised his investors huge returns on their capital, and had to find gold, spices, or slaves to make good. On Hispaniola, each Indian over 14 was obliged to bring in a certain quota of gold every three months. Indians failing to meet their quotas were punished by having both hands cut off, and usually then bled to death. Since there was very little gold on the island, most either fled or were killed. When the spices looked unpromising and the gold didn't materialize fast enough, Columbus shipped the Arawaks themselves to Spain to be sold in the slave markets of Seville, thus inaugurating an Atlantic slave trade that became one of the worst crimes in human history. . . .

Columbus himself returned to Europe in disgrace, and appears to have died without understanding that he had not landed in the Orient. But . . . [the] winners get to write the histories, and a gala Columbus anniversary extravaganza represents a serious perversion of what really happened.

Charles Sugnet
Joanna O'Connell

1. According to this article, why was Columbus traveling around the world?
2. What is meant by the statement "the winners get to write the histories"?
3. What do you think the authors of this article were trying to show by mentioning that Columbus "appears to have died without understanding that he had not landed in the Orient"?

Journal Suggestions

- Think of any instance you can of the winners writing the history. What would the same history look like if the losers wrote the history?

- Think of the last time you had a disagreement with someone. Try to write out the position of the other person as you think they would describe it. In other words, try to put yourself in the other person's shoes. Do you feel more sympathetic now to their position than you did before?

Do Not Disturb

Before you read, consider the following questions:

1. Do you know any traditional beliefs about how the earth was formed or how different races of human beings came about? Exchange your information with your classmates.
2. What do you know about the aborigines in Australia? Share your information with your classmates.

This reading describes the conflict surrounding the Australian government's plan to build a pipeline under a stream the aborigines of Australia consider sacred.

Bob Bropho returned to Bennett Brook last week, to the banks of the shallow stream that winds through the suburb of Lockridge on the northeastern side of Perth, capital of the state of Western Australia. With his grandchildren beside him, he stood in silence for several minutes. To Bropho and many of Australia's 170,000 other aborigines, Bennett Brook is the sacred resting place of Wagyl, the mythical rainbow snake with multiple legs and a horse's mane. Wagyl plays an important role in that part of aboriginal folklore known as dreamtime, the period of creation. In the days when the world was still unformed, legend has it, the giant serpent slithered across the coastal plains of Western Australia, carving out its hills and valleys.

According to aboriginal belief, Wagyl lies asleep, its memory revered and its presence deeply respected, beneath Bennett Brook. Now the great snake's slumber is threatened by a pipeline bringing natural gas to Perth and the populous southwest corner of the state from the underwater reservoirs of the Indian Ocean, 1,000 miles to the north. The plans call for one segment of the line, a twelve-mile spur to a gas plant in East Perth, to be buried in the ground under Bennett Brook. Many aborigines are outraged. Says Bropho: "Imagine the hurt we felt when they said they were going to dig a big hole and open our mother's guts and put a gas pipe in there."

The aborigines warn that if Wagyl is disturbed, the river system will dry up, the water will turn bad, and there will be sickness and death among their people. They want the pipeline to be built over the brook. The State Energy Commission argues that burying the pipeline is the safest option; besides, another gas line already runs under Bennett Brook, along with a water main and telephone lines. Responds Bropho: "In those days, aboriginal people were left in the dark. They were powerless. But now we have learned what to do to make the white man listen."

Indeed they have. The aborigines won an injunction in the state supreme court last November to prevent further work on the pipeline until the matter is settled. As a result, the uncompleted spur now stops on one side of Bennett Brook and resumes on the other bank. The injunction was continued last week. Said Justice Barry Rowland: "I cannot leave this matter without expressing the hope that it is not beyond the wit or resolve of all parties to get together quickly to see if they can accommodate the aspirations of all."

While the commission and state government pondered their next move, the aborigines declared that they had no intention of giving in. Said Bropho: "It's no good white society saying Wagyl is dead. People could say that about Jesus Christ. We are not dealing with beliefs of 200 years or 2,000 years ago. We are dealing with beliefs from the beginning of time."

Time, July 28, 1986

1. What are the issues involved in this case? How does each side defend its position?
2. How valid are the arguments of each side?
3. At what point does the advance of "progress" or modernization have to stop, if ever, when it conflicts with what humans hold sacred?
4. Which side should win this case? Can you think of any way to resolve the problem?
5. Do you know of any other case where traditional beliefs and modernization clashed head on? Which side won? What was the result?

Journal Suggestions

- Are there any remnants in your culture of strong traditional beliefs like those of the aborigines? Describe them.
- In your culture, are there any creatures like Wagyl that people believe in or used to believe in? Describe what the creature looks like and what it does. What significance does the creature have in traditional beliefs?

Sacred Places

Five Hundred Years after Columbus More Than Sixty Native American Spiritual Sites across the Country Face Their Greatest Threat Ever

Before you read, consider the following questions:

1. Do you know of any situation in which one group's spiritual needs conflict with another group's desires? Describe the situation.
2. Why do you think most religions have sacred places? Do you have places in your culture that are considered sacred or holy?

Nearly all human groups consider certain places special, even sacred. For many Native Americans, the land where they have lived, where their ancestors are buried, and where they continue to honor nature is sacred. But these same places are now U.S. territory, and most white people in the United States do not consider these places sacred. Instead they may, for example, see this land as rich in mineral wealth and want to dig up the land to reach this wealth. In many places in the country Native Americans are fighting legal battles to prevent the destruction of places that they consider holy. This article describes some of this battle.

The canyon wakes at twilight. As the rocks lose their heat, the wind kicks up in all directions, and, for a moment, its fitful whistling sounds like chanting voices. But the power of suggestion is strong in this deep tributary of the Grand Canyon, where the Havasupai Indians have been living for more generations than anyone can count. It only takes a few days down here to start seeing spirits in the shadows, and ghosts in the rocks. . . . Rex Tilousi, one of the Havasupai's most venerated spiritual elders, [has just made] a long trip home from the U.S. Court of Appeals in San Francisco. He has spent the week arguing, as he has for years, that the government's plan to allow a uranium mine at a sacred site north of the Havasupai's holy Red Butte would wreak an irrevocable spiritual and physical catastrophe upon his people.

···················

The fight to save sacred places is becoming for American Indians of many tribes a full-time job. The U.S. Forest Service wants to let oil companies drill for oil and natural gas in the windy Badger Two Medicine site of northern Montana, where Blackfeet seek visions now as they did five centuries ago. A seven-telescope observatory is about to be built on the San

Carlos Apache's Mount Graham, and a proposed recreational reservoir threatens to inundate a Western Shoshone burial ground in Nevada. The Forest Service plans to turn the Big Horn Medicine Wheel in northern Wyoming—an ancient, timekeeping circle of stones common to about a dozen Plains tribes—into a major tourist attraction, complete with a visitors' center. The National Park Service wants to turn Rainbow Bridge, the southern Utah site that figures in the Navajo creation story, into more of a tourist center than it has already become. The list goes on.

"Conservatively, we're talking about sixty to seventy sacred-lands disputes in the country," says Jerry Flute of the Association on American Indian Affairs. These encroachments are driven by the same economics that are damming rivers and razing forests coast to coast. Only, for Indians, what's being destroyed is the anchor of an ancient spirituality—the equivalent of Mecca to Muslims or of Jerusalem to Christians and Jews. . . . "We have fewer and fewer sacred sites that haven't been harmed, altered, encroached upon, or destroyed," says Steven Moore, a staff attorney for the Native American Rights Fund. . . . "There's a cumulative effect, too. The more sacred sites are destroyed, the weaker the community of Indians becomes, and the easier it is to destroy their sacred sites."

Indians talk about the attack on their sacred lands as cutting right to the quick of who they are. "You people left the graves of your grandfathers and brought with you everything you thought was important," says Buster Yellow Kidney, a sixty-two-year-old Blackfeet in northern Montana who spends half his time on the road as a kind of Indian revivalist, performing ceremonies all over the country to bring the people back in. "The land of the grandfathers wasn't important to you, but it is to us." The European newcomers built churches, into which they retreated so that sight of the land wouldn't interfere with their prayers. But to Yellow Kidney and others like him, the land is the religion, and vice versa. "It's not like a church—that if it burns down you can rebuild it again, and there you've got your church," says Clay Bravo. "If you lose your sacred site, it's gone forever, and you can't be whole."

•••••••••••••••••

Sacking temples is a time-honored way to debase a conquered people, and, when a sacred butte in Arizona is bulldozed for a gravel pit, many Indians see it as just that. "Our fate has always been the same as the land's," says Russell Means, a former leader of the American Indian Movement. . . . "White America's eradication of the land meant eradication of the Indians. It's part of the same damn genocide."

While the disgrace that most non-Indian visitors would notice first on many reservations is poverty and neglect, Indians are far less likely to complain about the economic abuse they've suffered than the cultural—including the decades of government policy that banned their languages, raided their ceremonies, stole their children, criminalized peyote, and has continued to allow the destruction of their sacred places. Native American religious and cultural practices are at least rhetorically honored, although not protected, by the American Indian Religious Freedom Act of 1978. AIRFA, however, is only a policy statement; nothing currently on the books guards the holy places by which many Native Americans define themselves. Some see the attack on their sacred sites as distinctly worse than other white onslaughts of insult and violence. They feel their very foundation is crumbling, and worry that, if the destruction of sacred places continues, the country could in a few generations be a land without Native Americans. . . .

Dan Baum

1. This article begins by describing countryside. What do you suppose is the purpose of this description?
2. Find the section of this article that compares Indian sacred lands and white people's churches. Describe this comparison in your own words.
3. Explain in your own words why these sites are so important to Native Americans.
4. What is meant by the last sentence of this text: "if the destruction of sacred places continues, the country could in a few generations be a land without Native Americans."

Journal Suggestions

- What is your reaction to this article? Who do you think will win in this dispute? Why? Is that who should win?
- If the dispute described here were taking place in your country, how would people react? Would they sympathize with the position of the Native Americans, or would they feel that leaving these lands alone means wasting their potential for producing wealth and entertainment?
- Religious intolerance seems to be a source of many conflicts among communities, and yet most major religions preach peace. How do you explain this contradiction?

➤ *Optional Writing Assignment*

> Both the articles "Do Not Disturb" (page 297) and "Sacred
> Places" describe native people struggling against changes that
> the dominant society is trying to force on them. Whose rights
> seem most important to protect—those of the native people, who
> are a minority in number, or those of the dominant, majority cul-
> ture? Explain why you feel this way.   ◄

Auto-cracy Is Being Exported to Third World

Bikes Make More Sense Than Cars for the People of Developing Nations

Before you read, consider the following questions:

1. Does your home town have a public transportation system? If so, describe its good and bad points.
2. Does the town or city in which you are now studying have a public transportation system? If so, describe its good and bad points.
3. Do you own a car? What problems are associated with owning a car?

This article describes the problems created by increasing desire for and dependence on cars instead of on transportation systems that create less pollution, such as bicycles. It then describes the advantages of using bikes, the resistance to using bikes, and a multinational program to promote the use of bikes.

One of the most common images of an advanced, Western-style culture is that of a bustling, traffic-filled city. Since their first appearance on American roadways, automobiles have become a symbol of progress, a source of thousands of jobs, and an almost inalienable right for citizens' personal freedom of movement. In recent decades, our oft-touted "love affair" with the car is being exported directly to the developing world, and it is increasingly apparent that this transfer is leading to disaster.

America's almost complete dependence on automobiles has been a terrible mistake. As late as 1950, a large percentage of the American public used mass transit. A combination of public policy decisions and corporate conspiracy saw to it that countless convenient and efficient urban streetcar and intra-city rail systems were dismantled. Our air quality now suffers from the effects of carbon monoxide, hydrocarbons, and other pollutants emitted directly from our cars. Our lives have been planned along a road grid—homes far from work, shopping far from everything, with hideous stretches of concrete and blacktop in between.

Developing countries are copying Western-style transportation systems down to the last traffic snarl. The problems caused by motorized vehicles in the West are often magnified in developing nations. Pollution control measures are either lax or nonexistent, leading to choking clouds of smog. Gasoline still contains lead, which is extremely poisonous to humans. Movement in some cities comes to a virtual standstill as motorized traffic competes with rickshaws, buses, bicycles, mopeds, and pedestrians.

In addition to pollution and congestion problems, auto safety is a critical issue in developing nations.

••••••••••••••••••

Given all the problems with motorized vehicles, it comes as no surprise that bicycles have emerged as a legitimate transportation technology for developing nations. They are relatively easy to manufacture, emit no pollutants, require minimal maintenance, and use no electricity or fossil fuels. They can be customized for a wide variety of uses, including carrying firewood and water (a task usually performed by women, often lugging huge bundles on their heads for miles) and serving as medical supply carriers and ambulances in remote areas (where the new mountain bike technologies are especially useful).

Marcia Lowe, in her article "The Bicycle: Vehicle for a Small Planet" in *Worldwatch Paper* (No. 90, Sept. 1989), points out that in developing countries, automobiles can cost as much as 30 times the annual per capita income and that most Third World people will "never sit inside—let alone own—an automobile." Smaller motorized vehicles, such as motorcycles and mopeds, are more attainable, but still pose pollution and safety hazards. Public transit systems, mainly buses, are not adequate for the number of riders and are often unable to navigate narrow or poorly conditioned roadways.

Besides providing critical access to services and personal door-to-door mobility, bicycles are an excellent source of jobs and foreign exchange in developing countries. Lowe cites the "mass of self-employed entrepreneurs"—including bicycle newspaper and food vendors, passenger-carrying rickshaw drivers, scrap recyclers, and delivery people—who constitute 20 to 70 percent of urban labor forces in some cities. Secondary opportunities arise for bicycle mechanics and repair stations. Bicycle manufacturing is another industry that can be developed with a small investment. Lowe points out that India has become a major bicycle producer and exporter, sharing its small-scale, labor-intensive manufacturing processes through joint-venture and license agreements with countries throughout Asia, Africa, and the Caribbean.

China may be the best example of a nation consciously promoting a bicycle-based transportation system. By providing guarded parking, plenty of repair services, and monetary incentives for cyclists, China boasts the world's largest percentage of bicycle commuters. The success has been so great that, according to Lowe, "The kingdom of bicycles now suffers from [bicycle] traffic jams," and planners are urging cyclists to use the bus more often.

Despite the bicycle's advantages for developing nations, many of them are actively campaigning against bicycle use. According to Michael Renner in his *Worldwatch Paper* (No. 84, June 1988) article "Rethinking the Role of the Automobile," Third World government policies favor private car ownership by the "tiny but affluent elite" and are "squandering scarce resources and distorting development priorities." He cites as an example [one country] where only one out of every 200 people owns a car, yet one-third of the country's import budget is devoted to fuel and transport equipment. Western-educated engineers and policy makers return home armed with both their degrees and an image of what a "successful" nation's transportation system looks like. It does not include bicycles. Other anti-bicycle motivations vary, but seem to fall into four general cultural or political arguments: 1) Bicycles interfere with motorized traffic; 2) Bicycles are suitable only for the poor and unskilled, and therefore advertise backwardness to foreign visitors; 3) Bicycle taxis are inhumane; and 4) Bicycle use is inappropriate for women because it is immodest and beyond their physical capabilities.

Working to dispel these anti-bicycle prejudices is the Washington, D.C.-based Institute for Transportation and Development Policy, which has pioneered bicycle use as part of a sustainable transportation strategy in developing nations. Since 1984, ITDP has established four programs, the best known of which is Bikes Not Bombs—a project whose 20 U.S. chapters donated more than 5,000 used bicycles to the people of Nicaragua for use by health, education, and other civilian workers. The ITDP newsletter *Bikes Not Bombs Campaign Update* (Vol. 6, No. 1, 1990) reports that the campaign is cooperating with a Nicaraguan non-profit group, the Organization of Revolutionary Disabled People, at a "bicycle and wheelchair assembly and repair shop in Leon, which now employs more than a dozen mechanics, many of them disabled veterans of the Nicaraguan revolution and war against the contras." The three other ITDP programs are Bikes for Africa, which recently received a grant to purchase bicycles and parts to assist women farmers and refugee outreach workers in Mozambique; Mobility Haiti, which uses all-terrain bicycles and carts for child survival health programs; and the Transportation Alternative Project, formed to press the World Bank to consider non-motorized transportation in its lending to developing countries.

For developed countries, dealing with the ravages of automobile-based societies is proving to be an awesome task. Developing countries can learn from the West's mistakes.

Mary Morse

1. What are some of the problems this article says are created by the use of cars as the primary means of transportation?
2. Despite all the problems caused by cars, why do the "tiny but affluent elite" groups mentioned in this article insist on continuing to drive cars?
3. What are some of the advantages of using bikes mentioned in the article? Are there other advantages not mentioned?
4. What reasons do people described in this article give for resisting the use of bikes? Can you think of other disadvantages of using bikes?

Journal Suggestions

- Do you own and ride a bike either in your home country or where you are now studying? Are you pleased with this situation? Why or why not?

- What is your reaction to an article written in the United States that promotes the use of bicycles in other parts of the world but does not mention the advantages of using bikes in the United States?

- What is your reaction to the idea that the rest of the world can or should learn from the mistakes of the West? Do you agree or do you feel that people learn best from their own mistakes?

- Nearly all of us have had bad experiences with one type of transportation or another. What is the worst means of travel you have ever experienced? Describe other funny or bad transportation experiences. What can be done to make traveling easier on people?

- Does the use of cars cause particular problems in your country? What are they? How can governments encourage the use of bikes among people who do not want to give up cars?

The Japanese Funeral Ceremony and the Spiritual World after Death

Before you read, consider the following questions:

1. What are the most important occasions when people get together in your culture? Weddings? Births? Young people's coming-of-age parties?
2. What are some of the special things that people in your culture do on these occasions?

In this article the student author describes what funeral ceremonies are like in Japan.

The Japanese funeral ceremony seems to be very different from the western funeral ceremony. It is rather complicated but is really interesting because the Japanese way of thinking after death can be observed through this funeral custom, which is based on Buddhism. The spirit of the dead person is supposed to stay in his house with his family for forty-nine days after he dies, so his family have several ceremonies to comfort his spirit during this period. Among those ceremonies, especially three seem to be regarded as the most important ones. They are (1) "Otsuya," which is held on the first evening after his death or on the next evening after his dying; (2) "Osoushiki," held the day after Otsuya; (3) "Shijukunichi-no-Houyou," held on the forty-ninth day after his death. This essay will focus on the concept of the world of death in Japan.

Otsuya is held to say "Good-bye" to the deceased from the early evening through the late time of the night. The word "Otsuya" is explained as "Through the night" in kanji, our Chinese characters. His family immediately prepares a specially decorative altar for him, and his coffin is put on the shelf in the middle of the altar. The family ornaments it with several flower baskets and some fruit baskets. In addition, they never forget to put his picture on the altar. He is smiling in it to visitors. His body is also surrounded by many chrysanthemums in the coffin. Thus, he is beautifully ornamented before he leaves for Heaven.

Many people come on this night. The relatives, his friends, his co-workers, neighbors and friends of his family members visit for Otsuya. On this night his soul is supposed to remain in his dead body, so all the visitors say good-bye to him in their minds while looking at his picture on the altar. Every visitor steps up to the altar one by one, burns incense, and makes a bow in front of it. (At this time they tell him the last good-bye.) This ritual is exactly the same one we use when we pray to Buddha in a temple. The dead person is supposed to become one of the Buddhas, not a real Buddha but a sort of Buddha at the moment of his death. This thought comes from the doctrine of Buddhism, which says all people can be absolved of all sins after death.

There is one more important event in this ceremony, Otsuya. A Buddhist priest chants sutra for the peace of his spirit in front of his altar and gives him a new name which he should be called by in Heaven. This new name is given as a result of considering his character and his achievement in his work; therefore, it is very meaningful. At the same time he gets a new birthday. From that time the day of his death called "Meinichi" is regarded as his birthday and is commemorated as such each year. "Meinichi" means "The Day of Life" in kanji.

On the next day of Otsuya, the family has a real funeral, "Osoushiki." This time, usually only his family and the relatives participate in it. Osoushiki is never held in the evening because it is supposed to be very bad to have an Osoushiki after it gets dark. Osoushiki seems to be more formal than Otsuya, even though it is carried out by his family and the relatives. All the visitors who participate in it should be dressed in black formal wear; women don't wear any accessory except pearls. Bright jewelry like diamonds and gold is completely avoided to express their deep sorrow at losing him. Everybody never laughs because laughing is regarded as impolite to him and is supposed to be indiscreet in this sad situation. Otsuya is a rather colorful and merry ceremony; on the contrary, Osoushiki is a serious and grand ceremony. All the people seem to give reverence to his spirit.

While a priest dressed in his most splendid clothes showing his high position among Buddhists is chanting a long sutra in the main hall of the temple, everybody keeps silent and droops his/her head deeply as if meditating. In the middle of the sutra, the priest asks them to pray to Buddha for his spirit. His family and the relatives step up to the small table set up at the back of the priests; then they burn incense and pray with their palms together.

After this rather long ceremony finishes, some of them see him off at a crematory, and others wait for the coming back home of his remains. At this time family members and the close relatives go to a crematory with his body.

The family has ceremonies on every seventh day until the forty-ninth day comes finally. On this day his spirit is supposed to leave for Heaven, departing from his family after staying with his family for forty-eight days. The family has a big ceremony like a Osoushiki again in a temple. This big ceremony is called

"Shijukunichi-no-Houyou," and this word means "The ritual on the forty-ninth day" in Japanese.

The concept after his leaving for Heaven from this world is interesting. His spirit flies into the sky and arrives at the riverside where this physical world is separated from the dead spiritual world. When he reaches this shore, he can find a boat which will carry him to the other side of the river in which there is a world of dead people. Once he crosses this river, he can't come back to this side again. He must become a dweller of the death world and will wait for the day of rebirth in this world.

Thus, the series of funeral services is carried out through a long period. His family can be gradually set free from anguish after he dies through this long period, so Japanese funerals seem to be held to comfort not only the spirit of the dead people but also their families. His family keeps going to his grave on his Meinichi every year and constantly keeps having ceremonies on the particular years until fifty years have passed. Japanese live closely with the spirits of dead people like this. Some people say that they can feel that the spirits of their ancestors or spirits of their ex-family members always protect them. It's a really mysterious world.

Masako Imamiya (Japan)

1. How are Japanese funeral ceremonies divided, according to this article?
2. Who is involved in the funeral ceremony in Japan besides the immediate family?
3. What is the significance of the forty-nine-day period?

Journal Suggestion

- In some cultures funerals are extremely solemn. In other countries, perhaps where people believe in an afterlife, funerals include a great deal of eating and drinking, almost like celebrations. How do people organize funerals in your country?

Japanese Miai

Before you read, consider the following questions:

1. Do you know what a "blind date" is? Have you ever had such an experience or known anyone else who has? How successful was the experience?
2. Do arranged marriages take place in your country? How are the marriages arranged?
3. What traditions are associated with weddings in your country? Do the couple and their guests wear special clothing? Does the event take place somewhere special?

This selection describes a system used in Japan to bring together a man and a woman who have not been able to find someone to marry within their own social group.

In Japan, we have a custom to help us find a good marriageable spouse. It is called *miai. Miai* is a meeting between a man and a woman on the understanding that they may choose each other as husband or wife. The meeting is arranged by a person who knows both parties. For instance, a teacher may try to match one of her former students with her niece, or a company executive may think his secretary and his friend's son will make a good couple. They exchange an account of their families and personal backgrounds and their photographs so that they can judge if the counterpart will be a good spouse. If the credentials are satisfactory on paper, they meet at the go-between's house or in a fashionable hotel lobby or restaurant. After an introductory chat, the go-between and his wife will leave the young couple to talk by themselves. They may go to a movie or disco, or go to a park for a stroll. After the meeting they report to the go-between on whether they want to meet again or not. After several such meetings, the couple agrees to marry.

The marriage after a process like this is called *miai kekkon,* an "arranged" or "interview" marriage. Although such an arrangement may strike people in the West as unusual and perhaps even undesirable, it is an extremely useful way to find a spouse if one has little social contact with members of the opposite sex.

Taisuke Akasaka (Japan)

1. Why do the Japanese use *miai* to get to know another person? What is the advantage of this system?
2. Use your own words to describe how this meeting takes place.

Journal Suggestions

- How do young men and women get to know each other in your country? Do young people date in couples or go out in groups? At what point in a friendship would you need to introduce your friend to your parents?
- What procedure do people follow to get their parents' consent for marriage in your country? Can a couple get married without their parents' consent?

Taking the Bungee Plunge
Are High-Risk Sports an Inexpensive Form of Therapy?

Before you read, consider the following questions:

1. Are people in your country interested in sports? What is the most popular sport at home? Why do you think it is so popular?
2. Have you ever done something for fun that you knew would be dangerous? Why did you do it? Describe the experience.
3. Have you ever watched a dangerous sport? Why do people like dangerous sports?

The title of this article refers to a fad called bungee jumping. Believe it or not, in this activity, a person is attached to an elastic cord and jumps off a high place head first. Although the person falls freely for some time, the elastic cord is designed to prevent the person from hitting the ground and being killed. The article here discusses the reasons people may have for engaging in such a strange and potentially dangerous form of fun.

. . . For many in the growing crowd attracted to bungee jumping, rock climbing, skydiving, and other high-risk weekend fun, these breathtaking activities have become a form of budget therapy. Life-imperiling sports that some would argue reflect a death wish are for them a life-affirming challenge.

Humans are inherently risk-taking creatures, contends Dan Bensimhon in *Men's Health* (April 1992). Most of our prehistoric past was filled with danger and uncertainty. The people who survived were those who thrived on risks. But today, adventure for the average person usually amounts to nothing more than deft negotiation of a jam-packed freeway. Thus, bungee jumping—the non-art of flinging yourself into mid-air with an ankle strapped to elastic—can be an exhilarating thrill in an otherwise dreary nine-to-five existence.

But for many enthusiasts the expectations are more disconcertingly far reaching. "Bungee jumping may be seen as a metaphor for life," claims enthusiast Cathy Hanesworth in an interview in *East Bay Express* (Dec. 13, 1991). "If you can prove to yourself that you can do something that is very scary, you can carry that confidence with you into any situation . . . because you have pushed your physical and mental limits farther than your comfort zone."

Some psychologists agree. Dangerous sport, they believe, boosts personal growth. Suspend yourself from a bridge today and commit to a long-term relationship tomorrow; dive out of a plane now, realize your dream of becoming the next Ella Fitzgerald later—or so the logic goes. As Bensimhon points out, experts who have studied risk taking say it develops character and courage, extends creativity, and helps establish a sense of possibility.

There's no denying that success at something new and challenging is an invaluable experience. But what are you really succeeding at when you parachute out of two-seater aircraft? With a bit of luck, you touch ground intact and sigh blissfully. Perhaps you become a conversation piece among friends for a nanosecond or two. But ultimately the only thing you've truly accomplished is *not dying*. Bruce Ogilvie, a pioneer in the field of sports psychology, believes that, for suicide-sport fanatics, "the immediate high is enough in and of itself. Risk taking isn't likely to transfer into other areas of life." To suggest that a confirmed bachelor will bungee jump his way into love, marriage, and 2.5 children "is at best a tenuous leap," he argues.

What the popularity of potentially fatal sports reveals is that in an I-want-it-now microwave culture, quick exercises in temerity become a stand-in for the time-consuming process of mastering a skill. Many of the thrill sports merely require you to say, "I want to take a chance. Where do I sign up?" We build sustainable confidence not by taking life-threatening risks but by gradually working at things we never thought we could achieve. "The best moments usually occur when a person's body or mind is stretched to its limits in a voluntary effort to accomplish something difficult and worthwhile," says University of Chicago psychology professor Mihaly Csikszentmihalyi in the San Francisco monthly magazine *The City* (Oct. 1991). The sensation of completing a bungee jump will probably come up short against the satisfaction gained from learning to speak a new language after months of study and practice. Nor could it compare—especially for those who grew up believing that the concept of hand-eye coordination was a vicious myth—to learning how to play tennis, row a boat, or knit a sweater. In the end, it's hard to believe that risking death is a meaningful way to embrace life.

Ginia Bellafante

1. What reasons does the article give for people's interest in such dangerous sports as bungee jumping?
2. According to the article, why are these sports especially attractive in modern times?

3. What is meant by an expression used in this article, "an I-want-it-now microwave culture"?

4. What kinds of activities does the author suggest are more meaningful than these high-risk sports? What arguments does she make to support her position?

Journal Suggestions

- What is your reaction to the information in this article? Write a journal entry in which you make comments or note anything you found interesting.

- Not all high-risk activities are life threatening. If you have left your home to study abroad, you are also taking a high risk. What kinds of risks are you taking by studying abroad?

- Some people become extremely wrapped up in sports, to the point of seeming to lose their common sense—for example, the violent soccer fans who fight each other and destroy property during soccer matches. How do you account for this type of behavior? Do you think it is something in the sport itself that creates or promotes violence in the spectators? What other factors may account for the violent behavior of some sports fans?

Darwin Revisited

Survival of the Fittest May Mean Survival of the Most Cooperative

Before you read, consider the following questions:

1. What do you know about Darwinism?
2. What animal species do you know of that seems to cooperate to improve the chances of all the group's members to survive? What do they do to cooperate with one another?

This article describes a challenge to the widely accepted idea that competition among individuals is the force that drives evolution. We can think of evolution as the natural changes in populations of organisms over time, creating new species. In this new analysis of how living things interact, cooperation for the survival of the whole group is thought to be more important than competition for the survival of individual members of the group. Finally, the article describes criticism of the way the West has thought of science and has used Western scientific methods to study living systems.

Life on earth is amazingly varied and complex: Widely disparate species of plants and animals occupy countless ecological niches throughout our biosphere. Science has long supposed that this proliferation came about through gradual changes in the individual organisms that best adapted to their environments. This view of life's evolution, expounded by Charles Darwin in 1859, was by the 1940s combined with the laws of genetics to form the evolutionary theory that reigns today: neo-Darwinism. A cornerstone of modern biology, neo-Darwinism has long been the target of religious groups. Recently, however, it has also been challenged from within the scientific community itself by heretics who believe that it's time to update our views of evolution.

Evolution, according to neo-Darwinians, proceeds as individual plants and animals born with mutations that enable them to better survive in their environments are then rewarded with greater opportunities to reproduce, allowing them to pass on their superior adaptations to their descendants—the survival of the fittest. While not questioning the fact of evolution, some scientists and philosophers are critical of Darwin's notion that natural selection acts on *individuals,* not on groups, that an organism's evolutionary stock rises or falls according to how it alone fares against the environment, not how it relates to its own population group.

The research of V. C. Wynne-Edwards, professor of natural

history at Scotland's University of Aberdeen, challenges this primacy of the individual. Throughout his career, reports the British magazine *The Ecologist* (May/June 1991), Wynne-Edwards has found that traits important to the survival of a group of animals are reinforced by natural selection more than traits benefiting any given individual. Studies of feeding territory among members of certain bird species, for example, reveal an arrangement that works best for the population as a whole. Conventional theory assumes that an aggressive individual takes and defends more territory, thereby being "the fittest." This aggressiveness, however, reduces the overall reproductive success of the group and thus weakens the overall survival rate of the group as a whole, including the aggressive individual. Wynne-Edwards claims that nature actually selects cooperation and compromise in many ecosystems. Survival of the fittest may really mean survival of organisms that can live best with one another.

Neo-Darwinism's shortcomings are related to its being mired in a 19th-century outlook, says Robert Wesson in his book *Beyond Natural Selection* (MIT Press, 1991). This mechanistic worldview was adapted wholesale from the early physical sciences. In the 20th century, insoluble paradoxes eventually forced physicists to abandon the view of the universe as a predictable mechanism. But neo-Darwinism, says Wesson, still clings to the illusion of predictability.

Other commentators find that the flaws of neo-Darwinism go right to its scientific bedrock. Edward Goldsmith writes in *The Ecologist* (March/April 1990) that "to understand evolution one must reject the neo-Darwinist thesis and indeed the Paradigm of Science it so faithfully reflects." Western science, he claims, rests on assumptions that are not appropriate for studying life. Science proceeds by reductionism, studying complex systems by separately analyzing their constituent parts. "This approach makes it impossible to understand life," writes Goldsmith, "since one of the most important features of living processes is their hierarchical organization." Goldsmith, like Wesson, also finds neo-Darwinism tainted with the notion of mechanism. He points out that studying organisms and ecosystems as though they behaved like machines forces us to ignore all the defining characteristics of living things—consciousness, intelligence, purposiveness, self-regulation, cooperation. Only by abandoning the paradigm of Western science, Goldsmith argues, can we make a start on understanding the true science of life.

James Marti

1. What does "survival of the fittest" mean?
2. How does this idea relate to the idea of competition?
3. What is the new view of evolution described here?

Journal Suggestions

- Do you think competition or cooperation is the stronger force in your own society? In the United States? Is this as it should be, or would we be better off if the other force were stronger? Do you think of yourself as more competitive or as more cooperative? Which would you rather be?

➤ *Optional Writing Assignment*

This article on Darwinism presents a new interpretation of the notion of "survival of the fittest." Assume that you are explaining both the old and the new interpretation to someone who has not heard of Darwinism. Use your own words and try to be as clear as possible. ◄

From *Black Holes and Baby Universes*

Before you read, consider the following questions:

1. Describe the way the scientific method works to establish the "facts" of science. What do scientists do?
2. What is a theory in science supposed to do?
3. Can you think of an old scientific theory that is no longer generally accepted? What happened?
4. If you have ever taken a class in physics, what do you know about Einstein's Theory of Relativity?

In this excerpt, Stephen Hawking, one of the greatest scientific minds of the twentieth century, discusses the relationship between scientific theories, experiments, and observations. He tells us that experiments, which many people think of as equal to the scientific approach, are not very important in physics. What is more important is that scientific theories be logical and consistent with themselves; that is, one part of the good theory cannot contradict another part, and the theory should correspond to our observations of reality. He argues that in theoretical physics, theories survive until they begin to no longer correspond to observations. When this happens, scientists are forced to develop a new theory that explains the observations better.

This seems simple enough. But, what may be especially difficult to understand about this idea, as Hawking explains it, is that the reality that scientists observe depends on the theory that they have. In other words, reality is not simply out there and real for anyone to see. We see a different reality if we have a different theory. Does this mean that reality is not really "out there" at all but rather, as some religions have said, reality is inside each of us, created by our own minds? Hawking rejects this idea, he says, because if we believe that reality is only in our minds and that there is no outside reality, we have no reason to ever do anything; we would live our lives by contemplating only our own thoughts—which is, of course, what holy people from many religions worldwide do. Nevertheless, if you think of science as cold hard facts, Hawking's discussion here may convince you that, at least in theoretical physics, science may have a closer relationship with philosophy than you may have thought.

In theoretical physics, the search for logical self-consistency has always been more important in making advances than experimental results. Otherwise elegant and beautiful theories have been rejected because they don't agree with observation, but I don't know of any major theory that has been advanced just on the basis of experiment. The theory always came first, put forward from the desire to have an elegant and consistent mathematical model. The theory then makes predictions, which can then be tested by observation. If the observations agree with the predictions, that doesn't prove the theory; but the theory survives to make further predictions, which again are tested against observation. If the observations don't agree with the predictions, one abandons the theory.

Or rather, that is what is supposed to happen. In practice people are very reluctant to give up a theory in which they've invested a lot of time and effort. They usually start by questioning the accuracy of the observations. If that fails, they try to modify the theory in an ad hoc manner. Eventually the theory becomes a creaking and ugly edifice. Then someone suggests a new theory, in which all the awkward observations are explained in an elegant and natural manner. An example of this was the Michelson-Morley experiment, performed in 1887, which showed that the speed of light was always the same no matter how the source or the observer were moving. This seemed ridiculous. Surely someone moving toward the light ought to measure it traveling at a higher speed than someone moving in the same direction as the light; yet the experiment showed that both observers would measure exactly the same speed. For the next 18 years people like Hendrik Lorentz and George Fitzgerald tried to accommodate this observation within accepted ideas of space and time. They introduced ad hoc postulates, such as proposing that objects got shorter when they moved at high speeds. The entire framework of physics became clumsy and ugly. Then in 1905 Einstein suggested a much more attractive viewpoint, in which time was not regarded as completely separate and on its own. Instead, it was combined with space in a four dimensional object called space-time. Einstein was driven to this idea not so much by the experimental results as by the desire to make two parts of the theory fit together in a consistent whole. The two parts were the laws that govern the electric and magnetic fields, and the laws that govern the motion of bodies.

I don't think Einstein, or anyone else in 1905, realized how simple and elegant the new theory of relativity was. It completely revolutionized our notions of space and time. This example illustrates well the difficulty of being a realist in the philosophy of science, for what we regard as reality is conditioned by the theory to which we subscribe. I'm certain that Lorentz and Fitzgerald regarded themselves as realists, interpreting the experiment on the speed of light in terms of Newtonian ideas of absolute space and absolute time. These notions of space and time seemed to correspond to common sense and reality. Yet nowadays those who are familiar with the theory of relativity, still a disturbingly small minority, have a rather different view. We ought to be telling people about the modern understanding of such basic concepts as space and time.

If what we regard as real depends on our theory, how can we make reality the basis of our philosophy? I would say that I'm a realist in the sense that I think there's a universe out there waiting to be investigated and understood. I regard the solipsist position that everything is the creation of our imaginations as a waste of time. No one acts on that basis. But we cannot distinguish what is real about the universe without a theory. I therefore take the view . . . that a theory of physics is just a mathematical model that we use to describe the results of observations. A theory is a good theory if it is an elegant model, if it describes a wide class of observations, and if it predicts the results of new observations. Beyond that, it makes no sense to ask if it corresponds to reality, because we do not know what reality is independent of a theory.

➤ *Stephen Hawking*

1. What is Hawking's definition of a good theory in physics?
2. What do you think Hawking means when he says, "If the observations agree with the predictions, that doesn't prove the theory"? If this is true, then what *does* prove a theory, if anything?
3. How do theories fall out of favor or become considered inaccurate or useless?
4. How do new theories become accepted?
5. Can you explain what Hawking means by saying, "we do not know what reality is independent of a theory"?

Journal Suggestions

- Sometimes common sense deceives us. What seems obviously to be true may not be true. An obvious example of this is that the earth looks flat, but very few people believe this now. Can you think of other examples where something that looks true is not and where our common sense deceives us?
- If you are interested in the study of the universe, what is the most interesting aspect of this field for you? What is the most interesting idea you have heard about the nature of the universe? What do you know, for example, about black

holes in space? Have you heard of the idea that the universe began with a "big bang"? What does that mean?

- Some aspects of physics seem extremely theoretical. Should these aspects be taught in school if they have no practical side to them? Why or why not? What kind of people do you think are attracted to very abstract subjects like theoretical physics?

- Some people might say that it does not matter what you think about something; what matters is what you do. In other words, practical science is more important than theoretical science. Do you agree or disagree? What role *does* theory play in our lives?

The Quality of Mercy

Not a Black-and-White Issue. An African American Victim's Story

Before you read, consider the following questions:

1. Have you ever been a victim of crime? How did you react? Do you feel that that was the best reaction?
2. Have you known anyone else who was a victim of crime? How did they react?

Insecurity has become an increasingly important concern for this country. Many people see the connection between the increase in crime here and the increase in unemployment and hopelessness as the rich get richer and the poor get poorer. The following text is a frightening story of an African American woman who is stopped by a gang of young men with a gun who are apparently attempting to steal her car. She escapes without harm because one of the young men urges the others not to rob a sister, that is, a fellow African American. When she later talks to the police, she realizes that she probably does not have the same ideas about this situation as the others do.

It's 10:30 on a Saturday night, and I am trying to drive up La Cienega, but even at this hour, the turgid flow of traffic is maddening. I decide to cut over to Crescent Heights, which should move faster. As I swing right onto Airdrome, a pedestrian steps in front of my car. This strikes me as very wrong, but I stop.

When the guy moves around toward my side, I see why it feels odd. He is a young, black kid, braced in a combat stance, and he is pointing a gun at me. Before the fear slams my senses shut, I register a baby face with dimples, a sensuous, pink mouth, and a Batman cap with the bill sideways on his head. But his eyes are what make me lose hope. He looks bored.

Panic wrestles with paralysis as I contemplate flooring it and running him down. But he would definitely shoot me, and I can tell from the size of the barrel that if he gets off even one round, it will be lethal.

He walks toward my door, and the closer he gets, the more I feel my system become drowsy with fear.

But my thoughts surge through a list of protests so naive that it surprises me. Having worked for years to transform my own black rage into something constructive, I had not realized I felt entitled to some kind of immunity. Instead, I am now staring down the cannon of this kid who is acting out *his* black rage.

Then two more guys appear, quiet as eels, a foot from the

door. I sense rather than see them, because I can't tear my eyes away from the escape route ahead. I struggle not to slide completely into shock. My unlocked car door swings open.

"Get out," the kid demands. His voice is close behind me to the left. The muscles at the base of my head twitch as he gently rests the gun barrel at the base of my brainstem. I fantasize the trajectory of the bullet passing through the left rear of my skull and exploding out my right temple. I know I should do exactly as he says, but I'm too scared to move.

Then I remember something familiar about this kid's stance. His teachers were probably cops. He has that same paramilitary detachment. Long ago, I was taught that when a jacked-up cop shakes you down, you keep your hands in plain sight and don't make any fast moves. That lesson was learned fighting for the civil rights of kids such as these. I hope now it will work to protect me from them.

Then another buried lesson surfaces. I was backpacking in Wyoming and had fallen asleep in the afternoon. I awoke at dusk to find a young mountain lion on a ledge above me. Somehow I knew that I must not look it in the eye or give in to my panicky impulse to tear off down the mountain. So I acted as if I were unaware of any danger. Once the lion had satisfied itself that I was neither a threat nor a source of food, it vanished. My hope, now, is to maintain a posture of active passivity. So I continue staring ahead.

"I *said* get out of the car, bitch," the kid snaps.

The layers of contempt in the word "bitch" make me wonder whether the plan is rape. I notice my legs cramp. I decide that exposing my entire body to his rage would be suicidal, so I don't move at all. But I have another problem. I'm angry. And that has to be contained.

I decide that I am not going to be punished for whatever it is these kids hate women for. When I realize that such puny resistance as I will offer may be effective, it gives me courage. This is not the first group of bullies I have faced. At the WASPy prep school I attended in rural Colorado, "nigger" was the nicest name they called me. It got so virulent I used to eat my meals on a tray in the lavatory. But one day I saw myself in the mirror, cowering on the can, scarfing down my lunch. And I realized this was the bottom. Nothing they could say to me could be worse than this, so I took my tray into the lunchroom.

From then on, it was open season. They went at me with a renewed vengeance. Then one evening before study hall, I once more lost my nerve. I just couldn't stand it, so I walked away from school—which could have gotten me expelled. They loved it. And that was it. I picked up a rock and decided to fight. And to my surprise, the chase ended, the name-calling stopped. Now, even though these kids are black, it feels just like my old home-town.

The first kid drags a jagged fingernail across my throat as he tries to yank me out of the car. But even though I haven't moved, I am no longer immobile. My grip on the steering wheel tightens, even as his pulling me slams my head against the roof of the car. After a halfhearted go at it, he stops and moves away from the car. There is whispering among the boys, and I pick up the phrase "Bitch must be crazy." I pray that I won't slide into hysterical laughter.

This standoff has gone on far too long. The cars passing behind me on brightly lit La Cienega sound so deliciously ordinary, I can hear the clicking of the traffic signal as the lights cycle from green to amber to red. Then I hear the guy who has been standing the farthest away approach the car. He croons. "Ah, man. Man, this is a sister. We can't be ripping off no sister."

I don't get it. Then I realize that, in the dark, they could not tell that I was black. But in this epidemic of black-on-black violence, I would never expect my race to protect me. If anything, it should make them rip me off with impunity.

But the compassion flowing toward me from this young man is unmistakable. He has interceded for me. And I am sure that he is taking a tremendous risk by doing so. I also know that this delicate dynamic could shift back in a breath. But I have to look at him anyway. "Thank you," I say, then floor it.

••••••••••••••••••

It's a good thing the car finds the way back home, because I can't remember how to get there. When I am finally safe, I only want to immerse myself in the mundane. I definitely do not want to call the police. But somebody else might be in danger. So I have to do something.

"Yes, officer," I say to the policeman who comes on the line. "I want to report an attempted, I don't know what, robbery or assault or . . . "

"Where did this happen, ma'am?"

"Over in Los Angeles, on Airdrome right off La Cienega."

"Sorry, ma'am. You'll have to call the Wilshire Division. We don't handle L.A. stuff in this precinct. You need to call this number and tell them what happened." The line goes dead.

Then the effort of holding myself together collapses, and I start shivering.

While I make some tea, I chide myself to gain perspective. That desk sergeant was not a therapist and my little incident, which ended well, will seem tame to him, given the calls he must field on a Saturday night in L.A. But I try the number he gave me.

"Wilshire District. Please hold."

I listen to a tape, which tells me to "Please hold during this recording." Then a male voice answers.

"Wilshire Division."

"I want to report a holdup tonight."

"Where did it happen?" I fill in the details. "So why didn't you just keep on driving?"

"Officer, he had this huge gun. I was certain he was going to blow me away if I moved at all."

"Yeah, well, why did you stop in the first place?"

"I stop for pedestrians." Mine was clearly the stupidest phone call he had received that evening.

"Well, what do you want to do?" he asks. "You want us to send somebody out there to talk to you, or what?"

"Look, I just wanted to report what happened in case they should try to hurt anyone else. I don't have any idea how the police department handles these things, so you tell me."

"You weren't hurt, right?"

"No," I say, "unless you think having a gun held to your head is hurtful."

He puts me on hold. When he comes back on five minutes later, he says, "Call the dispatch commander and have them send out a patrol car. I'm going to transfer you now."

"Wait," I say. "What's that number in case I get disconnected?"

He tells me the number, transfers me and I get disconnected. When I call back, the recording I listened to earlier repeats itself eight times. Now the voice is that of a woman, a black woman. Hope for understanding, maybe even some empathy, comes back.

"You wish to make a report?" she asks.

"Please," I say.

"What was the location of the incident?"

I give her the information. Then I notice her tone shift when I tell her that the one kid let me go because I was a "sister."

"These kids were black?"

"Yes," I reply, and before I can say anything else, she interrupts me. "Will that be all?"

I can't quite let it go. So I ask her, "What do you think of how I handled this situation?"

"Listen, lady, anybody who'd drive around in L.A. at night without their door locked is crazy and, second, you ought to have run those fools down. Then we could have sent a cruiser to take them to the morgue. You can believe they would have done the same to you. I don't understand you stopping in the first place."

I feel dumb. She does have a point. My door should have been locked, but . . . I prepare to launch into a self-defensive diatribe, when it hits me that this black woman, and the cops I spoke to before, and the kids who tried to hold me up would all concur that I have been the fool this evening. And that she can't hear me any more than they could have. So I decide to let it rest.

She tells me that she will send a cruiser out, but since I can't identify any suspects, I shouldn't expect much.

Rita Williams

1. Can you tell why this woman left a main street and began to drive on another street?
2. Why didn't she drive away when she first saw the young man with the gun?
3. Look back at the section in which she describes her high school life. Describe in your own words what happened to her there.
4. What lesson does it seem that she learned in high school?
5. What does she mean at the end when she says that everyone else involved in this incident probably thinks she has been a fool?

Journal Suggestions

- What is your reaction to this story? Write a journal entry commenting on anything in this incident you find interesting.
- People react differently in threatening situations. What do you think you would have done if you had been this woman?
- What is your reaction to the fact that one of the gang members saved the woman from the robbery because they were all African American? While many people seem to believe that violence in this country usually takes place between people of different races, in fact, in most personal crime (like murder, assault, or robbery) the victim and the criminal are the same race. What is your reaction to this information? Why do you think Williams used the subtitle "Not a black-and-white issue"?
- What do you think creates situations in which human beings attack other human beings? Are all these situations different, or do they have a common underlying cause? Is the cause related to human nature or to the environment in which people live?

From *Eight Little Piggies*

Chapter 19: Ten Thousand Acts of Kindness

Before you read, consider the following questions:

1. Do you think of human beings as basically good or as basically evil?
2. If you think that human beings are born neither good nor evil, what is it that makes people behave in good or evil ways?
3. Can good people do evil things and vice versa, or is the behavior of most people consistently good or evil?

Stephen Jay Gould is a professor at Harvard University, where he studies and lectures on the evolution of life over millions of years. But most people know him through his wonderful essays on science and on what the study of science can tell us about ourselves as we live and make decisions in our modern world. You may find his style of writing somewhat difficult to read but just read for his basic argument, which should seem fairly clear.

History is made by warfare, greed, lust for power, hatred, and xenophobia (with some other, more admirable motives thrown in here and there). We therefore often assume that these obviously human traits define our essential nature. How often have we been told that "man" is, by nature, aggressive and selfishly acquisitive?

Such claims make no sense to me—in a purely empirical way, not as a statement about hope or preferred morality. What do we see on any ordinary day on the streets or in the homes of any American city—even in the subways of New York? Thousands of tiny and insignificant acts of kindness and consideration. We step aside to let someone pass, smile at a child, chat aimlessly with an acquaintance or even with a stranger. At most moments, on most days, in most places, what do you ever see of the dark side—perhaps a parent slapping a child or a teenager on a skateboard cutting off an old lady? Look, I'm no ivory-tower Pollyanna, and I did grow up on the streets of New York. I understand the unpleasantness and danger of crowded cities. I'm only trying to make a statistical point.

Nothing is more unfamiliar or uncongenial to the human mind than thinking correctly about probabilities. Many of us have the impression that daily life is an unending series of unpleasantnesses—that 50 percent or more of human encounters are stressful or aggressive. But think about it seriously for a moment. Such levels of nastiness cannot possibly be sustained. Society would devolve to anarchy in an instant if half our overtures to another human being were met with a punch in the nose.

No, nearly every encounter with another person is at least neutral and usually pleasant enough. *Homo sapiens* is a remarkably genial species. Ethologists consider other animals relatively peaceful if they see but one or two aggressive encounters while observing an organism for, say, tens of hours. But think of how many millions of hours we can log for most people on most days without noting anything more threatening than a raised third finger once a week or so.

Why, then, do most of us have the impression that people are so aggressive, and intrinsically so? The answer, I think, lies in the asymmetry of effects—the truly tragic side of human existence. Unfortunately, one incident of violence can undo ten thousand acts of kindness, and we easily forget the predominance of kindness over aggression by confusing effect with frequency. One racially motivated beating can wipe out years of patient education for respect and toleration in a school or community. One murder can convert a friendly town, replete with trust, into a nexus of fear with people behind barred doors, suspicious of everyone and afraid to go out at night. Kindness is so fragile, so easy to efface; violence is so powerful.

This crushing and tragic asymmetry of kindness and violence is infinitely magnified when we consider the causes of history in the large. One fire in the library of Alexandria can wipe out the accumulated wisdom of antiquity. One supposed insult, one crazed act of assassination, can undo decades of patient diplomacy, cultural exchanges, peace corps, pen pals—small acts of kindness involving millions of citizens—and bring two nations to a war that no one wants, but that kills millions and irrevocably changes the paths of history.

Yes, I fully admit that the dark side of human possibility makes most of our history. But this tragic fact does not imply that behavioral traits of the dark side define the essence of human nature. On the contrary, I would argue, by analogy to the ordinary versus the history-making in evolution, that the reality of human interactions at almost any moment of our daily lives runs contrary, and must in any stable society, to the rare and disruptive events that construct history. If you want to understand human nature, defined as our usual propensities in ordinary situations, then find out what traits make history and identify human nature with the opposite sources of stability—the predictable behaviors of nonaggression that prevail for 99.9 percent of our lives. The real tragedy of human existence is not that we are nasty by nature, but that a cruel structural asymmetry grants to rare events of meanness such power to shape our history.

•••••••••••••••••

I am not, by the way, asserting that humans are either genial or aggressive by inborn biological necessity. Obviously, both kindness and violence lie within the bounds of our nature because we perpetuate both, in spades. I only advance a structural claim that social stability rules nearly all the time and must be based on an overwhelmingly predominant (but tragically ignored) frequency of genial acts, and that geniality is therefore our usual and preferred response nearly all the time.

•••••••••••••••••

This is not an essay about optimism; it is an essay about tragedy. If I felt that humans were nasty by nature, I would just say, the hell with it. We get what we deserve, or what evolution left us as a legacy. But the center of human nature is rooted in ten thousand ordinary acts of kindness that define our days. What can be more tragic than the structural paradox that this Everest of geniality stands upside down on its pointed summit and can be toppled so easily by rare events contrary to our everyday nature—and that these rare events make our history. In some deep sense, we do not get what we deserve.

The solution to our woes lies not in overcoming our "nature" but in fracturing the "great asymmetry" and allowing our ordinary propensities to direct our lives. But how can we put the commonplace into the driver's seat of history?

Stephen Jay Gould

1. What is Gould's basic argument?
2. Does Gould believe that humans are basically selfish and aggressive, kind and generous, or something else?
3. If Gould is correct and acts of kindness occur much more frequently than acts of aggression among humans, why does this not *seem* to be the case? Why do we believe that humans are cruel rather than kind?
4. What are some of the examples of acts of cruelty and their consequences that Gould mentions?
5. Why does Gould say that this is an essay about tragedy?

Journal Suggestions

- How do you react to Gould's arguments? Are you convinced by his argument or not? Do you believe that human beings as a species are basically kind or cruel? What about individual human beings?

- Think of your experiences yesterday. Did you witness more kindness than aggression as Gould predicts, or did you witness the opposite?

➤ *Optional Writing Assignment*

Rita Williams in the previous essay recounts her story of a terrifying encounter with a gang. Stephen Jay Gould tries to argue that although the effects of violence are far reaching, violence is rare among humans compared with the many acts of kindness humans perform for one another. Choose one of the following questions to write on.

1. Use Gould's ideas about violence and kindness to explain the behavior of Williams, of the members of the gang, and of the policewoman whom Williams speaks to on the telephone. Do you think Gould is right in the case of Williams's experiences?

2. Think about your own experiences with or information about violence. How does the discussion in either of these two texts fit with your own experience and knowledge?

◄

Excerpt 1 from *Savage Inequalities*

Chapter 2: Other People's Children

Before you read, consider the following questions:

1. How do schools in your country get money to operate, to hire teachers, to buy equipment, and to maintain buildings?
2. Are all schools funded by the central government, or do different sections of your country provide money for education in that district only?
3. Who makes decisions about what will be taught in schools and which teachers will be hired? Are these national or local decisions?

Savage Inequalities is a shocking account of the differences between rich and poor schools in this country. The author, Jonathan Kozol, visited school districts around the country and talked with administrators, teachers, students, and parents about their schools. Because schools in this country receive their money from local, not national, taxes, rich neighborhoods have much more money to spend on schools than poor neighborhoods have. Some people, particularly those whose schools have a great deal of money, have argued that money is not really what makes a school good or bad. Instead, they blame bad schools on the bad attitudes of students, who don't really want to learn, and parents, who don't really care about their children's education. Yet Kozol provides a great deal of evidence that less money prevents school officials from buying books for the library, hiring more teachers to reduce the number of children in each classroom, and hiring more qualified, more dedicated teachers.

In this excerpt, Kozol takes us into three schools: Goudy, a poor elementary school in Chicago's inner city; New Trier, a rich high school in the suburbs of Chicago; and Du Sable, a poor high school in the inner city of Chicago. His descriptions are based on his visits to each of these schools and his discussions with the people he found there.

Far from the worst school in Chicago, Goudy's building is nonetheless depressing. There is no playground. There are no swings. There is no jungle gym.

According to Bonita Brodt, a writer for the *Chicago Tribune* who spent several months at Goudy during 1988, teachers use materials in class long since thrown out in most suburban schools. Slow readers in an eighth grade history class are taught from 15-year-old textbooks in which Richard Nixon is still president. There are no science labs, no art or music teachers. Soap, paper towels and toilet paper are in short supply. There are two working bathrooms for some 700 children.

These children "cry out for something more," the *Tribune* writes. "They do not get it."

"Keisha, look at me," an adult shouts at a slow reader in a sixth grade class. "Look me in the eye." Keisha has been fighting with her classmate. Over what? As it turns out, over a crayon. The child is terrified and starts to cry. Tears spill out of her eyes and drop onto the pages of her math book. In January the school begins to ration crayons, pencils, writing paper.

Keisha's teacher is a permanent sub who doesn't want to teach this class but has no choice. "It was my turn," the teacher says. "I have a room of 39 overage, unmotivated sixth and seventh graders. . . . I am not prepared for this. I have absolutely no idea of what to do."

• • • • • • • • • • • • • • • •

The bleakness of the children's lives is underlined by one of Goudy's third grade teachers: "I passed out dictionaries once . . . One of my students started ripping out the pages when he found a word. I said, 'What are you doing? You leave the pages there for the next person.' And he told me, 'That's their problem. This is my word.' "

• • • • • • • • • • • • • • • •

Children who go to school in towns like Glencoe and Winnetka do not need to steal words from a dictionary. Most of them learn to read by second or third grade. By the time they get to sixth or seventh grade, many are reading at the level of the seniors in the best Chicago high schools. By the time they enter ninth grade at New Trier High, they are in a world of academic possibilities that far exceed the hopes and dreams of most schoolchildren in Chicago.

"Our goal is for students to be successful," says the New Trier principal. With 93 percent of seniors going on to four-year colleges—many to schools like Harvard, Princeton, Berkeley, Brown and Yale—this goal is largely realized.

New Trier's physical setting might well make the students of Du Sable High School envious. The *Washington Post* describes a neighborhood of "circular driveways, chirping birds and white-columned homes." It is, says a student, "a maple land of beauty and civility." While Du Sable is sited on one crowded city block, New Trier students have the use of 27 acres. While Du Sable's science students have to settle for makeshift equipment, New Trier's students have superior labs and up-to-date technology. One wing of the school, a physical education center that includes three separate gyms, also contains a fencing room, a wrestling room and studios for dance instruction. In all, the school has seven gyms as well as an Olympic pool.

The youngsters, according to a profile of the school in *Town and Country* magazine, "make good use of the huge, well-equipped building, which is immaculately maintained by a custodial staff of 48."

It is impossible to read this without thinking of a school like Goudy, where there are no science labs, no music or art classes and no playground—and where the two bathrooms, lacking toilet paper, fill the building with their stench.

....

Average class size is 24 children; classes for slower learners hold 15. This may be compared to Goudy—where a remedial class holds 39 children and a "gifted" class has 36.

Every freshman at New Trier is assigned a faculty adviser who remains assigned to him or her through graduation. Each of the faculty advisers—they are given a reduced class schedule to allow them time for this—gives counseling to about two dozen children. At Du Sable, where the lack of staff prohibits such reduction in class schedules, each of the guidance counselors advises 420 children.

The ambience among the students at New Trier, of whom only 1.3 percent are black, says *Town and Country,* is "wholesome and refreshing, a sort of throwback to the Fifties." It is, we are told, "a preppy kind of place." In a cheerful photo of the faculty and students, one cannot discern a single nonwhite face.

....

It is part of our faith, as Americans, that there is potential in all children. Even among the 700 children who must settle for rationed paper and pencils at Goudy Elementary School, there are surely several dozen, maybe several hundred, who, if given the chance, would thrive and overcome most of the obstacles of poverty if they attended schools like those of Glencoe and Winnetka. We know that very few of them will have that opportunity. Few, as a result, will graduate from high school; fewer still will go to college; scarcely any will attend good colleges. There will be more space for children of New Trier as a consequence.

The denial of opportunity to Keisha and the superfluity of opportunity for children at New Trier High School are not unconnected. The parents of New Trier's feeder districts vote consistently against redistribution of school funding. By a nine-to-one ratio, according to a recent survey, suburban residents resist all efforts to provide more money for Chicago's schools.

....

After lunch [at Du Sable High School, with an entirely black student population] I talk with a group of students who are hoping to go on to college but do not seem sure of what they'll need to do to make this possible. Only one out of five seniors in the group has filed an application, and it is already April. Pamela, the one who did apply, however, tells me she neglected to submit her grades and college-entrance test results and therefore has to start again. The courses she is taking seem to rule out application to a four-year college. She tells me she is taking Spanish, literature, physical education, Afro-American history and a class she terms "job strategy." When I ask her what this is, she says, "It teaches how to dress and be on time and figure your deductions." She's a bright, articulate student, and it seems quite sad that she has not had any of the richness of curriculum that would have been given to her at a high school like New Trier.

The children in the group seem not just lacking in important, useful information that would help them to achieve their dreams, but, in a far more drastic sense, cut off and disconnected from the outside world. In talking of some recent news events, they speak of Moscow and Berlin, but all but Pamela are unaware that Moscow is the capital of the Soviet Union or that Berlin is in Germany. Several believe that Jesse Jackson is the mayor of New York City. Listening to their guesses and observing their confusion, I am thinking of the students at New Trier High. These children live in truly separate worlds. What do they have in common? And yet the kids before me seem so innocent and spiritually clean and also—most of all—so vulnerable. It's as if they have been stripped of all the armament—the words, the reference points, the facts, the reasoning, the elemental weapons—that suburban children take for granted.

··················

"It took an extraordinary combination of greed, racism, political cowardice and public apathy," writes James D. Squires, the former editor of the *Chicago Tribune,* "to let the public schools in Chicago get so bad." He speaks of the schools as a costly result of "the political orphaning of the urban poor . . . daytime warehouses for inferior students . . . a bottomless pit."

The results of these conditions are observed in thousands of low-income children in Chicago who are virtually disjoined from the entire worldview, even from the basic reference points, of the American experience. A 16-year-old girl who has dropped out of school discusses her economic prospects with a TV interviewer.

"How much money would you like to make in a year?" asks the reporter.

"About $2,000," she replies.

The reporter looks bewildered by this answer. This teen-age girl, he says, "has no clue that $2,000 a year isn't enough to survive anywhere in America, not even in her world."

This sad young woman, who already has a baby and is pregnant once again, lives in a truly separate universe of clouded hopes and incomplete cognition. "We are creating an entire generation of incompetents," a black sociologist observes. "Her kids will fail. There is a good chance that she'll end up living with a man who is addicted or an alcoholic. She'll be shot or killed, or else her children will be shot or killed, or else her boyfriend will be shot or killed. Drugs will be overwhelmingly attractive to a person living in a world so bare of richness or amenities. No one will remember what we did to her when she was eight years old in elementary school or 15 years old at Du Sable High. No one will remember that her mother might have tried and failed to get her into Head Start when she was a baby. Who knows if her mother even got prenatal care? She may be brain-damaged—or lead-poisoned. Who will ask these questions later on? They will see her as a kind of horrible deformity. Useless too. Maybe a maid. Maybe not. Maybe just another drain upon society."

•••••••••••••••••

The focus in this book is on the inner-city schools; inevitably, therefore, I am describing classrooms in which almost all the children are black or Latino. But there are also poor and mainly white suburban districts and, of course, some desperately poor and very isolated rural districts. Children in the rural districts of Kentucky, northern Maine, and Arkansas, for instance, face a number of the problems we have seen in East St. Louis and Chicago, though the nature of the poverty in rural schools is often somewhat different. The most important difference in the urban systems, I believe, is that they are often just adjacent to the nation's richest districts, and this ever-present contrast adds a heightened bitterness to the experience of children. The ugliness of racial segregation adds its special injuries as well. It is this killing combination, I believe, that renders life within these urban schools not merely grim but also desperate and often pathological.

Jonathan Kozol

1. What strikes you the most about each of these three schools: Goudy, New Trier, and Du Sable?
2. What are the most striking differences to you between the rich school, on the one hand, and the two poor schools, on the

other, in terms of physical setting, availability of equipment, and availability of staff?

3. What evidence does Kozol give which suggests that even if students at Du Sable High School were better educated in academic subjects, they still would have a hard time competing with students from New Trier to get into college?

Journal Suggestions

- What is your reaction to the descriptions and information in this article? Comment on any aspect of the article you found interesting.

- Do you think it is better to have a national educational system or to allow regions to determine for themselves what they need in their schools? What might be some advantages and disadvantages of each approach?

- Do you believe that students like Pamela and Keisha have a real chance to escape from their backgrounds of poverty and lack of education, or do you think that it is too late for them, especially Pamela, to recover? Do you believe that with effort people can do anything they want to do, or do you believe that sometimes the structures of society are so powerful that no matter how hard some people try, they can never succeed? Or might it be the case that those very structures of society change some people in such a way that actually makes them unable to really try?

History Proves It: Other Systems of Naming Work

Before you read, consider the following questions:

1. Who decides on children's first or given names in your country? The parents, the grandparents, tradition?
2. How do people in your country get their last or family names?
3. Have you noticed any difference between the way naming operates in your country and in other countries.

The issue of how to name children, particularly what last name or family name to give, is of interest in the United States because many people feel that the system here, in which children get their father's last name, is unfair. People question why it is not equally acceptable for children to have their mother's last name, for example. This essay points out that giving children the last names, or surnames, of their fathers is by no means a universal way of naming children. To prove this point, the essay discusses the ways that humans have used to name themselves in different times and places. Some examples of systems are: patrilineal, like that in the United States; matronymic, in which a child might be called, for example, "John, son of Mary" or "Ann, daughter of Mary"; or patronymic, in which a child would be, for example, "John, son of Tom" or "Ann, daughter of John." But there are even more possible ways of handling names.

Many arguments for our system of passing the father's last name on to children come down to "if there were a better way to name ourselves, someone would have thought of it before and put their new system into practice." Just because our parents didn't come up with something other than this patrilineal practice doesn't mean that we shouldn't. Besides, it hasn't actually been around that long, nor has it been or is it now universally practiced in the Western world.

No surnames of any kind were used in Europe until about the 11th century, and they didn't become common until the end of the 16th century. Women first started taking their husbands' names around the 13th century; among aristocratic families, women did so for prestige.

With the development of commerce, there was an increasing need to distinguish among, say, all the men named John, in order to establish who owned a piece of property, for instance. Originally, surnames varied among people in the same family (one person might even have several different names in one lifetime as she or he changed occupations). The family names of today evolved from those individualized surnames.

But many isolated communities did not readily adopt this system of surnames.

....

For example, while for centuries the communities around them were using patronymical last names, the Jews in the ghettos of Central and Eastern Europe didn't use fixed surnames. It wasn't until the late 18th and early part of the 19th century that Jews had to choose or were given family names. Even when they did begin using last names, European Jews did not universally adopt the last name of their fathers. Very frequently children would be given their mother's birth name rather than their father's.

Norwegians also used patronymics while other European communities had converted over to the last name systems that resemble the one we use today. When Norwegians immigrated to the United States in the mid-19th century, they had to convert their patronymics and the names of their homeland family farms, which were also used as surnames, into patrilineal last names—hence, the large number of Hansens and Petersens. Relationship-to-father names are still in use in Iceland and in the Shetland Islands.

Author Una Stannard believes that the practice of giving children their father's surnames sprang from people's ignorance of the facts of life. It was thought that males contributed the seed of life, while the female womb provided the soil in which the seed grew. It wasn't until 1827 that the female ovum was discovered, and even then it was thought to be merely a source of nutrition. Since the female role in generation was thought to be negligible, it seemed only logical that children would receive their names from their fathers, who were seen as the sole progenitors.

Historical and cross-cultural examples of other naming systems abound, and some of them have attractive features. They provide concrete evidence that it's quite possible for people to live with last name systems that vary greatly from our current one.

For example, the practice prevalent in medieval France was to give female children their mother's birth name and male children their father's birth name. Many contemporary communities in Iceland and the Soviet Union use patronymics in combination with a patrilineally inherited family name. In Russia, for example, if a father's name is Ivan Sokolov, then the son's name would be Viktor (first name) Ivanovich (patronymic) Sokolov (family), and the daughter's name would be Katya (first name)

Ivanovna (patronymic meaning daughter of Ivan) Sokolova (family name with feminine ending). A person is typically addressed by his or her first name and the patronymic.

The present-day naming systems of Spain, Portugal, and other Latin countries are more equitable than our system, and they prove that primary families (one generation consisting of parents and children) can be perfectly stable without the glue of the same last name.

Here's how the Spanish system works: When children are born—males or females—they are given a legal name that they will officially use for life. That name consists of a first name and *two* fully functional surnames. Almost universally the first surname comes from the father and the second surname comes from the mother (husbands and wives have different last names). However, it is generally the first surname (which looks like a middle name to us) that carries more social weight. Even though the surname of the father is passed on to subsequent generations and the surname of the mother isn't, a person bears, and never loses or changes, both his father's and mother's surnames.

Sharon Lebell

1. Besides patrilineal, matrilineal, matronymic, and patronymic, what other systems of naming does this article mention?
2. Why did the need for surnames come about, according to the article?
3. Why does the author say that the Spanish and Portuguese system of naming is more fair than the patrilineal system used in the United States?

Journal Suggestions

- How does the naming system work in your country or in other countries you know about? Are there systems you know of that are not mentioned in this article? Of the systems mentioned here or those you know of, which seem the best to you? Do you think this is an interesting or important issue or not?
- If you could name your own children according to any system you wished, which would you choose? What would the advantages and disadvantages of that system be?

➤ *Optional Writing Assignment*

This article describes several different ways human societies have used to name themselves and their children. Using both the information in this article and your own experience with systems for naming in your culture, discuss the ways you think are best and explain why you feel this way. ◄

From *The First Four Minutes*

Before you read, consider the following questions:
1. When you first meet people, what makes you like or dislike them? The way they look? How intelligent they seem? How entertaining they seem? How interested they are in you?
2. Have you ever formed a first impression of someone that eventually proved to be completely wrong? Do you know of any occasion when someone formed an impression of you that was completely wrong?
3. What is the best kind of first impression to make?

According to this reading, the first four minutes after meeting someone are crucial in determining whether the two of you will become friends. The best approach to take when you meet someone new is to give that person your complete attention for the first four minutes. Act friendly and self-confident during that period to convey a good impression of yourself. The reading states that learning how to interact with people should be an important part of our education.

Did you ever wonder what makes some people become friends and others not? According to Dr. Leonard Zunin, whether or not people become friends is at least partly determined by the way they interact when they first meet, that is, in their first "contact." In his book *Contact: The First Four Minutes*, Zunin discusses contacts with "strangers, friends, lovers, children, bosses, blind dates, plumbers, teachers, politicians — the whole cast of characters in your individual world." But the most interesting part of his thesis is the idea that the first four minutes of contact can be crucial in determining how the rest of the interaction and perhaps the whole relationship will go.

Part of Zunin's research consisted of observing strangers interact. These observations made it clear that four minutes was the average time which lapsed before these strangers decided to continue the interaction or to separate. For example, when two people are introduced for the first time, it is normal for them to chat for a few minutes before moving away to talk to someone else. Although most people are behaving unconsciously, they would feel uncomfortable and impolite if they did not spend those first few minutes interacting with the new person, but they do not feel required to spend longer than 3–5 minutes. They will only continue the contact if there is some reason to do so.

What does that mean for the average person? A relationship can only develop if both parties are interested in pursuing it. So, how can you let someone know that you are interested? If you want to start new friendships, Zunin says, "Every time you meet someone in a social situation, give him [or her] your undivided attention for four minutes." Perhaps you have been, for example, at a party. You are introduced to a man who spends his time looking over your shoulder or around the room instead of at you as though he were looking for someone more interesting to talk to. Zunin's findings suggest that you will lose interest in that person because of his behavior, and you will not bother to seek his friendship. In other words, it is important to give your undivided attention for the first four minutes of contact with anyone you would like to make into a friend.

Furthermore, if you want to be well liked, Zunin's advice is to act self-confident, friendly, and happy. People like people who like themselves. But what if in fact you are not self-confident but shy and insecure? Isn't it dishonest to pretend to be someone you are not naturally? The answer is that we become shy or self-confident partly because of the way we have been socialized. In other words, we are not necessarily born shy or insecure, and therefore, we can learn to become more self-confident. Zunin feels that learning how to interact well with people is such an important social skill that it should be taught in school. Besides, acting self-confident will give you the success in social situations that will actually make you be more self-confident.

Finally, Zunin claims that the first four minutes of contact are important even for family members. Because we have a long history with members of our families, they will understand and forgive us if we do not always behave as they would like, and negative interactions in the first few minutes are not irreversible, of course. Nevertheless, if you haven't seen your family for a while, it is unwise to immediately begin talking about problems and complaints when you first see them. If you talk instead about pleasant subjects, they are more likely to be happy with you and to be able to deal well with the problems later.

If you have your doubts about the usefulness of Dr. Zunin's advice, at least give his suggestion a try. The next time you are at a party or other social gathering, do your best to seem self-confident, attentive, and happy with yourself during the first few minutes of contact. You may find the rewards well worth the effort.

Condensed from The First Four Minutes *by Leonard Zunin*

1. Find the section that raises the question of honesty in human relations. Can you reconstruct the argument made? Do you agree that we should try to seem friendly and self-confident even if we do not honestly feel this way?

2. What kinds of behavior in the first four minutes are likely to produce a bad impression?
3. Find the section about relationships among friends and relatives. What advice is given there?
4. Do you think schools should spend time teaching interpersonal relationships? Have you ever studied or discussed such topics in school?
5. Do you think the author wanted you to get only information from this reading?

Journal Suggestions

- If this selection interested you, use it as the basis for a journal entry. Comment on, react to, or make note of information you found in the selection.

- We all have our public selves and our private selves, and our cultures play a role in determining how much of our private selves we will show in public. How open are people in your culture about showing their personal sorrows and joys? Do people from your culture show their emotions quickly and easily, or do they hide their emotions, especially negative emotions? Are people in your culture demonstrative of their affection for others in public? That is, do they kiss, hold hands, or hug in public?

Nonverbal Communication

Before you read, consider the following questions:

1. What do you suppose *nonverbal communication* means?
2. Look at the subtitles in this selection. Now write down four questions you expect to find answered in this selection.
3. Read the three short statements at the beginning of the reading by the teacher, the college student, and the customer. What is each statement meant to show?

This selection discusses how we human beings communicate a great deal of information to one another without using words and sometimes without consciously realizing how we are communicating. For this communication, we use our faces, our bodies, and our sense of personal space. In addition, the reading points out that these means of communication vary from one culture to another, just as verbal languages vary.

Teacher: I've been a teacher for ten years and I can always tell when students don't know an answer in class discussion. They either look down at their notes, stare out the window, or fix their shoelaces—but they never look me in the eye.

College Student: Mary says she likes me, but I don't know how she really feels about me. We've gone out three times and she rarely laughs at my jokes or smiles at me. She always looks bored when I talk to her.

Customer: Jane was at the store trying to decide which television set to buy. A loud, overeager salesman approached her, waved his hands in her face, and nearly stood on her feet. She became so uncomfortable that she left the shop.

Language studies traditionally have emphasized verbal and written language, but recently have begun to consider communication that takes place without words. In some types of communication people express more nonverbally than verbally. If you ask an obviously depressed person, "What's wrong?", and he answers, "Nothing. I'm fine," you probably won't believe him. When an angry person says, "Let's forget this subject, I don't want to talk about it any more!" you know that he hasn't stopped communicating. His silence and withdrawal continue to convey emotional meaning.

One study done in the United States showed that in the communication of attitudes, 93 percent of the message was transmitted by the tone of the voice and by facial expressions, whereas only 7 percent of the speaker's attitude was transmitted by words. Apparently, we express our emotions and attitudes more nonverbally than verbally.

Cultural Differences in Nonverbal Communication. Nonverbal communication expresses meaning or feeling without words. Universal emotions, such as happiness, fear, and sadness, are expressed in a similar nonverbal way throughout the world. There are, however, nonverbal differences across cultures that may be a source of confusion for foreigners. For example, feelings of friendship exist everywhere but their expression varies. It may be acceptable in some countries for men to embrace each other and for women to hold hands; in other countries these displays of affection may be shocking.

What is acceptable in one culture may be completely unacceptable in another. One culture may determine that snapping fingers to call a waiter is appropriate; another may consider this gesture rude. We are often not aware of how gestures, facial expressions, eye contact, and the use of space affect communication. In order to correctly interpret another culture's style of communication, it is necessary to study the "silent language" of that culture.

Gestures. Gestures refer to specific body movements that carry meaning. Hands can form shapes that convey many meanings: "That's expensive," "Come here," "Go away," and "It's OK" can be expressed nonverbally using only hands. The gestures for these phrases may differ among languages. As children we imitate and learn these nonverbal movements and often use them to accompany or replace words. When traveling to another country, foreign visitors soon learn that not all gestures are universal. The "OK" gesture in the American culture is a symbol for money in Japan. The same gesture is obscene in some Latin American countries. (This is why the editors of a Latin American newspaper enjoyed publishing a picture of former President Nixon giving the OK symbol with both hands!)

Facial Expressions. Facial expressions carry meaning determined by contexts and relationships. For instance, the smile, which is typically an expression of pleasure, has many functions. A man's smile at a policeman who is about to give him a ticket does not carry the same meaning as the smile he gives to a young child. A smile may show affection, convey politeness, or disguise true feelings. Pain is conveyed by a grimace, which also signifies disgust or disapproval. Surprise, shock, or disbelief can be shown by raising the eyebrows. A wink given to a friend may mean "You and I have a secret" or "I'm just kidding." Between a man and a woman, a wink can be flirtatious. Our faces easily reveal emotions and attitudes.

The degree of facial expressiveness also varies among individuals and cultures. The fact that members of one culture do not express their emotions as openly as members of another does not mean they do not experience emotions. Rather, there are cultural restraints on the amount of nonverbal expressiveness permitted. Given individual differences, it is difficult to make generalizations about a cultural style of communication. Americans express themselves facially in varying degrees. People from certain ethnic backgrounds in the United States may use their hands, bodies, and faces more than other Americans. There are no fixed rules, although it is considered negative or suspicious to have a "deadpan" expression or a "poker face." Some people can be "read like a book"; others are difficult to read.

Eye Contact. Eye contact is important because insufficient or excessive eye contact may create communication barriers. It is important in relationships because it serves to show intimacy, attention, and influence. As with facial expressions, there are no specific rules governing eye behavior except that it is considered rude to stare, especially at strangers. It is, however, common for two strangers to walk toward each other, make eye contact, smile and perhaps even say "Hi." The strangers may immediately look away and forget that they even had any contact. This type of glance does not mean much; it is simply a way of acknowledging another person's presence. In a conversation too little eye contact may be seen negatively because it conveys lack of interest, inattention, or even mistrust. The relationship between mistrust and lack of eye contact is stated directly in the expression, "Never trust a person who can't look you in the eyes."

Space. Unconsciously, we all carry with us what have been called "body bubbles." These bubbles are like invisible walls which define our personal space. The amount of space changes depending on the interpersonal relationship. For example, we are usually more comfortable standing closer to family members than to strangers. Personality also determines the size of this space. Introverts often prefer to interact with others at a greater distance than extroverts. Cultural styles are important too. A Japanese employer and employee usually stand farther apart while talking than their American counterparts. Latin Americans and Arabs tend to stand closer together than Americans when talking.

For Americans, distance in social conversation is about an arm's length to four feet. Less space in the American culture may be associated with greater intimacy or aggressive behavior. The common practice of saying "Excuse me," or "Pardon me" for the slightest accidental touching of another person reveals an American attitude about personal space. Thus, when a person's "space" is intruded upon by someone, he or she may feel threatened and react defensively. In cultures where close physical contact is acceptable and desirable, Americans may be perceived as cold and distant.

Culture does not always determine the messages that our body movements convey. Contexts, personalities, and relationships also influence them. Therefore, no two people in any one society have the same nonverbal behavior. However, like verbal language, nonverbal communication cannot be completely separated from culture. Whether we emphasize differences or similarities, the "silent language" is much louder than it first appears.

Deena R. Levine
Mara B. Adelman

1. What does "silent language" refer to in the last sentence?
2. According to the reading, what do human beings express through nonverbal rather than verbal communication?
3. Can you give any examples, either from the reading or from your own experience, of forms of nonverbal communication that are acceptable in one culture but shocking or confusing in another?
4. What differences in gestures, eye contact, and body space have you noticed between your own culture and what you have seen in the United States?
5. What gestures do you use to indicate the following?
   That's expensive.
   Come here.
   Go away.
   It's OK.

How do you call a waiter in a restaurant? How do you show the height of a child? Of an animal? How do you show that you are listening to and agree with what someone is saying? What gesture do you use to show that you are talking on the telephone? Eating? Drinking? What part of a person's body do you look at when he or she is speaking to you?

Journal Suggestions

- If the information in this reading interested you, comment on it in your journal.
- Do an informal survey of friends from your own country, from the United States, and from other countries to see what cultural differences in nonverbal communication they have noticed. Then write a journal entry explaining what you found out.

How to Spot a Liar

Before you read, consider the following questions:

1. What do you think is the answer to the question "How can you tell if someone is lying?"
2. Are there certain things that you yourself do if you are not telling the truth? What are they? Do you get nervous, for example?

This article describes differences in people's behavior, actions, and expressions that can reveal when they are not telling the truth. The author also mentions some behaviors which seem to indicate that someone is lying but in fact take place as much during truth telling as lying. In any case, it is easier to tell if someone you know well is lying than it is to tell if a stranger or a practiced liar is lying.

It's not easy to tell when someone's lying to you. But most liars feel a little bad about their deception, whether it's complimenting Grandma on her tasteless cake or covering up a major scandal. And often that twinge of guilt, anxiety, or fear is strong enough to give lies away.

The tone of a person's voice, for example, is one of the best cues. "People's voices often get noticeably higher in pitch when they lie," says Bella DePaulo, a University of Virginia psychologist who studies videotapes of people telling lies and telling the truth. "And they're more likely to stammer or stumble over words."

Liars also often sound distant when they're making something up, using few descriptive phrases or hand motions. In one of DePaulo's studies, students pretending to like a person they in fact disliked said such things as, "Yeah, I really like her because she's a good person." Liars also tend to lace their speech with denials and hedging such as, "I didn't read the book very carefully, so I'm not sure," or, "I don't remember for sure who I played against in the tournament." And they're prone to frequent blinking and fidgeting, such as head scratching or nail biting. Even clever, confident people exhibit such "leaks" because it's extremely hard for anyone to control face, voice, and body movements—all while spinning a convincing line of bull.

An even more subtle behavior betrays lies as well. Take for example that momentary look of panic that flashes across your face right after you hear something like, "Hey! What are you doing here? You told me you were going to a doctor's appointment."

The face can also exhibit flashes of glee, hatred, sadness—any emotion, when it's strong enough.

Psychologist Paul Ekman, author of *Telling Lies*, observed these microexpressions, as he calls them, while studying videos of nursing students talking about two films—one showing pastoral scenes and one showing gruesome surgical procedures. Ekman had the students describe the nature film accurately and then attempt to portray the surgery film as equally pleasant. Fleeting expressions of disgust and dismay punctuated the descriptions of the surgery film, but not of the nature film.

With a little practice, Ekman says, you can see microexpressions in the faces of almost anybody lying when strong emotion is involved. Listening for a higher voice pitch as well, his researchers can tell when someone is lying about 85 percent of the time, he says.

Many behaviors we *think* are signs of deception are not. "Shifty eyes, for example, are not a good sign that someone is lying," DePaulo says. When people speak slowly, take a long time to answer questions, shift their gaze or their posture, or don't smile much, they're *perceived* to be deceptive, she finds. "Actually, these behaviors are as likely to show up during lie-telling as during truth-telling," she says.

And facial expressions—the obvious ones—can be very misleading, because most of us are pretty good at covering a lie with, say, a quick smile or a stern look. DePaulo has found that, without special training, most people who try to detect deception by concentrating only on the face do no better than if they'd guessed randomly.

Nonetheless, the more reliable clues that Ekman and DePaulo describe do give you a way to compare people's normal behavior with the way they act when you suspect they're lying. Say you suspect your spouse or lover of having an affair. You might ask: Does she play with her hair this much when talking about a man she's not interested in? Does his voice usually quiver like this when he's talking about another woman who's just a friend?

Sizing up a suspected liar you don't know well is especially difficult, because you're not familiar with how the person acts when relaxed. Good interviewers try to get job applicants comfortable with affable small talk before popping something like, "So, why was it you left your last job?" Trial lawyers often use similar tactics to catch witnesses off guard.

Many smooth-talking liars have prepared responses for these questions, but their stories may sound flat. "It's the difference between, 'I went to the window. I looked out. I saw the car,'" says Ekman, "and, 'I'd stumbled over a chair on the way to the bathroom—I'd slept late, you see, and I couldn't find my glasses—so I went to look over by the window.'"

Unfortunately, *real* smooth talkers don't just prepare—they go into sales. And shady salespeople are skillful enough with their pitches that lies are virtually undetectable. Bella DePaulo and her brother Peter DePaulo, a marketing professor at the University of Missouri at St. Louis, asked 107 college students to watch videos of salespeople describing products and to figure out which people were lying and which were being truthful. No matter what clues the students looked for, none could do better than if they'd guessed haphazardly.

"The only way to tell for certain," says Peter DePaulo, "is to know the answers to your questions before asking them."

Benedict Carey

1. What are some of the clues that can tell you if someone is lying?
2. What seems to be the best clue that someone is lying?
3. What are some of the false clues that might make people think another person is lying even if that person is telling the truth?
4. From the discussion in this article, does it seem that facial expressions are a good clue or a bad clue as to whether or not someone is telling the truth?
5. According to the article, what might be the purpose of friendly conversation at the beginning of a job interview?

Journal Suggestions

- What is your reaction to the information in this article? Was any of the information new to you?
- Think of the last time you know that someone lied to you. How did you know? What is the best way you have found to determine if someone is telling you the truth or not?
- In your country, what do people say is the best way to tell if someone is lying? Is that different from what you learned in this article or the same? For example, many people in the United States become suspicious if the person they are talking to looks away; if you are telling the truth, you are expected to look the other person in the eye. In your country is it considered important to look into the other person's eyes

when talking, or might that be a sign of, perhaps, disrespect?

➢ *Optional Writing Assignment*

Using the information from "Nonverbal Communication" and "How to Spot a Liar," discuss how nonverbal communication patterns in your own country differ from those described in these articles as common in the United States.   ◄

Primate Studies and Sex Differences

Before you read, consider the following questions:

1. Do male and female animals behave differently? What kinds of differences have you ever noticed in what kinds of animals?
2. If you have noticed differences, at what age do the differing behaviors begin?
3. Do you think that this behavior is natural or learned?

This article discusses behavior in primates, those animals that are most like human beings, such as monkeys, chimpanzees, and apes. The author notes that differences in the way that male and female primates behave have been assumed to reflect innate, or inborn, differences between the genders. It has also been assumed that if those differences are natural to primates, they are also natural to human beings. But the author disagrees with those assumptions, stating that scientists who have studied primate behavior have been prejudiced in their approach to these studies and have failed to see the behavior of these animals in its proper context. The author then argues that the behaviors that scientists have been calling natural, innate, or biological may, in fact, be behaviors learned as part of the animals' socialization process within their social group.

If we want to get to the heart of male/female sex differences, we must be able to separate the biological from the learned (sociocultural). Comparing cultures can only take us so far—there are human possibilities which *no* culture that we know of has yet instituted. Because we don't find a particular behavior in any culture now or in the past does not mean the behavior is impossible. If we can imagine it, it is possible. So comparing sex roles in various cultures does not give us anything approaching a total picture of the potentialities of either males or females. Since in most cultures we find females subservient to males, it is often assumed that there is a biological or physiological basis for this. Anthropologists, ethnologists, and psychologists have recently turned to primate studies as a way of finding out the "truth" about sex differences. They have done this in two ways: first by observing the natural behavior of nonhuman primates in the wild, and second by tampering with the balance of male and female hormones in the animals and then observing their behavior.

On the *first* point, it has been observed that male monkeys and apes seem to be more aggressive than females. They initiate, and participate in, more rough-and-tumble, dominance-type interactions. The females show more interest in infants, try to hold them, care for them, etc. From this sort of observation some researchers have concluded that aggressiveness and nurturance are biologically-based characteristics of males and females respectively, in all primates both human and nonhuman. This is an extremely poor use of the evidence; it is both anthropomorphic and ethnocentric. The major factor which is being overlooked is that these primates under observation *live in a social group*. Animal behaviorists have been emphasizing for years the importance of the social group, and the extent to which most primate behavior is *learned*. It is inexcusable to emphasize the importance of this learned behavior in all other contexts, and to ignore it when considering sex-role behavior. Monkey and ape socialization must begin as early as it does in humans. Has any observer of primate behavior in the wild investigated the following questions: How soon does the mother recognize the sex of her newborn infant? How does she recognize it—by smell, by the sight of genital organs? Does she treat male and female infants differently once she has recognized their sex? How soon do other members of the troop recognize the infant's sex? Do they react differently to males and females? . . .

Surely monkeys and apes can tell a male from a female at a fairly early age. To the human observer the animals all look alike at first, but familiarity soon brings recognition of each animal as an individual, and as male or female. If a human is able to make observations such as more aggressiveness in the males, more nurturance in the females, we must assume that the primates under observation can distinguish between the sexes at least as well! At some point the primate social group begins to train its members for their adult roles, including their sexual roles. To my knowledge, no researcher has ever raised any of the above questions. They have simply observed male/female differences in behavior, *in a social group*, and gone on to make completely unwarranted assumptions about biology.

There is evidence (from the Japanese studies) that the offspring of less dominant animals are much less likely to grow up to be dominant themselves. In other words, they begin to *learn submissiveness* at an early age. If this is true, there is a very strong basis for inferring that they also learn their sex roles at an early age. . . . It has often been observed that female primates who did not receive the proper socialization, or who are isolated from others of their kind, make very poor mothers. They tend to reject the infant, fail to care for it properly, sometimes deliberately kill it when it does not simply die from neglect. This has usually been taken as a sign of pathology, because of course any "normal" primate mother cares for her infant. What has never been suggested in this context is that the nurturing female role is *socially learned*, and that without this social learning it is perfectly natural for the female primate to fail to care for her infant. It is not natural (instinctive) for her, any more than for a human female, to be nurturing unless she has been taught this behavior by her social group.

In sum, the observation of primate behavior in the wild which has been done so far gives us no sort of argument for the "instinctive" or biological nature of observed differences in male/female sex-role behavior.

The *second* sort of "biological" evidence comes from experiments where the balance of sex hormones was tampered with. It was observed, for instance, that when female monkeys were shot full of male hormones they became more aggressive. This has been taken as evidence to "prove" that males are naturally (instinctively) more aggressive and females more passive. All it actually proves is that females with an overabundance of male hormones act more aggressively. . . . We might hypothesize that the hormone balance affects smell, so that the injected females begin to smell more like males. If this is the case, then their social group would treat them as males, and they would accordingly be differentially socialized. This has never been investigated. When looked at closely this biological "proof" of sex differences also withers away.

It seems to me that all these rather desperate attempts to prove from biology that human males are naturally aggressive, while human females are naturally passive and nurturing, are ethnocentric strivings designed to find scientific support for a status quo which is now being threatened. It is obvious that if any large number of females in our culture reject the submissive, dependent, nurturing role they have traditionally played, massive social upheaval will follow. That is beginning to happen already, and many members of our culture (both male and female) do not wish to face the implications or the consequences of this sort of social change. So attempts are made to prove "scientifically" and "biologically" that females are naturally destined to be passive and dependent. To approach any topic with such massive preconception and bias contradicts the ideals (though not always the practice) of scientific investigation. On a subject such as male/female differences, which is both scientifically and humanly important, every effort should be made to recognize and eliminate our cultural biases from the research design and from the interpretation of results.

Even if it could be demonstrated that there is a biological predisposition for the sorts of male/female differences discussed above, it would mean very little in modern society. Many biological tendencies are overcome by cultural and social conditioning—that is part of being human. Most of our "instinctive" behavior is under cortical control. We may want to have sexual intercourse with almost every individual of the opposite sex we see; we may want to kill the person who makes us angry; but we don't do these things. We behave, in other words, in "unbiological" ways. Any argument from biological fact to cultural necessity must be made with extreme care. The discovery of a biological predisposition is one thing: what we choose to do about it culturally is another. Because someone is stronger than I, does that mean I must let him beat me up? To limit female options in our society because of some sort of biological or pseudo-biological argument is to fail to understand the nature of human life, of our society, *culture and* biology.

Sally Linton

1. What are the two methods that researchers have used to study gender differences in primate behavior?
2. What have these researchers concluded about gender differences?
3. How does the author dispute or argue with each of these pieces of evidence?
4. What do you think the author's purpose is in this article?
5. Where in the article can you see this purpose most clearly suggested?

Journal Suggestions

- What is your reaction to the information in this article? Do you agree with the author that primate behavior must be studied in its natural social context, or are you convinced by the arguments that gender differences are innate in primates?
- Do you feel that we can learn about human beings by observing animal behavior, or do you believe that humans are different enough from animals that nothing really meaningful can be concluded about humans by observing animals? Why do you feel this way?
- If you have ever spent time close to an animal, such as a pet dog or cat, have you ever noticed that the animal sometimes

behaves in a way that seems human to you? Can you describe that behavior?

- If we were to establish beyond a doubt that gender differences in the behavior of human beings reflect natural, biological differences, what difference would or should this information make in the way human beings organize their social lives in the modern world?

Abraham Lincoln

Before you read, consider the following questions:

1. Who was Abraham Lincoln? Think of everything you know about him. Where did you get this information?
2. Lincoln was elected president of the United States in the mid–nineteenth century. What kind of image do people who run for president want to project of themselves to convince the public to vote for them? Do you think the desirable image today is different from the desirable image in the nineteenth century?

Abraham Lincoln (1809–65) was the U.S. president who signed the Emancipation Proclamation, which led the way to the eventual abolition of slavery in the United States. The Southern states so opposed Lincoln's election to office that they threatened to break off from the rest of the United States and become a separate country. When Lincoln was elected, the Southern states did in fact secede, beginning the U.S. Civil War (1860–65). Lincoln has become legendary for his simplicity, integrity, and compassion, particularly since he held office during the bloody and painful Civil War. Lincoln was eventually assassinated, shot to death as he sat watching a theater performance.

The following short autobiographical sketch was written just before Lincoln was elected president, in 1859. In it, Lincoln talks about his parents and grandparents and their simple background. He describes his own boyhood on the farm, his education, and the history of his political life from being a lawyer to running for office to losing interest in politics. Then he mentions the Missouri Compromise (1820–21), which was the resolution of a conflict between Southern slave states, which wanted Missouri to allow slavery, and Northern nonslave states, which wanted no more new states to allow slavery. The public debate on this issue drew Lincoln back into political life and eventually to the presidency.

I was born February 12, 1809, in Hardin County, Kentucky. My parents were both born in Virginia, of undistinguished families—second families, perhaps I should say. My mother, who died in my tenth year, was of a family of the name of Hanks, some of whom now reside in Adams, and others in Macon County, Illinois. My paternal grandfather, Abraham Lincoln, emigrated from Rockingham County, Virginia, to Kentucky about 1781 or 1782, where a year or two later he was killed by the

Indians, not in battle, but by stealth, when he was laboring to open a farm in the forest. His ancestors, who were Quakers, went to Virginia from Berks County, Pennsylvania. . . .

My father, at the death of his father was but six years of age, and he grew up literally without education. He removed from Kentucky to what is now Spencer County, Indiana, in my eighth year. We reached our new home about the time the state came into the Union. It was a wild region, with many bears and other wild animals still in the woods. There I grew up. There were some schools, so called, but no qualification was ever required of a teacher beyond "readin', writin', and cipherin'" to the rule of three. If a straggler supposed to understand Latin happened to sojourn in the neighborhood, he was looked upon as a wizard. There was absolutely nothing to excite ambition for education. Of course, when I came of age I did not know much. Still, somehow, I could read, write, and cipher to the rule of three, but that was all. I have not been to school since. The little advance I now have upon this store of education, I have picked up from time to time under the pressure of necessity.

I was raised to farm work, which I continued till I was twenty-two. At twenty-one I came to Illinois, Macon County. Then I got to New Salem, at that time in Sangamon, now in Menard County, where I remained a year as a sort of clerk in a store. Then came the Black Hawk War; and I was elected a captain of volunteers, a success which gave me more pleasure than any I have had since. I went the campaign, was elated, ran for the legislature the same year (1832), and was beaten—the only time I ever have been beaten by the people. The next and three succeeding biennial elections I was elected to the legislature. I was not a candidate afterward. During this legislative period I had studied law, and removed to Springfield to practice it. In 1846 I was once elected to the lower House of Congress, but was not a candidate for reelection. From 1849 to 1854, both inclusive, I practiced law more assiduously than ever before, always a Whig in politics, and generally on the Whig electoral tickets, making active canvasses. I was losing interest in politics when the repeal of the Missouri Compromise aroused me again. What I have done since then is pretty well known.

If any personal description of me is thought desirable, it may be said I am, in height, six feet four inches, nearly; lean in flesh, weighing on an average one hundred and eighty pounds; dark complexion, with coarse black hair and gray eyes. No other marks or brands recollected.

Abraham Lincoln

1. What general impression do you get of Lincoln, his personality and his background? Keep in mind that the man who wrote this was running for president of a country. What image of himself do you think Lincoln meant to convey?
2. What character traits does Lincoln seem to value?
3. What might people admire about the man from this description? What might people find negative or undesirable about this man?
4. Do you think that Lincoln's life as he describes it was difficult or easy? What gives you that impression?
5. How much formal education did Lincoln receive? At what two places in this autobiographical sketch does he mention education beyond his initial training? What kind of tone does he use to refer to his education?
6. What other things might you want to know about this man if you were deciding whether or not to vote for him?

Journal Suggestions

- If this autobiographical sketch by Abraham Lincoln interested you, comment, react, or note interesting parts in a journal entry.
- What kinds of qualities do you consider important for the leader of a country? List these qualities as they come to your mind, then rank them according to the order of their importance.

From *Two Years in the Melting Pot*

Before you read, consider the following questions:

1. What is your current living arrangement? Are you living alone, with roommates, with a host family? With relatives? How has this arrangement worked out for you?
2. Are there many people where you are now who speak your native language? Do you try to avoid speaking your native language and spending time with people from your country, or do you spend a good deal of your time with them? Which do you think is better?

This excerpt comes from a book by Liu Zongren, a Chinese journalist who spent two years living and studying in Chicago. His account is very honest, and often critical of the United States and of U.S. culture. His account is also full of insight, often funny, and sometimes painful. At the time that this excerpt takes place Liu is living in a suburb just north of Chicago with an American family, the McKnights, and he is having a difficult time. He misses his wife and child, he feels depressed, and he does not feel comfortable in the household where he is living. There are simply too many cultural differences between himself and his hosts. He is clearly experiencing culture shock. At one point he almost gives up and goes back to China. But he decides to stay. In this excerpt we see Liu trying other strategies to make himself feel less alone in the United States; he transfers to another school and moves in with other Chinese.

Meanwhile more and more areas of my life were becoming meaningless. Two months had passed and I did not seem to be able to adjust very well to living in the McKnights' house. I wasn't sure whether I could survive for two years under these conditions. I began to wonder if it might be better for me to live with other Chinese. Before leaving China, I had decided not to speak Chinese at all in the United States, in order to make faster progress with English. And in these two months I had spoken more English than I had in all the fourteen years since I had been studying the language. Nevertheless, I now began to yearn to speak my own language again.

Professor McKnight kindly gave me the telephone number of a Chinese student at Northwestern, who gave me another number of a group of five Chinese living in an apartment west of the campus. They asked me to visit them on Saturday night. I knew none of them, but they looked, acted, thought, and spoke Chinese, and I felt comfortable and warm just being among my own people. After that, I went to their place every weekend, sometimes staying overnight. Perhaps I was speaking Chinese too much of the time, but with the tension gone I could relax, watch TV, and catch a lot more of the dialogue than at the McKnights'. With these new friends I felt more safe and secure.

I tried going to more classes, as a way to pass the time. In the beginning, I would wait for the professor of the class to arrive to inform him that I was there to sit in. Later, I just went in and found a seat. Nobody seemed to care who was or wasn't there. Still the days were too long. For hours I would sit in a corner of the library, making every effort to focus on the books assigned to me by Professor Thompson. The words blurred as my thoughts drifted to the airplanes that passed overhead every half hour or so. Through the window I could see the snow melting under the early spring sun. Energetic, merry young people in pairs, and in threes and fours, hurried along in animated conversation. If only I could be one of them! I envied the students with oriental features who had American friends. By now I concluded that it was impossible for me to make friends with American students. There were too many differences between us. The age difference alone gave us different interests.

I tried to approach some professors. Professor Swashlose, who taught News Media and U.S. Government, had told the class that he was a believer in communism in the 1960s, and my impression from his lectures was that he was still interested in socialist countries. Since I came from a socialist country, I thought we might have something to talk about. I made an appointment to talk with him. However, the two talks in his office, each lasting about twenty minutes, made it clear that I wasn't making friends with this professor, either. No matter how friendly he tried to be, he gave me the impression that he was the professor and I was the humble student. The same age as I, he sat behind a big desk filling his pipe constantly, just as he did behind the lectern. I stumbled with my words, more because of my reaction to his status than because of my poor command of English.

Professor Swashlose, however, was a sensitive man in comparison to Professor Davis. This preeminent teacher at Medill had forty students in his News Writing class. Professor Thompson had particularly asked me to sit in on this class to learn the basic skills of news writing. Every morning at ten o'clock I slipped in to sit in a back seat, never daring to speak.

One day Professor Davis was lecturing on how to use question marks, saying that, according to the A.P. style, putting punctuation outside the quotes was the rule. According to *China Reconstructs* the rule is to put them inside. I knew in such matters there are different rules and that most writers don't really care. That day, however, I was tempted to speak out in class. I wanted to test my courage. I raised my hand, immediately conscious of the stares of the other students. I began to hope he would not see me.

"Well, go ahead," this sixtyish professor snapped.

Ignoring my pounding heart, I told him my magazine places punctuation inside the quotes.

"Your magazine? What's your magazine?"

I told him.

"Never heard of it" he said. "I don't care whose rule it uses. You take my class, you listen to my rules."

Perhaps he was trying to be humorous, but I didn't think it was funny. All I recognized was his sarcasm. My face flushed, and my heart raced at a wild speed. "I am a foreigner," I wanted to say. "How dare you treat me so shabbily. If I have said something wrong, you, as the teacher, should correct me politely. This is the first time in one and a half months I have spoken in your class, and you embarrass me like this?" Oh, how I wished I could say those words aloud. I was furious and I felt frustrated, but I remained silent. "Under others' eaves you have to bend your head," a Chinese proverb says.

I began to wonder if I were attending the right school. Perhaps I should go elsewhere. There were several other universities in the Chicago area that were said to be good schools.

It was not an easy decision. I felt I was letting Ron [Liu's American friend who had helped him come to the United States] and the McKnights down, after Ron had taken the trouble to get me into a good journalism school, and the McKnights had tried to please me. I wrote a letter to Ron, asking his opinion.

He replied: "I'm sorry you're having such a rough time. If you think it is your living situation that's creating the problem, then by all means, move. I assure you that neither Dean Cole nor the McKnights will be offended. Cole has nothing whatsoever to do with where you live, and the McKnights will certainly respect your judgment that you need a Chinese space in which to reassemble your thoughts after each day in an alien world. You're a grown man, and in America those kinds of decisions are entirely your own to make." He also said, "I think it is fairly common, when living in a foreign culture for the first time, to ride an emotional roller-coaster, with great highs and deep lows. That certainly has been my experience in China. For a long time you were my only real connection to China, and it was only on those occasions when I thought you had let me a little further into your life that my general state of gloominess was temporarily dispelled."

After a lot of mental struggle, I decided to transfer to the University of Illinois at Chicago Circle. . . .

In thinking about what to do with my future here, I had come to the conclusion that what I needed was a bridge person, one who could close the gap for me between the culture of China and the United States. There were a thousand things I was eager to know. The rest of my time in the United States would hardly be long enough to learn about the culture. I didn't want to be confined just to a classroom. I could take a hundred books back to read in my own country, but I couldn't take people with me. I had to know them here.

It hadn't taken long for me to realize that my language was not as much of an obstacle to learning as was my cultural heritage. Even if I could have understood all the words people were using in their conversations, I often had no idea what they were talking about. I could follow a conversation but could not take part in it because I knew so little about the subject. The gap was often so great that I thought we must be using different forms of logic in our thinking. As the Chinese say, "You can't grasp his mind."

Really, I should not have felt such great culture shock. For years I had been reading American novels, *Newsweek*, *Time* and *The Reader's Digest*. I was much more aware of American life than most other visiting Chinese scholars. I had had American teachers in school and had been exposed to American colleagues in my office. Perhaps the Japanese are right when they tell a foreigner who is unable to comprehend some of their ideas, "If only you were born Japanese, you would understand." I was born Chinese and so I think in a Chinese way.

My other difficulty was that the language used in daily life was quite different from that used in books. A foreigner can usually find the definition of a written word or phrase in the dictionary. However, many phrases used in daily conversation can be learned only through exposure to an environment in which people speak them constantly. Until one has learned how, it is even difficult to know how to order a dinner in an American restaurant. I heard of one Chinese professor who, having taught English for twenty years in a Chinese foreign language institute, didn't know how to order in a restaurant when he went to England with a delegation. As a translator, I needed this live language and experience. Chicago is a place saturated with lively English; Evanston was too quiet and too upper-middle class.

••••••••••••••••

To a certain extent I was pleased that I was finally learning to be more aggressive, to make my own choices, and to overcome the Chinese reluctance to say no to other people. . . . But before I had told the McKnights that I had decided to leave, I hesitated for several days. I worried that I would be letting them down if I left their house. And in the end, I didn't give them a straightforward reason; I only stressed the dullness of the school.

On a Saturday morning, Zheng Zhenyi came to Evanston to help me move. I can't put into words how I felt then. Bitter, miserable, regretful?—I didn't know. The McKnights probably were relieved that I was leaving. I must have become a bore to them—a depressed character hanging around their otherwise complacent life. They saw me off, without the many polite words that Chinese usually use when saying goodby to a guest. The white house stood quietly against the gray sky; the grass beside the sidewalks was turning tenderly green.

••••••••••••••••

The train rumbled southward. It was Saturday and it was cold. The few passengers were wrapped in heavy coats, even though the car was heated. I began to realize that something was missing. I was here to learn about America and now I was moving away from an American family to live with Zheng Zhenyi and other Chinese. Where would I find the chance to speak English?

When the McKnights had said that I should feel free to come back to their house whenever I wanted to, I told them, a bit too bluntly, that if I didn't feel better in the new place I would go back to China. There wouldn't be any coming back. As the Chinese saying goes, a good horse doesn't graze backwards.

Liu Zongren

1. From the excerpt you have read here, what impression do you get of the American professors Liu writes about here? Have you had similar experiences?
2. Why does Liu say that the real obstacle to learning English for him was not language but cultural heritage? What do you think that means?
3. Why do you think that Liu was so reluctant and hesitant about moving out of the McKnight household?

4. What impression do you have of the McKnights from this description?

Journal Suggestions

- What is your reaction to this excerpt? Are you tempted to read more? Comment on any aspect of this text that you find interesting.

- What do you think of Liu's need to be with other Chinese? Have you had a similar experience? What do you think accounts for the need to be with other people from your own country, even if they are strangers?

- What do you think of Liu's comments about learning English? Do you think he has been doing the right thing in order to learn the most he can? Have you ever had the experience of listening to a conversation, understanding all the words, and yet not really understanding what the people are talking about? How can you explain this?

➤ Optional Writing Assignment

Lincoln's biography was prepared for a clear purpose, to allow voters to know him better before they decided whether or not to vote for him. Liu writes about only a short time in his life while he was in the United States. Based on your reading of these two short excerpts from two men's very different lives, describe these two people. What impressions do you get of their personalities? Do they seem similar in any way?   ◄

Who Are Smarter—Boys or Girls?

Scientists Probe the Roots of Abilities That Seem Linked to Sex

---

Before you read, consider the following questions:

1. If you went to a coeducational school as a child, did boys or girls generally seem smarter? Were boys or girls generally better behaved? What do you imagine was the reason for this?

2. Who is better in math, boys or girls? Who is better in language? Who is more sensitive? Who is more aggressive? Are these characteristics innate, or do children learn to behave in certain ways? Are there exceptions? What happens to the exceptions?

This reading from Current Science *discusses the differences between boys and girls in the United States from the point of view of intelligence. It points out that girls start school more prepared physically and mentally than boys. Later, however, men get better jobs. The reading explores the idea that society teaches little boys to be independent and aggressive even from the time they are very young. Little girls are taught to be dependent and obedient; society does not reward them for being aggressive and independent. Little girls respond by not developing that side of their nature, while boys do not develop the gentle side of their nature.*

Only boys are good at science.
Girls have better vocabularies than boys.
Girls have good memories.
Boys are good at building things.

Now wait. Don't start those letters to the editors yet. You may not like what you've just read. But it's true. There are exceptions, but here are the facts. On the average, males score higher on tests that measure mathematical reasoning, mechanical aptitude, and problem-solving ability. Females show superior ability in tests measuring vocabulary, spelling, and memory.

Although these test scores are the facts, they are not unchangeable—not anymore. For scientists are learning that no one is locked into certain abilities at birth because of sex. Says one scientist, "Nothing is impossible for a human being to be or do if he or she really wants it."

Studying the Baby. Scientific studies have focused on observing and testing young babies to trace the development of different abilities.

A scientific team headed by Jerome Kagan, Harvard psychologist, is studying the thinking ability of $11\frac{1}{2}$-month-old children. The test is a simple one. The baby, while seated on its mother's lap, watches a "show" on a puppet theater stage.

In Act I of the show an orange cube is lifted from a blue box and moved across the stage in a zigzag path. Then it is returned to the box. This is repeated six times. Act II is similar, except that the orange block is smaller. Baby boys do not react at all to the difference in the size of the cube, but girls immediately begin to babble and become excited.

The scientists interpret the girls' babbling and excitement as meaning they are trying to understand what they have just seen. They are wondering why Act II is odd and how it differs from Act I. In other words, the little girls are reasoning.

This experiment certainly does not definitely prove that girls start to reason before boys. But it provides a clue that scientists would like to study more carefully. Already it is known that bones, muscles, and nerves develop faster in baby girls. Perhaps it is early nerve development that makes some infant girls show more intelligence than infant boys.

Scientists have also found that nature seems to give another boost to girls. It is usual to find baby girls talking at an earlier age than boys do. Scientists think that there is a physical reason for this. They believe that the nerve endings in the left side of the brain develop faster in girls than they do in boys. And it is this side of the brain that strongly influences an individual's ability to use words, spell, and remember things.

By the time they start school, therefore, little girls have a head start on boys. Memorizing, spelling, and reading are just what they're good at.

Boys Learn Aggression. But what has been happening to baby boys all this time? They have been developing that secret weapon called *aggression*. This secret weapon makes them strivers, go-getters, independent.

What produces this aggression in little boys? Male hormones play a part. But the mother seems to make the biggest contribution.

A team of psychologists discovered this by placing mothers and their one-year-old babies in a special observation room filled with toys. Then they took notes on everything the mothers or babies did. This is a sample of those notes, taken during the observation of a boy and his mother.

"Baby leans against mother. Looks up at her. She speaks to him. She turns him around. He walks away, picks up toy cat.

Goes to mother, drops cat, and leans against her. Looks up at her. She turns him around."

From these notes and from interviews with the mother, the scientists concluded that while the mother keeps her daughter close she unconsciously trains her son to investigate—to become a problem solver.

A Second Lesson. As the boy grows, he gets another boost in his aggression lessons—the "be-a-man" problem. As a baby and a young child, he spends most of his waking hours with his mother. His first strong attachment is to his mother. He models himself after her.

But soon he begins to get some confusing commands from his mother. "Don't be a sissy!" "Boys don't cry." "Boys don't walk like that." And so there is a new problem. He is somehow different from his model. But what is the difference? All he hears are "don'ts." He struggles to find out what the "do's" are.

When the little girl and boy meet in the first grade, it is the old story of the tortoise and the hare all over again. While the girl collects A's in spelling, the boy is working at problems— "how to get a C in spelling," "how to be a man." Like the tortoise, the boy plods ahead, gaining more and more experience in problem solving. Like the swift-footed hare, the girl glides through the first few grades, losing the chance to learn problem solving at an early age.

Aggression Runs Our World. In the world we live in, the aggressive person is usually the one who gets the big salary, the good job, the prizes. And since men are trained at an early age to be aggressive, they are the ones most often picked for the key positions.

But many believe this situation is wrong. They think women have an equal contribution to make in science and industry. Teachers and scientists suggest that girls be given aggression lessons in school. This does not mean that every little girl should learn to box. Games that teach competition and problem solving are one suggestion.

Another scientist believes that boys may get too much training in aggression. A little more affection from their mothers might make them gentler. And the world needs gentleness, just as it needs aggression.

Current Science

1. In what ways do little girls have an advantage over little boys when they both start school at age five or six?

2. Recount Kagan's experiment conducted with the babies and mothers.
3. Why don't little girls do better in the real world if they do better in school than little boys?
4. Do you agree with the conclusions reached in this selection?

Journal Suggestions

- If this reading interested you, respond to it in a journal entry. Comment, react, or note any interesting information.
- Would you rather be a male or a female in your society? Whose life is better? What are the advantages and disadvantages of each one? Do you think more men would want to be women or to live women's lives or more women would want to be men or lead men's lives? Why?

Are Men Born with Power?

Before you read, consider the following questions:

1. What do you think accounts for the fact that males seem to dominate most human societies?
2. Can you name any situations you are aware of in which males are subordinate to females? What accounts for this situation?

In the following essay the author, a research anthropologist, discusses biological explanations for males' historical dominance over females. Her approach focuses mainly on brain chemistry.

Why did ancient agricultural societies become patriarchies instead of matriarchies? Why didn't women seize the rule? The brute force necessary to drive the plow and the strength required in warfare both suffice to answer this question. But I think at least one more primary factor was involved in the florescence of patriarchy and the decline of women's worlds—biology.

In every single society where ranks are prevalent, men hold the majority of the authoritative roles. In fact, in 88 percent of 93 societies canvassed, *all* local and intermediate political leaders are men; in 84 percent of these cultures men hold *all* the top leadership positions in the kin group too. This is not because women are barred from these positions. In many of these cultures—such as the United States—women are permitted to seek influential positions in government. Today greater numbers of women are indeed running for office. But even now women do not seek political positions with anything near the regularity that men do.

•••••••••••••••••

[As] one who takes science seriously, I cannot ignore the possibility that biology plays a role in the acquisition of rank. In fact, several lines of reasoning support this conclusion.

The brain is indeed sexed before birth by fetal hormones. There is a clear link between testosterone and aggressive behavior in animals and people. High rank is also associated with high levels of male hormones in men and monkeys. Also, women in many cultures assume more leadership positions after their childbearing years are over. There certainly are cultural reasons for this. Released from the constant chores of rearing young, postmenopausal women are certainly liberated to pursue activities outside the home. But there may be a biological reason for their assertiveness as well. Levels of estrogen decline with menopause, unmasking levels of testosterone. Nature has concocted a chemical that possibly contributes to the drive for rank.

There may be another chemical in the cocktail too—serotonin, another of the brain's molecules. The highest-ranking male vervet monkey in a troop, scientists have established, has consistently higher levels of serotonin in his blood. Even when male monkeys are artificially administered serotonin, their rank goes up; and male monkeys given drugs that inhibit the secretion of serotonin experience a drop in rank.

Among human males the same correlations prevail. Officers in college student groups show higher levels of serotonin in their blood than do nonofficers, as do leaders of college sports teams. These simple correlations seem not to be exhibited in women. And scientists preliminarily conclude that women and female nonhuman primates exhibit a more complex behavioral and physiological system of dominance.

Nevertheless, there seems to be a rather direct correlation between testosterone and rank—as well as some evidence that other brain substances contribute to the biology of hierarchy.

Helen Fisher

1. The author gives several pieces of evidence to suggest that the dominance of males in society is caused by testosterone. What are they?
2. What does the presence of serotonin correlate with in monkeys and humans?
3. Because the same correlations do not occur in women, what conclusions do researchers draw about women and brain chemistry?

Journal Suggestions

- What is your reaction to the information in this essay? Are you convinced or do you feel that the situation might be more complex than simple issues of chemistry? Comment on any aspect of this essay that you find interesting.
- If the conclusions that the author draws from brain chemistry are correct, what does that suggest about how human beings should live? Should we try to do something to reduce the testosterone in excessively aggressive men? How much aggression is excessive? Should women try to increase the amount of testosterone in their bodies?

- If you were to assume that brain chemistry is, in fact, the major cause of the kind of behavior that creates leaders, would this fact make you feel less impressed with leadership qualities? In other words, if people become leaders because of natural chemical gifts instead of effort or wisdom, would this make you think less highly of leaders?

➤ *Optional Writing Assignment*

In "Who Are Smarter—Boys or Girls?" and "Are Men Born with Power?" two different explanations for differences in male/female behavior are given. The first article gives an explanation based partly on biological differences but mostly on the way boys and girls are treated. The second article concludes that biochemical differences have the most impact on the way dominance (including male dominance over females) creates hierarchies among primates. Which position seems most convincing to you? Use summaries, paraphrases, and quotations from the articles to support or explain your position. Be sure to cite the articles as necessary in your text and prepare a bibliography.   ◄

From *Savage Inequalities*
Chapter 2: Other People's Children

Before you read, consider the following questions:

1. When you started school, did you expect to study at a university or college some day? Did your family expect you to continue your education beyond high school? What kind of profession did they expect you to enter?
2. How do young people in your country decide what they will study in elementary and secondary school? Are there exams that put children on a particular educational track that they must follow, or are children free to select any courses they like?

In this section of Savage Inequalities *Kozol discusses the kinds of limitations placed on children who must attend poorly funded, educationally inferior schools. First he describes the practical argument that because children in inner-city schools are not trained well enough to go to college, they should be trained in schools for the jobs they will eventually hold, even though these jobs are the least prestigious, lowest-level jobs in society. Wealthy suburban children can get the education that they will need to fill the jobs of lawyer and doctor. Kozol then responds to this argument by pointing out that those who make this type of argument are the same people who reject the idea of spending more money on educating inner-city schoolchildren enough so that they will be qualified to go to college. He says that if society expects little from the children in poor schools, then the children themselves and their parents will also expect little from them and, as a result, are likely to get little. The wealthy parents and their privileged children, on the other hand, expect to get the best education and later the best jobs and will accept nothing less.*

A recent emphasis of certain business-minded authors writing about children in the kinds of schools we have examined in Chicago urges us to settle for "realistic" goals, by which these authors mean the kinds of limited career objectives that seem logical or fitting for low-income children. Many corporate leaders have resisted this idea, and there are some who hold out high ideals and truly democratic hopes for these low-income children; but other business leaders speak quite openly of "training" kids like these for nothing better than the entry-level jobs their corporations have available. Urban schools, they argue, should dispense with "frills" and focus on the "the basics" needed for employment. Emphasis in the suburban schools, they add, should necessarily be more expansive, with a focus upon college preparation.

Investment strategies, according to this logic, should be matched to the potential economic value of each person. Future service workers need a different and, presumably, a lower order of investment than the children destined to be corporate executives, physicians, lawyers, engineers. Future plumbers and future scientists require different schooling—maybe different schools. Segregated education is not necessarily so unattractive by this reasoning.

Early testing to assign each child to a "realistic" course of study, the tracking of children by ability determined by the tests, and the expansion of a parallel system for the children who appear to show the greatest promise (gifted classes and selective schools) are also favored from this vantage point. In terms of sheer efficiency and of cost-benefit considerations, it is a sensible approach to education. If children are seen primarily as raw material for industry, a greater investment in the better raw material makes sense. Market values do not favor much investment in the poorest children.

One cannot dispute the fact that giving poor black adolescents job skills, if it is self-evident that they do not possess the academic skills to go to college, is a good thing in itself. But the business leaders who put emphasis on filling entry-level job slots are too frequently the people who, by prior lobbying and voting patterns and their impact upon social policy, have made it all but certain that few of these urban kids would get the education in their early years that would have made them *look* like college prospects by their secondary years. First we circumscribe their destinies and then we look at the diminished product and we say, "Let's be pragmatic and do with them what we can."

The evolution of two parallel curricula, one for urban and one for suburban schools, has also underlined the differences in what is felt to be appropriate to different kinds of children and to socially distinct communities. "This school is right for this community," says a former director of student services at New Trier High. But, he goes on, "it certainly wouldn't be right for every community." What is considered right for children at Du Sable and their counterparts in other inner-city schools becomes self-evident to anyone who sees the course of study in such schools. Many urban high school students do not study math but "business math"—essentially, a very elemental level of bookkeeping. Job-specific courses such as "cosmetology" (hairdressing, manicures), which would be viewed as insults by suburban parents, are a common item in the segregated high schools and are seen as realistic preparation for the adult roles that 16-year-old black girls may expect to fill.

Inevitably this thinking must diminish the horizons and the aspirations of poor children, locking them at a very early age into the slots that are regarded as appropriate to their societal position. On its darkest side, it also leads to greater willingness to write off certain children. "It doesn't make sense to offer something that most of these urban kids will never use," a businessman said to me flatly in Chicago. "No one expects these ghetto kids to go to college Most of them are lucky if they're even literate. If we can teach some useful skills, get them to stay in school and graduate, and maybe into jobs, we're giving them the most that they can hope for."

"Besides," a common line of reasoning continues, "these bottom-level jobs exist. They need to be done. Somebody's got to do them." It is evident, however, who that somebody will be. There is no sentimentalizing here. No corporate CEO is likely to confess a secret wish to see his children trained as cosmetologists or clerical assistants. So the prerogatives of class and caste are clear.

Some years ago, New Trier High School inaugurated an "office education" course that offered instruction in shorthand, filing and typing. "It was an acknowledged flop," the *Washington Post* reports. Not enough students were enrolled. The course was discontinued. "I guess," a teacher said, kids at New Trier "just don't think of themselves as future secretaries."

Jonathan Kozol

1. What does Kozol think about the idea that high schools should train poor children in low-level job skills?
2. What is Kozol's reaction to the idea that low-level jobs must be done by someone and so it is logical for these poor children to eventually take these jobs?
3. Why was the course in office education eventually dropped from the curriculum at New Trier High School?

Journal Suggestions

- What is your reaction to the argument in this text? Do you agree with Kozol that limiting our expectations of certain people in society and limiting their opportunities is unfair? Or do you agree with the argument that someone must eventually do low-level jobs in society and so these poorer students should be trained to do them?

- How do you think you would have reacted and developed if people around you had expected you to eventually be able to get only a low-level, low-paying job? What kinds of expectations did your friends and family have for you when you were young? What kinds of schools did you attend? Did you know children whose parents set low expectations for them? What happened to them?

Is There a Doctor in the Classroom?

New Questions about the Necessity of a Ph.D. for College Teachers

Before you read, consider the following questions:

1. What is a Ph.D. or a doctorate?
2. Do any of your teachers now have Ph.D.s?
3. What advantage do you think having a Ph.D. would be for a teacher?
4. What advantage do you think it would be for a student to be taught by a teacher with a Ph.D.?

Getting a Ph.D. is the highest academic achievement in the United States. In most cases only professors with Ph.D.s are hired by universities. However, the Ph.D. is a research degree, not a teaching degree. This means that many of the professors in colleges and universities have been trained to do research but have not been trained to teach. In fact, research is considered much more prestigious than teaching, as is shown by the differences in salaries paid to researchers and teachers. This article discusses the question of whether or not it is a good idea to hire people with a Ph.D. for institutions in which the main responsibility is not research but teaching.

We're all familiar with the stereotypical absent-minded professor so distracted by his research that he (and it is usually a he) cannot function in daily life—let alone relate to his students. The stereotype may be funny, but the assumption at its heart suggests a serious question that could affect the future of higher education: Is the traditional doctoral program, with its emphasis on specialization and research, necessarily the best or only way to train college professors?

Sociology professor Lionel S. Lewis of the State University of New York (SUNY) at Buffalo and Philip G. Altbach, professor and director of SUNY Buffalo's Comparative Education Center, are among the minority of educators who say no. In a controversial critique of doctoral education in the American Association of University Professors' magazine, *Academe* (May/June 1992), they argue that the esteemed Ph.D. degree—that long-established rite of passage to professorship—may be ideal for a career in research but is superfluous and even inappropriate for the majority of academics, who are primarily teachers.

Their argument is logical—and convincing. Consider, for instance, that the Ph.D. regimen offers very little instruction in

teaching or communicating with students. Course work is concentrated in a single discipline or subdiscipline, and the cap-
stone of the degree—the doctoral dissertation—is an intense exercise in independent study within a carefully delimited area of
knowledge.

Yet despite the emphasis on research, most American academics with Ph.D.s essentially do none. "The American academic
profession is largely a teaching profession," write Lewis and
Altbach. "And in any case, the overwhelming majority of
American faculty work in institutions that cannot provide them
with scientific equipment, library facilities, and other resources
to carry on pathbreaking research."

Contrary to the "publish or perish" myth that helps to legitimate the importance of Ph.D.s, even those few academics who do
conduct original research seldom publish, report Lewis and
Altbach. According to a 1989 study of faculty at two- and four-
year colleges by the Carnegie Foundation for the Advancement
of Teaching cited by Lewis and Altbach, 28 percent of faculty had
never published an article, and 47 percent had published nothing in the past two years. Fifty-seven percent had never published a book or monograph, while close to half identified themselves primarily as teachers and 27 percent leaned toward
teaching. Only 6 percent focused primarily on research.

Despite findings such as these, the century-long dominance
of the Ph.D. in higher education has made it difficult, if not impossible, for new models of doctoral training to succeed. Decades
ago an effort was made to institute a broader-based doctor of
arts degree as an alternative to the increasingly specialized
Ph.D., but the reform failed when students continued to prefer
the more prestigious doctorate and colleges and universities continued to require it.

In the 1990s, academia may have no choice but to reconsider.

•••••••••••••••••

News of a long-anticipated faculty shortage fills professional
journals. As *Minnesota*, the University of Minnesota Alumni
Association magazine (March 1990), reports, Howard Boen and
Jack Schuster, authors of *American Professors: A National
Resource Imperiled*, predict that 500,000 of the nation's 700,000
faculty members will retire within the next two decades, and
most of them will have to be replaced.

Even if the faculty shortage doesn't materialize, tuition
hikes are prompting students to question the research emphasis
at large universities, and some colleges are responding by begin-

ning to pay more than lip service to the importance of teaching.
. . . Stanford president Donald Kennedy has urged faculty
tenure committees to value "forms of scholarship related to
teaching"—including textbooks, instructional software programs and books, and even videos aimed at popular audiences—
and has proposed ongoing evaluations of tenured professors,
"who now have little incentive to attend to the improvement of
teaching." Yet Stanford has not considered alternatives to the re-
search-driven Ph.D. requirement.

In a telephone interview, Altbach predicted that until a court
case determines that a Ph.D. is not a necessary requirement
for teaching, most universities are unlikely to think about
changes. . . .

·················

Despite these questions, few alternative models of doctoral
education have yet been proposed. Lewis and Altbach suggest
looking toward British and German models that require more
teaching experience and a less rigorous dissertation for those
whose primary goal is teaching.

Laurie Ouellette

1. What is the main reason that the Ph.D. degree may not be an
   appropriate requirement for most college professors?
2. The article cites a number of statistics about professors' publishing. What are these statistics intended to show?
3. Why did the more teaching-oriented doctor of arts degree not
   replace the Ph.D. as a requirement for college teaching, according to this article?
4. What evidence is there that schools may have to reconsider
   dropping the Ph.D. as a requirement for teaching?

Journal Suggestions

- What is your reaction to this article? Have you studied in
  many classrooms taught by someone with a Ph.D., either at
  home or where you are now studying? Did you consider
  these people to be good teachers?
- What do you think are the most important things a professor should know in order to be a good teacher? Can these
  things be taught in teacher-training classes?
- Are you planning to get a Ph.D.? If so, do you plan to teach
  or mainly to do research? If you are planning to teach, do

you think that the research you do for your Ph.D. and later will help you in your teaching in any way? How?

- Is a Ph.D. required to teach in a university or college in your country? If not, what is required? Do those requirements seem appropriate to you?

Voices from the College Front

Makes No Difference If It's Black or White, College Is a Different World. Here's What Some Students Have to Say About Life on Campus Today

Before you read, consider the following questions:

1. Are there schools in your country attended only by certain racial or ethnic groups or socioeconomic classes? How does this system work?
2. Would you feel comfortable being the only person of your racial or ethnic group or social class in college?

This article is a series of short statements by African American college students discussing their reasons for choosing to attend college in predominantly black or predominantly white schools and their experiences there. These students raise issues of extreme importance to African American young people. Most white people in the United States are aware of the problems of racism, but many are completely unaware of other problems young African Americans face, such as the importance to young black people of acting black so that they will not be accused by other black people of trying to be white; the fact that young black people have often learned to hate themselves for being black; the difficulty of studying in a culture that does not value and therefore does not teach their cultural values, history, or literature; the difficulty of cross-racial tensions and misunderstandings.

> *In the spring of my sophomore year at Harvard University, I was almost arrested in my own dormitory for attempting to take my computer to my nearby home. My younger brother had come in with me to help me carry it, and on our way out the door the security guard stopped us. He told us not to move, that we weren't going anywhere. My brother was able to motion for my mother and younger sister, who were waiting in the car, to come in. My mother tried to talk to the guard, but to no avail. He called for backup. At least four squad cars arrived on the scene immediately. At that point it didn't matter that we were a family, that I was a Harvard student, that my mother—herself a Harvard graduate—was a parent dressed in a sophisticated business suit, that my sister was only in seventh grade or that my brother was a sophomore in high school. None of this made a difference. All that mattered was that we were Black. I relay this incident because I learned from it a painful lesson: that my education,*

*my family, my person, my life even, do not carry the same
weight or have the same value as those of other students,
White students, on this campus.*

*In the narratives that follow, Black college students at
various Black and White institutions across the country
speak openly and honestly about their schools, their
experiences, their relationships with their peers and, most
important, the issues that concern them as members of a
generation with the potential and the responsibility to make
substantial changes in the lives of Black people.*

Olukemi Adewole, *1993 graduate, Northwestern University,
Evanston, Illinois, theater major*
I chose Northwestern because of its theater department
primarily and its location. I attended a racially mixed high
school, although I didn't have very many African-American
friends. When I got to Northwestern, I was determined to
integrate myself into the Black community. Before
matriculating I visited the school during a weekend when
there weren't too many other "prefreshmen" on campus, so I
was able to get more of a sense of how the Black community
really was. There were a lot of activities going on, and it felt
really positive.

I would say most of the Black students that come here
have gone to predominantly White schools and may not have
lived around other Black people or have had very many
Black friends, which was my situation. So you make a
decision that you want to be really involved in the Black
community.

But one of the problems some people have with that is
feeling that you have to prove yourself or your Blackness by
wearing this or that, or talking like this or that. This creates
a pressure to conform to those outward expressions of
"Blackness" in order to show that you're "down." People who
don't fit into this mold or who don't do these things feel
looked down upon or excluded. I'm not saying that only students who grew up in predominantly White environments
act in certain ways. It can't be as cut-and-dried as that. It's
just the way different people choose to do it [express their
identities]. However, I think things have been getting better
in that respect over the past year and a half.

I think the main advantage of being at this institution is
the exposure it has given me to reality in terms of the kinds
of people I'll be dealing with and the real situations I might
find myself in. College in itself is a fantasy. But I think, for

example, at a predominantly Black school you're more sheltered to an extent. I mean, when you get out there in the world, you're going to be dealing with White people. I just think attending a predominantly White school has helped me to be a little bit more realistic, and I stress a little bit more realistic.

Sushama Austin, *sophomore, Fisk University, Nashville, English major*

I chose to come to Fisk because my dad is a Fisk alumnus, but, more important, because I wanted to have a Black college experience. I knew it was a good school academically, but I chose Fisk more for social reasons. I attended predominantly White Catholic schools in Washington, D.C., and Michigan during high school. I had the hardest eleventh- and twelfth-grade years. The people at my school were really prejudiced, and the kids were not very nice to me. I had a difficult time proving myself and making friends there. It was so frustrating. I was ready for a change. I was ready to be around more people who looked like me. I told my parents last year that I never thought what color I was would actually be that big of a problem in my life—at least not to the extent that it was. I know I can't run away from racism, but at least now I know how it feels to be in an environment with mostly people of color.

····················

I think Fisk is a really good school academically. The expectations are high, and there's a lot of competition. You really do have to work. One of the things that makes it so nice, though, is that the school incorporates an African-American perspective. I love English—that's my major—but I've never enjoyed it as much as I have this year. So many Black writers were brought to my attention that I didn't even know about. I knew about the famous ones like James Baldwin and Toni Morrison, but there are writers I don't think I would ever have had the chance to experience in any other institution.

For me, it's a real experience to be here because I get to see the Black race at its best and celebrating its best. I've never been in an atmosphere, academically speaking, where you celebrate your best, and the best are these Black people who are just as bright and intelligent as everybody else.

I find it refreshing that if you're smart, you're smart because of who you are. You're not highlighted as "Oh, she's a smart Black student" or "She's doing so well for a Black student." I'm in a place where I'm not judged as much on race or color, and in that way I feel relieved. If I've grown any, I think it would be from that relief. I've been able to be more outspoken. I used to be shy, and it's been easier for me to make friends here with people I feel are going to be important to me even after I leave this place.

Cornell Womack, *1993 graduate, Georgetown University, Washington, D.C., history and drama major*
Where I ended up going to school was very much influenced by the fact that I come from a familial structure that really had no understanding of what it meant to go to college. Nobody in my family had gone to college. Nobody had any real knowledge of how to apply to schools, what schools to apply to, what it meant to go to certain schools. So I wound up applying to names that I had heard of. I applied to Princeton, Yale, West Point and Georgetown, and I got into all of them. I wound up at Georgetown, where I found an environment that was elitist and socially segregated. There was dialogue and talk of inclusiveness, but for all intents and purposes, socially, Blacks and Whites didn't really mix.

There is an undeniable Black community at Georgetown, which is formed as much through necessity as it is through threat. The threat is of exclusion from the Black community, and the necessity comes from the fear of being lost in Whiteness. It's a support system, in the absence of an academic or administrative support structure, where we can go to one another and socialize and not have to operate that "other part" of our consciousness that Du Bois [W.E.B.] talks about. bell hooks asks the question, "Does anybody question the fact that White people hang out together most of the time?" We always put things in these oppositional terms to see a deviance, and not what is a naturally occurring pattern in other ethnic groups. It's always difficult when you have a Black community on a predominantly White campus, because it then tends to become more defensive and more concerned with issues of getting the White structure to accept it. That may be energy wasted, and energy that probably would not have been spent, at least not in the same way, on a predominantly Black campus.

In terms of the processes of development I've gone through, I had to admit at some point in my life, as I think all Black people have to admit, that I have been taught to hate myself. It took a hell of a long time for me to be able to say that, yes, I have internalized my oppression. I have taken personal and emotional time to heal from the process of coming to this knowledge.

Liana Johnson, *1993 graduate, Vassar College, Poughkeepsie, New York, astronomy major*

I went to a high school that was approximately 80-percent Black. I was in the upper tenth percentile, and people thought that since I studied so hard and made good grades I was trying to be White. Sooner or later this entered my subconscious and I had that perception that if they felt that way, then maybe it was true, maybe only White people were smart. It was different when I came to Vassar because I was able to be around people who had the same academic interests I had. I don't think I've ever really felt alienated here because the Black women all help to keep one another sane. Some people in the outside community looking at us think that we're segregating ourselves. They don't understand that we have something in common and want to be around one another. I think one thing I learned at Vassar is to be more tolerant of differences. But I also learned to recognize when I'm being put down and to speak up when I find that something is wrong. I don't think I would have done anything like that before I came here.

••••••••••••••••••

Nicole Tarpley, *senior, Brandeis University, Waltham, Massachusetts, African-American studies and sociology major*

Brandeis is a predominantly Jewish institution. The academic calendar is set up around Jewish holidays. There are Jewish dorms. There is a kosher cafeteria. As a Black person here it is difficult to feel at home both academically and socially. There are about 100 to 150 Black people, and we pretty much stick together. I don't really socialize with the White students, so this is an important outlet for me. There are some people, however, who would say that it is not really a cohesive community. But I think that's because people have their own agendas and social priorities. I happen to get along with most of the Black students, so I don't think it's a problem.

It seems at times, though, that the presence of a Black community presents a threat to the wider campus population, based on their perception that we're separating ourselves. I remember one event during Black History Month when we invited a brother from the Nation of Islam to speak at the Intercultural Center on campus. His topic was the African-American male. But earlier that day some Jewish students were distributing flyers, saying that this event should be boycotted because the Nation of Islam is anti-Semitic. A group of them, outnumbering the Black students themselves, came in protest to the discussion. They were very rude and insulting. Some of them accused us of creating racial tension. I felt that this was an intrusion on our space and event.

A lot of times I wish I had gone to a predominantly Black institution. I think the social atmosphere would have been much more satisfying. Academically I could have found a wider range of courses that look more in depth at the African-American experience.

Anastacia Hill, *junior, University of North Carolina, Chapel Hill, North Carolina, African-American studies and mass communication major*

··················

I spoke to several civil-rights activists who fought during the sixties, and they said that they were fighting for an equal chance and an equal opportunity. I'm fighting for all that, but I'm fighting for the truth this time—for my history to be taught. We can't live together in America, unified, unless we first understand where we all come from and learn to respect and appreciate one another's cultures. If you can't learn to appreciate someone's culture, then you can't learn to appreciate that person as a person.

Natasha Tarpley

1. What lesson did Natasha Tarpley, the author of the first section of this article, learn from the experience with her computer at Harvard?
2. What are some of the reasons these students gave for attending predominantly black schools?
3. What are some of the reasons these students gave for attending predominantly white schools?
4. What do you think Cornell Womack meant by the statement that all black people have been taught to hate themselves?
5. What do you think it means to act black?
6. What does it mean to act white according to these students?
7. Why does it seem so important to these students to study black literature and history?

Journal Suggestions

- When people speak of American culture, they really mean the culture of white Americans. Were you surprised by anything you read in these students' statements? Were you aware of the special kinds of problems that minority groups experience besides obvious problems of racism? Comment on any aspect of these students' statements that you found interesting.

- What is the dominant racial group at the school where you are now studying? What other groups are represented? Do these groups socialize with one another, or do they seem to seek out only members of their own race for social interaction? If they do not mix much racially, why do you think these groups stay with members of their own race? Is this a good or bad situation?

- What is the situation in your home country? Is your country racially mixed? Do these groups interact much? Are the histories and cultures of all of these groups taught in schools? Can you apply any insights you gained from this article to the situation in your own country?

➤ Optional Writing Assignments

Using the Kozol text from *Savage Inequalities* for information, discuss the question of whether or not giving more money to schools is enough to improve children's education in public schools.

Using the article called "Is There a Doctor in the Classroom?" on professors with Ph.D.s teaching in colleges and universities, discuss the question of whether or not it is an advantage to be taught by a person with a Ph.D.

Using the students' thoughts in "Voices from the College Front" about the situation of African American college students in both black and white institutions, discuss the issue of whether or not black students should choose to attend predominantly black colleges and universities. ◄

A View from Other Cultures:
Must Men Fear "Women's Work"?

Before you read, consider the following questions:

1. What is considered "women's work" in your culture? What is "men's work"?
2. What reasons do you think there might be for dividing work into women's and men's work?

This article discusses three different theories that attempt to explain why women's work is considered inferior to men's work. The first theory has to do with the idea that women are closer to nature than men and so not as evolved, complicated, or civilized. The second interprets women's work as private rather than the more public and so more important work men do. And the last is a complicated psychological theory related to the development of little boys. It says that in order to grow into normal men, boys need to separate themselves as much as possible from their mothers. In order to separate themselves from their mothers, they must learn to avoid anything related to females or to female activities. The author then describes another type of division of labor that is less degrading for women.

Anthropologists have found that around the world whatever is considered "men's work" is almost universally given higher status than "women's work." If in one culture it is men who build houses and women who make baskets, then that culture will see house-building as more important. In another culture, perhaps right next door, the reverse may be true, and basket-weaving will have higher social status than house-building.

Anthropologists agree that biology is not a sufficient explanation of male dominance. Following are three different theories anthropologists have suggested to account for the universality of male dominance and female subordination.

- *Nature Versus Culture:* In all cultures women are seen as closer to nature than men, whereas men are seen as more involved with culture than women. Since the cultural is universally valued more than the merely natural, women, by being closer to nature, are therefore devalued.

   Women are considered closer to nature than men because their bodies share the same reproductive functions as non-human female mammals. These involve more time, energy, and bodily risk than men's reproductive role. Men therefore have more freedom and energy to invest in technology, trade, games, arts, politics, and religion.

And since women spend more time with young children, who are born incontinent and unsocialized and thus seem more like animals, women are also seen as more connected to nature because of their care of "unacculturated" children. Because of this, women are often seen as more "childlike" themselves.

- *Domestic Versus Public:* Although women's reproductive activities do not inevitably force them to keep their activities close to home, women are more apt than men to do domestic tasks that are easily combined with child care. For the same reason men are more likely to engage in "public" activities that take them out of the home and away from the children. These public, male-dominated activities almost always have commanded more cultural respect than the domestic, less visible activities of women.

- *Object Relations and Family Life:* Psychologists have traced the process by which children become aware of being male or female. It is not until around age three that a child is able to reason that he or she is either a boy or a girl, and always will be. From that time on, one of a child's developmental tasks is to become emotionally secure and happy about being either a boy or a girl.

  Here is where the role of mothers as almost exclusive child rearers begins to matter. Both little girls and little boys are naturally attracted by the nurturance and apparent power of the mother, and want to be like her. But a little boy soon finds out that he can't grow up to be like Mommy. He must be like Daddy—the big male person he sees only a short time mornings and evenings.

  The boy is caught in a double-bind in that he cannot stay attached to his mother; yet his role model for imitation is largely absent. Thus his sense of being securely male is less solid and he may nurse deep and unconscious doubts about his ability to cope with the male role.

  But as the boy grows older, he begins to realize that being male is supposed to be a privilege, and if men are "real men" they are socially more important than women. Already somewhat insecure in his masculinity, he must now try all the harder to prove to himself and the world that he is a real man.

  How to do this? The safest way is to have as little to do with women and their activities as possible, to repress and deny any "womanly" qualities or impulses in himself. In ex-

treme cases he may do this by openly scorning or even mis-
treating women. Or a man may simply avoid women except
when he has domestic and sexual needs to be filled, spending
the rest of his time in visibly and exclusively male groups.
Or paradoxically, he may idealize women, "placing them on a
pedestal." This too keeps them at a safe distance, but is often accompanied by impossible demands of "womanly perfection" from them as well.

••••••••••••••••••

Whatever strategies are used, they allow an insecure man to
mask what amounts to an unconscious "dread of women." His
earliest associations are still of a mother who seemed all-power-
ful. When combined with his early deprivation of an available
male role model, the result may be a deeply repressed yet powerful conviction that women can somehow strip him of his masculine identity.

In this way we can see how masculine insecurity perpetu-
ates itself from generation to generation. The underfathered boy
develops a fragile, ambivalent male identity. To compensate for
this insecurity in adolescence and adulthood, he distances himself from women and "women's work." And what is most obviously women's work? Caring for young children. So he avoids
nurturing contact with his own sons and unwittingly contributes
to *their* development of insecure masculinity, dread of women,
and woman-rejecting behavior.

Is there any escape from this vicious circle? Since cultures
differ in the extent to which they emphasize the private/public
split, it may be instructive to look at one culture that minimizes
the gender roles between men and women. I will draw on my
own research experience with the Pygmy nation of Central
Africa, who live as hunter-gatherers.

Among the Pygmy there are some gender role differences,
but the smallness and mobility of the group require close cooperation among all members. Women and children help with some
of the hunting, and a woman can call on her husband to care for
an infant while she is cooking. Grandparents of both sexes care
for toddlers while both parents hunt and gather. Here the pub-
lic/private split has very little relevance.

Of particular interest is the fact that hunter-gatherers' flexibility in gender roles and cooperation is accompanied by greater
intellectual similarity between men and women.

What can we learn from this about our own situation? Some
cultural anthropologists say that it is imperative to move in two
directions: Men must be integrated into the domestic sphere,
sharing in the socialization of children and performing domestic

tasks; and women must participate equally with men in the public world of work and culture. Only then can women's status be elevated.

Such changes do not turn men into women and women into men. What is vital in upgrading the status of women's work is not eliminating the presence of gender roles, but rather the degree of proximity, cooperation, and role flexibility that men and women share. In fact, even when men and women do perform a common task—such as child care—they approach it rather differently, and many of these stylistic differences turn out to be very much worth preserving.

Mary Stewart Van Leeuwen

1. Describe in your own words the three theories presented here.
2. According to this article, why do men in some cultures put women on pedestals—that is, idealize them?
3. How can a boy begin to prove that he is a "real man," according to this article?
4. What is different about the division of labor in the Pygmy culture that the author describes?
5. Why do men fear women's work, according to this article?
6. What is the answer to the question of the title: Must men fear women's work?

Journal Suggestions

- What is your reaction to the content of this essay? Are you convinced by the three explanations given for the fact that women's work is considered not as valuable as men's work? Comment on any aspect of this essay that you found interesting.

- How does your culture fit into the descriptions here? Is women's work considered inferior and undesirable for a man to do? Are women paid as much as men for the kind of work they do? Are there jobs in your culture that used to be strictly men's work that are now done by women as well? Do men in your culture care for children, or is that usually women's work? How old are children when they start doing work that is considered either strictly women's or strictly men's work?

- The division of labor between the two sexes is made somewhat differently in different cultures. Think about the way labor was divided between your mother and father, your aunts and uncles, your male and female neighbors, or even between you and your own brothers and sisters. Who took care of the children? Who did the daily work in the house? Did this division of labor seem fair and reasonable to you? What are your own beliefs about how human work should be divided between the two genders?

On Kids and Slasher Movies
Do Kids Need Horror to Deal with Everyday Life?

Before you read, consider the following questions:

1. Do you remember seeing any very frightening movies when you were young? Did you enjoy them?
2. Does violence in movies create violence in children?

This essay is a description of the author's experience in a store where he sees a young boy having his mother buy him the costume and weapon used by a violent killer in a popular movie. The author is shocked that the reminder of such violence should be considered a toy and sold to little children. He then wonders about the link between violence in life and violence in the media and the question of why this child seems to want and even need such a toy.

It's a simple thing, really. I shouldn't take it so seriously, I realize that. For it was only a child, a boy of about 10, buying a toy. For Halloween. This was the toy:

A sinister white mask and a quite convincing little rubber meat cleaver. Packaged together in cellophane. It's the "costume" of a maniac killer from one of the slasher movies. The boy wants to play at being a faceless, unstoppable murderer of innocent people (mostly women). At this moment, in this Woolworth's, that's this boy's idea of fun.

Understand that I didn't stand there and decide intellectually that this simple and small event is, when all is said and done, the worst thing I've seen. My body decided. My intestines, my knees, my chest. It was only later that I tried to think about it.

This boy's eagerness to "play" maniac killer is an event worse than the Bomb, worse even than Auschwitz. . . . The boy is certainly not committing a crime. The toy's merchandisers are within their rights. To legislate against them would be to endanger most of our freedoms. The mother buying the toy is perhaps making a mistake, perhaps not. Without knowing the boy, and knowing him well, who's to be certain that it isn't better for him to engage in, rather than repress, such play? The mother did not put the desire for the toy in him. Three thousand years of Judeo-Christian culture did that. Nor has the mother the power to take that desire from him. Nobody has that power. If he can want the toy at all, then it almost doesn't matter whether the toy exists or not. Doesn't the boy's need for such play exist with or without the toy?

Nor would I be too quick to blame the boy's desire on television and slasher films. The Nazis who crewed the camps and the scientists who built the bomb did not need television and slasher films to school them in horror. In fact, the worst atrocities from the pharaohs to Vietnam were committed quite ably before the first slasher film was made. Keeping your child away from TV may make *you* feel better, but can any child be protected from the total weight of Western history?

In a world shorn of order, stripped of traditions, molting every decade, every year, a dancing, varicolored snake of a century—pointless violence is evident everywhere, on every level. Professional soldiers are statistically safer than urban women; senseless destruction is visited on trees and on the ozone and on every species of life. No one feels safe anywhere. This has become the very meaning of the 20th century.

So I am in a Woolworth's one day and I feel a sort of final horror as I watch a boy buy a psycho-killer toy so that he can pretend he's an unstoppable maniacal murderer. What is so horrible is that this boy is doing this instinctively, for his very survival. In order to live, in order not to go mad, this boy is acclimating himself to the idea of the killer-maniac, because killer-maniac energy is so present in his world. He's trying to inoculate himself through play, as all children have, everywhere, in every era. He thus lets a little bit of the energy into him— that's how inoculations work. Too little, and he is too afraid of the world—it's too terrifying to feel powerless amid the maniacal that's taken for granted around him; to feel any power at all he needs a bit of it inside him. But if he takes in too much, he could be swamped.

How horrible that he is forced to such a choice. You'd think it would be enough to stop the world in its tracks. And what can we do for him? Struggle for a different world, yes, but that won't change what's already happened to him. What can we do for that boy except be on his side, stand by his choice, and pray for the play of his struggling soul?

Michael Ventura

1. What is it that the boy wants to buy?
2. What does the author use as evidence that the media are not the cause of violence in the world?
3. What is the author's opinion of the mother's buying the toy for the boy?

Journal Suggestions

- What is your reaction to this essay? Would you have been as horrified as the author was if you had seen the boy buying this toy? Do you agree with the author's idea that the reason children want these types of toys is in order to harden themselves to the horrible events that they hear about in the real world? Comment on any aspect of this essay you found interesting.

- Should parents buy their children toys that the children want but that the parents disapprove of? What might be the reaction of children who want a toy like the one described here but are not permitted to buy it? How can the parents decide what are appropriate toys for their children? Would you have allowed your child to buy this toy?

- Many children enjoy watching or hearing scary stories about ghosts or other frightening creatures. Why do you think this is so? Have you ever felt this way? Do you still enjoy those kinds of stories?

Public Enemy Number One?
Media Violence Accounts for, at Most, a Small Fraction of Violence in Society

---

Before you read, consider the following questions:

1. Do you think that violence in the media causes people to behave more violently?
2. Are movies in your country censored for violence at all? What about television?

In this article, the author makes the argument that criticizing violence in the media as a cause of violence in the real world is an excuse for not looking at the real causes of violence in the world, such as poverty and child abuse. But criticizing violence in movies and in song lyrics and trying to censor these is much easier than attacking the real social causes of violent behavior. The author cites research studies which seemed to show that watching violence in movies did make children behave slightly more violently, but then he cites statistics that show much more clear connections between violent behavior and harmful social conditions. The author suggests that violence in the media is the result, not the cause, of violence in real life.

Forget about poverty, racism, child abuse, domestic violence, rape. America . . . has discovered the real cause of our country's rising violence: television mayhem, Guns N' Roses, Ice-T and Freddy Krueger.

No need for family support policies, justice system reforms or grappling with such distressing issues as poverty and sexual violence against the young. . . . Just when earnest national soul-searching over the epidemic violence of contemporary America seemed unavoidable, that traditional scapegoat—media depravity—is topping the ratings again.

••••••••••••••••

"The average American child," she [columnist Ellen Goodman] writes, "sees 8,000 murders and 10,000 acts of violence on television before he or she is out of grammar school." Goodman, like most pundits, expends far more outrage on the sins of TV and rock 'n' roll than on the rapes and violent abuses millions of American children experience before they are out of grammar school.

••••••••••••••••

Popular perceptions aside, the most convincing research, found in massive, multi-national correlational studies of thousands of people, suggests that, at most, media violence accounts for 1 to 5 percent of all violence in society. For example, a 1984 study led by media-violence expert Rowell Huesmann of 1,500 youth in the U.S., Finland, Poland and Australia found that the amount of media violence watched is associated with about 5 percent of the violence in children, as rated by peers. Other correlational studies have found similarly small effects.

But the biggest question media-violence critics can't answer is the most fundamental one: is it the *cause*, or simply one of the many *symptoms*, of this unquestionably brutal age? The best evidence does not exonerate celluloid savagery (who could?) but shows that it is a small, derivative influence compared to the real-life violence, both domestic and official, that our children face growing up in '80s and '90s America.

When it comes to the genuine causes of youth violence, it's hard to dismiss the 51 percent increase in youth poverty since 1973, 1 million rapes and a like number of violently injurious offenses inflicted upon the young every year, a juvenile justice system bent on retribution against poor and minority youth, and the abysmal neglect of the needs of young families. The Carter-Reagan-Bush eras added 4 million youths to the poverty rolls. The last 20 years have brought a record decline in youth well-being.

Despite claims that media violence is the best-researched social phenomenon in history, social science indexes show many times more studies of the effects of rape, violence and poverty on the young. Unlike the indirect methods of most media studies (questionnaires, interviews, peer ratings and laboratory vignettes), child abuse research includes the records of real-life criminals and their backgrounds. Unlike the media studies, the findings of this avalanche of research are consistent: child poverty, abuse and neglect underlie every major social problem the nation faces.

And, unlike the small correlations or temporary laboratory effects found in media research, abuse-violence studies produce powerful results: "Eighty-four percent of prison inmates were abused as children," the research agency Childhelp USA reports in a 1993 summary of major findings. Separate studies by the Minnesota State Prison, the Massachusetts Correctional Institute and the Massachusetts Treatment Center for Sexually Dangerous Persons (to cite a few) find histories of childhood abuse and neglect in 60 to 90 percent of the violent inmates studied—including virtually all death row prisoners. The most conservative study, that by the National Institute of Justice, indicates that some half-million criminally violent of-

fenses each year are the result of offenders being abused as
children.

Two million American children are violently injured, sexually abused or neglected every year by adults whose age aver-
ages 32 years, according to the Denver-based American Humane
Association. One million children and teenagers are raped every
year, according to the 1992 federally funded *Rape in America*
study of 4,000 women, which has been roundly ignored by the
same media outlets that never seem short of space to berate violent rap lyrics.

Sensational articles . . . devoted pages to blaming music
and media for violence—yet . . . ignored this study of the rape
of millions of America's children. . . .

[If] as media critics claim, media violence is the, or even just
a, prime cause of youth violence, we might expect to see similar
rates of violence among all those exposed to similar amounts of
violence in the media, regardless of race, gender, region, economic status, or other demographic differences. Yet this is far
from the case.

Consider the issue of race. Surveys show that while black
and white families have access to similar commercial television
coverage, white families are much more likely to subscribe to violent cable channels. Yet murder arrests among black youth are
now 12 times higher than among white, non-Hispanic youth,
and increasing rapidly. Are blacks genetically more susceptible
to television violence than whites? Or could there be other reasons for this pattern—perhaps the 45 percent poverty rates and
60 percent unemployment rates among black teenagers?

And consider also the issue of gender. Girls watch as much
violent TV as boys. Yet female adolescents show remarkably low
and stable rates of violence. Over the last decade or so, murders
by female teens (180 in 1983, 171 in 1991) stayed roughly the
same, while murders by boys skyrocketed (1,476 in 1983, 3,435
in 1991). How do the media-blamers explain that?

Finally, consider the issue of locale. Kids see the same
amount of violent TV all over, but many rural states show no increases in violence, while in Los Angeles, to take one example,
homicide rates have skyrocketed.

The more media research claims are subjected to close
scrutiny, the more their contradictions emerge. It can be shown
that violent people do indeed patronize more violent media, just
as it can be shown that urban gang members wear baggy
clothes. But no one argues that baggy clothes cause violence.
The coexistence of media and real-life violence suffers from a

confusion of cause and effect: is an affinity for [that is, an interest in] violent media the result of abuse, poverty and anger, or is it a prime cause of the more violent behaviors that just happen to accompany those social conditions? In a 1991 study of teenage boys who listen to violent music, the University of Chicago's Jeffrey Arnett argues that "[r]ather than being the cause of recklessness and despair among adolescents, heavy metal music is a reflection of these [behaviors]."

The clamor over TV violence might be harmless were it not for the fact that media and legislative attention are rare, irreplaceable resources. Every minute devoted to thrashing over issues like violence in the media is one lost to addressing the accumulating, critical social problems that are much more crucial contributors to violence in the real world.

••••••••••••••••

Virtually alone among progressives, columnist Carl T. Rowan has expressed outrage over the misplaced energies of those who have embraced the media crusade and its "escapism from the truth about what makes children (and their parents and grandparents) so violent." Writes Rowan: "I'm appalled that liberal Democrats . . . are spreading the nonsensical notion that Americans will, to some meaningful degree, stop beating, raping and murdering each other if we just censor what is on the tube or big screen. . . . The politicians won't, or can't, deal with the real-life social problems that promote violence in America . . . so they try to make TV programs and movies the scapegoats! How pathetic!"

Without question, media-violence critics are genuinely concerned about today's pandemic violence. As such, it should alarm them greatly to see policy-makers and the public so preoccupied with an easy-to-castigate media culprit linked by their research to, at most, a small part of the nation's violence—while the urgent social problems devastating a generation continue to lack even a semblance of redress.

Mike Males

1. How much real-life violence is attributable to media violence, according to the Huesmann study mentioned in this article?
2. What kinds of changes have occurred in the lives of young people in the past 20 years, according to this article?
3. What do nearly all prisoners condemned to death in the United States seem to have in common?
4. Give evidence from this article which argues against the idea that media violence causes real-life violence.

Journal Suggestions

- What is your reaction to the information and arguments in this article? Before reading this article, did you believe that violence in media probably created violence in real life? Do you still believe this, or have you changed your mind? Comment on any aspect of this article you found interesting.

- Are people in your culture exposed to violence in the media? What do people in your culture say about the causes of violence in real life and the connection between real-life violence and media violence?

ALTERNATIVE WRITING ASSIGNMENT FOR CHAPTER 1

➤ *Writing Assignment 1.2: Technological Changes*

Writing
Assignment 1.2

Imagine that you are taking a history class called Problems of Industrialization. In this class you are studying the negative effects of technology as industrialization occurs around the world. First discuss with your class any changes you have noticed in your lifetime in which the introduction of modern technology has resulted in negative side effects.

Now read the text on page 303.

Reading
"Auto-cracy Is Being Exported to Third World," page 303

Here is a writing assignment you might get in this history class:

> Based on the article called "Auto-cracy Is Being Exported to Third World," write a short paper on the following topic:

> Modern technology has brought many positive changes in our lives, but with these advances have also come losses. Describe a change of this type that has occurred in your country. Compare the past situation with the present situation. What was the situation like before? What is it like now? What problems have these changes created?

This paper is due in one week.   ◄

To complete this assignment follow the directions for Writing Assignment 1.2 in Chapter 1. To help you think about the topic for this alternative assignment, read the following suggestions for journal entries.

Journal Suggestions

Chapter 2 will get you started keeping a writing journal.

• What is the most unusual mode of transportation in your country? Who uses this type of transportation? Is it an old, traditional form like riding on a mule or horse, or is it an ultra-modern form like Roller Blades or skateboards? What are its advantages and disadvantages?

• The popular culture, the economy, and sometimes the political ideas of the United States have had an effect on many other parts of the world. Have you seen this influence in your own country? How has this influence affected the tastes or the opinions of people in your country?

Again, follow the directions for Writing Assignment 1.2 in Chapter 1. When you are ready to start your first draft, you should have several important items in front of you:

the text of the article "Auto-cracy Is Being Exported to Third World,"

the directions for the assignment,

your invention lists,

your responses to the Journal Suggestions, if you wrote them,

your first draft,

your ideas about who will read this paper and why, and

your classmates' reactions to your writing.

If you find that you are having problems with this assignment, return to any of the parts of the process you have just gone through and try again. Different people approach the solution to their problems with a piece of writing in different ways. You may want to do one or more of the following:

• reread the text of the article on "Auto-cracy"
• gather more ideas and see how other people have written about similar topics by reading something related to this subject—for example, articles in this Appendix that discuss changes forced on traditional societies by the majority culture

Readings
"Do Not Disturb," page 297
"Sacred Places," page 299

• discuss the text with someone
• create a new list of ideas

- get more feedback from another classmate
- perhaps even put everything aside and write a whole new first draft

Do these activities in any order that you think will help you write the best paper you can.

➤ *APPENDIX B*

Editing Exercises

In this section you will find a series of short texts that contain grammatical, mechanical, and word form errors frequently made by advanced non-native writers. You can sharpen your editing skills by trying to find and correct the errors in the articles. Do one or more of these exercises just before you are ready to edit one of your own papers.

Before you begin to edit a text, read it through completely at least once to be sure you understand the meaning of the entire article. The number of errors is indicated for each text. Corrections appear in Appendix C.

When Babies Cry

New parents will be interesting in a recent discovery discussed in a well-known medical journal. As hospital personnel work in maternity wards are aware for a long time now, infants crying in the nursery have quite an effect on calm babies. When the calm infants hear the sound of other infant crying, they too begin to sob. In reported experiment, psychologists were making recordings of newborns crying; then have let the infants listen to the sound of their own cries. Amazing, most of infants stopped crying as soon as they heard themselves on tape. Furthermore, if the infants had not been crying, listen to their own cries did not make them begin. Other observations had shown that the cries of older babies will not cause the newborns to start crying. Thus, researchers have conclude that newborns are capable of making distinction between their own crying and that of other babies, furthermore, they react differently depending who the baby's crying they hear, their own, that of another infant, or that of an older baby. The exact mechanism by which this discrimination has been occurred, however, remains a mystery.

17 errors

Information taken from *Le Progres Egyptien*, Saturday 26 July 1986, p. 2.

Women Executives and Daddies

What makes some women success in a man's world where few women even operate? Is it genetic? Are success women just a character type? According to a study done on 25 top women executives, presidents and vice-presidents of major corporations, the answer is apparent no. But these women do have several fascinate feature in common. All 25 women were the first born in their families, a position gave them both extra privileges and responsibilities. Second, none of this women wished they were boys when they were youngs. They were all quite happy to be girls, except when people told them they were doing things girls shouldn't do. These girls were ignored people who told them to wear dresses, to be passive, not to engage in sports, or to be interest in cook instead of in building things. But the most important element in this picture was their relationship with their fathers. In each case their fathers encouraged them to do as they pleased regardless of what did society say. This does not mean their fathers treated them like boys or wished they were boys. On the other hand, their fathers admired their feminine while never assuming that their femininity should avoid them from striving for experience and freedom. All these fathers also spent time with these girls, playing sports with them, going for walks, or just talk. Furthermore, whereas boys may become rivals for their fathers, these girls were apparently never threat to their fathers. Therefore, these fathers prouded very much when their girls were competitive successful in any area. It seems clear that the combination of the close comradeship and continual encouragement of their fathers gave these women the strong and the sense of self-worth that allowed them to succeed where a few women do.

20 errors

Information taken from Gail Sheehy, *Passages* (New York: Dutton, 1976).

The Successes of Debi Thomas

Debi Thomas is the first Black ice skater to win a senior national championship. Her interest in skating has begun when she was only three years old and her mother took her to the Ice Capades. She became very excited during the show that she begged her mother for a pair of skates. Although she became an excellent skater as a child, but she didn't win any competitions until she was 12. Because she was determined to become a great skater, she quit school in the 8th grade in order to be able to spend all her time training. But in her next competition, she had only taken 4th place. Disappointing in her performance, she decided to go back to school. If she couldn't success as a skater, at least could still work hard for a good education. For four years in high school she studied hard all day and then every day after school spent hours to train for figure skating competitions. Her big chance came in 1985–86. First she accepted at Stanford University as a medical microbiology major, one of the most difficult major at the university. Next her hard work in the skating rink was finally reward when in 1986 she won the U.S. Senior Ladies' Figure Skating Championship. As she pursues her study in biochemistry, microbiology, and immunology in order to become an orthopedic surgeon specialize in sports medicine, Debi remains confidence that she can do anything she sets her mind to do.

15 errors

Information taken from *Sports Illustrated* 17 March 1986, vol. 64, no. 11, pp. 54–61.

Musical Faces

Everyone knows that some people are left handed and the rest are right handed, but not everyone realizes that their faces also display left or right dominance. Been left or right handed does not seem to correlate to any other psychological characteristics, but researches seem to show that left-faced people have a special talent for music.

By studying computerized images of lip and jaw movements, psychologist Karl U. Smith had been able to determinate that everyone shows a preference for one or other side of the face and that this preference is probably with us from birth. As with handedness, most people are right faced. But then Smith analyzed his findings by professions and found that, amazing as may seem, 98 percent of the opera singers he observed were left faced. In addition, he watched video tapes of current well-known musicians performing and look at paintings of famous musicians of the past, like Beethoven, Wagner, Liszt, Brahms, and once again his investigation showed that this musicians were predominantly left faced.

Smith explains that facedness is related to brain hemisphere dominance, with the left side of the brain controls the right side of the body and the right side of the brain controlling the left side of the body. Current theories of brain dominance hold that the right side of the brain controls holistic, creative, artistic functions. Whereas the left side of the brain is appeared to handle linguistic and analytical functions. Furthermore, the right side of brain controls total performance such as the ability to sing. Thus, this researchers' findings fit in with these theories. Artists have right brain, therefore left face, dominance.

Next time you smile at yourself in the mirror, check to see which side of your mouth moves first. If the left side appears dominant, you may had discovered the sign of a hidden talent for the music.

15 errors

Information taken from "The Sign of Music Read in the Face," R. J. Trotter, *Psychology Today*, March 1985, p. 18.

Going to School at Home

Although most states have compulsory education laws mandating education for all children, how these children are educated is not established by law. Either by choice or by necessity, an estimated 20,000 families have decide not to send their children to school but rather educating them at home.

In some cases, the families simply live too far away from the nearest school for the youngs to attend daily, in other cases, the parents' religious convictions make them uncomfort with send their children to schools. For the most part, however, home-schooling movement arises out of a dissatisfaction with what formal schooling does to children. Schools are accuse of discouraging independence thinking, of dampening motivation, and put too much pressure on children while they encourage competition and the desire to get good grades rather than to learn. Educator John Holt, an advocate of home schooling, has tried to reform education in this country from within for years until he finally gave up on a system that he says crush creativity and the desire to learn by forcing young students into molds that they accommodate the system rather than the individual learner. He says schools creating fear and anxiety in children which paralyze them intellectually just as laboratory rats paralyze by reward/punishment systems. Instead of teach children to think independently, schools had turned children into "praise junkies" interested mainly in getting good grades, not in learning.

Parents are happy with the home-schooling system maintain that their children often move faster through the curriculum than would in classrooms but, more importantly, that the children retain their interest in learning and their intellectual curiosity while covering the same subjects as their peers are cover in school. In almost all case of home schooling, parents make arrangements to submit educational plans to local school authorities for approval.

While home schooling may not be the answer for everyone and although it does have its critics among educators and counselors, but for some students at least, home schooling seems to fill a need quite well.

22 errors

Information taken from "The Home-Schooling Alternative," Eileen Garred, *USAir* September 1985, pp. 10–13.

➤ *APPENDIX C*

Answers to Exercises

POSSIBLE ANSWERS TO "IMPOSTOR PHENOMENON," CHAPTER 9

Do you ever secretly feel that your academic success is the result of luck rather than the result of your own intelligence? If so, you may be suffering from the "impostor phenomenon." People suffering from this psychological condition do not believe that they are really intelligent despite their academic successes at school. Moreover, these people feel guilty because they believe that they have deceived their teachers into thinking they are intelligent, while they themselves feel deep down that they are not.

The impostor phenomenon occurs mostly among young women, especially among beginning graduate students, women who are obviously intelligent. These women usually grew up in one of two types of families. In the first type of family, some other family member was designated "the smart one" in the family and the girl with the impostor feelings was designated as something else. Thus, whenever that girl was successful academically she felt as though she were tricking people. She felt sure she wasn't the intelligent one in the family. After all, that's what her family had always told her.

The second type of family is the high achiever type that believes success or achievement comes easily and naturally for superior people. As a result of this attitude in the family, children may become afraid to admit that their achievements have come from hard work. For example, one young woman who suffered from impostor feelings never let her family see her studying because they had told her that really smart people don't need to study. Consequently, she felt that if she studied and got good grades, she was tricking people into thinking she was intelligent. She knew she couldn't really be intelligent, because she had to study and she had been told that intelligent people don't have to study.

Even though their academic achievements prove their intelligence, these women cannot think of themselves as intelligent. Instead they think of themselves as cheaters, hiding from the world the truth that they are not as good as they seem, that they are only impostors.

LOGICAL CONNECTORS, CHAPTER 9

These logical connectors are grouped into general categories by meaning. However, the meanings of the words in the same category are not necessarily interchangeable. Check with your instructor if you are unsure of exactly which word in a category to use. Furthermore, remember that the prepositional expressions (*in addition to, despite*, etc.) must be followed by a noun phrase or a gerund (verb ending in *-ing*). Adverbial subordinators (or clause markers) must be followed by a clause containing a subject and conjugated verb. This list is not complete, but it will give you a variety of connectors to choose from.

Adverbs	Prepositional phrases	Adverbial subordinators	Coordinators
Additions:			
moreover	in addition to ____		and
in addition	besides ____		or
furthermore	other than ____		
besides			
Similarities:			
also	like ____		
likewise			
in the same way			
similarly			
Contrary-to-Expectations, Contradictions, Surprises:			
however	despite ____	although	but
nevertheless	in spite of ____	even though	yet
on the other hand		whereas	
on the contrary			
Illustrations:			
for example			
for instance			
Results:			
therefore	as a result of ____		
thus			
as a result			
in this way			
consequently			
so			

Adverbs	Prepositional phrases	Adverbial subordinators	Coordi-nators
Reason, Purpose:			
	as a result of _____	since	for
	in order (+infinitive phrase)	inasmuch as because so that	
Condition:			
otherwise		if when in the event that whether (or not) unless	
Sequence in Time/Space:			
first, second, third, (etc.)			
finally	before _____	before	and
afterward	after _____	after	
next	until _____	when while	

Further Explanation:

in fact (=this is going to be a more striking example of what I just said)
actually (=this is the real truth)
likewise (=in the same way as just mentioned)
after all (=this is the obvious reason behind what was just mentioned; this makes
    what I just said predictable)
in other words (=the same idea but in different words)

Conclusions:

in short

in summary

in sum

all in all

in conclusion

Corrected Version of Editing Test, Chapter 9

When I left my home and parents to begin my studies abroad, I was told that going abroad was going to be the most thrilling experience of my life. Studying in a foreign country was going to build my character, enhance my sense of responsibility, and give me new horizons to look forward to. I have been living here only since September, but I see that what living abroad also does is to take away that period of carelessness, that spirit of freedom that is so special to teenagers.

Leaving home and parents to study abroad was a striking experience. It was not only my family I was leaving but also my friends and the places I knew: a whole part of my life. Once in the U.S., I had to face the problems of a new language, new friends, in short, a new way of life. Even though a beginning is always difficult, all these changes are very enriching. I have been told many times that after overcoming all these obstacles, people feel much better, much stronger than they did before they faced these difficulties. My answer to these claims is that as a result of my experiences here I will certainly have more confidence. The problem is, however, that the timing was wrong for me. It would have been better for me to wait until I'm older. Trying to make new friends, to speak a new language, and to face all the problems of a new culture when you have no one to confide in makes you grow—not stronger—but older than you really are. You realize this when you talk to people who are your own age. You see that their concerns are quite different from yours. What they have to worry about is what fraternity they will join or what they will do on Friday night. There are not enough similarities between them and you. A gap has formed between you and your own generation.

Moreover, it is not only a new culture that you now have to face but also new responsibilities. There is no one but yourself to take care of you. *You* have to be sure that your phone bill is paid on time and that your money has been spent conscientiously. You cannot bring your dirty clothes home during the weekend to your mother's house and ask her to wash them for you because your studies are consuming most of your time or just because you do not feel like washing them yourself. Although you don't want to worry about all these details yourself, you must. If you feel sick, you cannot just call your mother and ask her what to do. You yourself will have to search for a doctor's phone number and call him. The successful completion of all these duties obviously requires a great sense of responsibility. Someone might object that whether we take these responsibilities at this time or at another, this is how life is going to be anyway and that it is never too soon to start learning. But at 17, 18, or 19, you still need to expend that "youthful energy" which is still boiling in you.

Being very mature and very responsible forces you to miss this freedom that you still need.

   All people should be given the chance to live their own ages fully.
Right now I would prefer being a teenager to being a mature adult.
For a fruit ripened too quickly loses its flavor.

Karen Moukheiber (Lebanon)   ■

ANSWERS TO EDITING TEST, CHAPTER 9

Part 1

1. *thrill* → *thrilling*. Use the adjective form to describe the noun. *The experience thrills me* becomes *The experience is thrilling* or *It is a thrilling experience.*

2. *in the foreign country* → *in a foreign country*. Use the in-definite article when the noun has not previously been identified. The definite article is usually used once the reader knows which specific country is being referred to.

3. *characteristics* → *character*. Usage error. *Characteristics* means features that distinguish or define. *Character* means personality or moral strength.

4. *see* → *offer/give me*. Parallelism. *Studying* was going to build, *enhance, and offer* . . . The subject of *see new horizons is I*, not *Studying.*

5. *am living* → *have been living*. Use present perfect with since in the time clause.

6. *needs* → *needed*. Past participle reduced from passive form. *A teenager needs freedom*, but *freedom is needed by a teenager*. Therefore: *spirit of freedom* [which is] *needed.*

7. *for studying* → *to study*. To show purpose, the infinitive is preferred unless there is a noun (not a noun derived from a verb) that might be used after the preposition: for an education.

8. *whole part of my life* → *a whole part of my life. Part* is a countable noun. Therefore, it must have an article in front of it or be plural.

9. *in U.S.* → *in the U.S.* Always use before United States or U.S.

10. *Even a beginning is always difficult* → *Even though a beginning is always difficult. Even* is not a clause marker;

it is a kind of intensifier. *Though* (or *although* or *even though*) is a clause marker.

11. *overcome* → *overcoming*. Use a noun form after a preposition: *after overcoming*. Or use a clause: *after you overcome.*

12. *this difficulties* → *these difficulties*. *Difficulties* is plural; demonstrative adjectives (*this, that, these, those*) agree with the nouns they modify.

13. *are* → *is*. Agreement. The subject of the verb is *answer*, not *claims*.

14. *confident* → *confidence*. Function category. Use the noun form after *to have* + *confidence* or change the verb: *to be confident.*

15. *had been* → *is*. Use past perfect only to emphasize the relationship between two past actions; past perfect indicates the action that occurred first in relation to another action. She came to the United States in the past, but she is not trying to show that action in relation to another action in the past.

16. *I would have been better to wait* → *It would have been better for me to wait*. It is not that *the woman would have been a better idea* but that *waiting would have been a better idea*. Thus: Waiting would have been better for me. Or, displacing the subject with the expletive *it*: It would have been better for me to wait.

17. *all the problem* → *all the problems*. *All* can be followed by an uncountable noun (all the difficulty); but if *all* is followed by a countable noun, the noun must be plural.

18. *you talk to people are you own age* → *you talk to people who are your own age*. Sentence structure. *People* is the object of *to*; it cannot at the same time be the subject of *are*. *Are* requires its own subject, the clause marker that corresponds to *people*: who (or possibly: that).

19. *age, you* → *age. You*. Run-on sentence or comma splice. *You realize* constitutes the beginning of a main clause. *You see* also constitutes the beginning of a main clause. Main clauses must be separated by a period or joined by a conjunction (for example: and).

20. *what will they do* → *what they will do*. Invert the subject and verb in a question. This is not a question; it is a noun clause. In a clause use normal word order.

21. *Similar interests are not enough* → *There are not enough similar interests*. When referring to the existence of a

previously unnoticed, unmentioned, or unknown object or situation, use *there is / are.*

22. *has form → has formed.* Verb form. Use the past participle form after *have / has.*

Part 2

23. *Moreover, not only a new culture . . . but also new responsibilities → Moreover, it is not only a new culture . . . but also new responsibilities.* Fragment. There was no independent subject and verb in the incorrect formulation.

24. *It is no one → There is no one.* When pointing out the existence of a previously unmentioned object or situation, use *there is / are.* In the incorrect sentence, *it is* seems to be answering the question: Who is it?

25. *has spent → has been spent.* Passive. *You have spent the money.* Or, *The money has been spent.*

26. *Dirties clothes → dirty clothes.* Adjectives never agree with nouns. Whether the noun is plural or singular, the adjective does not change.

27. *to the house of your mother → to your mother's house.* When referring to something belonging to a person, use *'s* instead of the *of* construction. Use the *of* construction for features of objects: the top of the building.

28. *the most your time → most of your time.* If the noun after *most* (or other quantity expressions, such as *much, many, few*) is modified by an article, demonstrative, or possessive, use *of. The most* is a superlative form not intended here.

29. *are not feel → do not feel.* After *to be,* use the present participle for continuous forms or the past participle for passive forms. The simple form cannot appear after any forms of *to be.* Use the simple present rather than the present continuous because the writer is referring to a repeated situation, not one situation in progress now.

30. *Although you don't want to . . . , but → Although you don't want to . . . , you.* Or *You don't want to . . . , but you.* Sentence structure. *Although* begins a clause that must be attached to an independent sentence. *But* joins two independent sentences. In the incorrect sentence, the two forms were mixed together. To correct this, either make two independent sentences joined by *but* or make one clause and one dependent sentence without *but*.

31. *could* → *can*. The *if* clause sets the tense and the mode: present real. *Could* is used in past real situations or present unreal. (*if you felt sick, you could not just call . . .*)

32. *The success completion* → *The successful completion*. Function category. *Success* is a noun. Use the adjective form to modify the noun *completion*.

33. *is obviously requiring* → *obviously requires*. Present continuous emphasizes action in progress at the present moment as opposed to simple present, which refers to repeated action or to a situation that is generally or always true.

34. *would* → *might*. *Would* implies too much certainty for this idea. *Might* implies the possibility of someone asking.

35. *other* → *another*. Treat *other* like a countable noun. It must be preceded by an article (*the, an*) or be plural (*others*).

36. *have still needed* → *still need*. The present perfect suggests a relationship between a past event and the present. This sentence refers to the present without any past event.

37. *"youthful energy" which it is boiling* → *"youthful energy" which is boiling*. In an adjective clause, the clause marker *replaces* the subject or object in the clause; it does not appear *in addition to* the subject or object.

38. *carelessness. This freedom that you still need* → *carelessness, this freedom that you still need*. Fragment. *This freedom that you still need* is not a complete sentence because there is no verb for the subject *This freedom*. This fragment must be attached to an independent sentence.

39. *should be give* → *should be given*. A verb after *to be* must be a present participle (for continuous) or a past participle (for passive). *Someone should give all people the chance* becomes *All people should be given the chance* in the passive form.

40. *I would prefer been* → *I would prefer being*. Use the gerund (*-ing*) form of a verb when the verb must act as a noun. *I would prefer [noun] to [noun]*.

ANSWERS TO BIBLIOGRAPHY EXERCISE, CHAPTER 11

I.

Bibliography

Conrad, Joseph. "The Secret Sharer." <u>Introduction to Liter-</u>
<u>ature: Stories</u>. 3rd ed. Eds. Lynn Altenbernd and Leslie
L. Lewis. New York: Macmillan, 1980. 97-126.
"Crime Bills up for Debate." <u>The Daily Beacon</u> [Knoxville, Ten-
nessee] 6 Feb. 1984: 2.
Greenward, John. "The Negotiation Waltz." <u>Time</u> 1 Aug. 1983:
41-42.
Kesey, Ken. <u>One Flew Over the Cuckoo's Nest</u>. New York: Signet,
1962.

II.

(Greenward 42)

(Crime 2)

(Kesey 131)

(Conrad 115)

ANSWERS TO DOCUMENTATION EXERCISE, CHAPTER 11

1. "But even more basic, this poverty twists and deforms the spirit" (Harrington 2).

2. Answers will vary. A possible answer might be: Obviously, these poor Americans are not poor in the same way as are citizens of other countries who barely keep from starving. (Harrington 1).

3. Answers will vary. A possible answer might be: Harrington refers to the many Americans who are "maimed in body and spirit, existing at levels beneath those necessary for human decency" (Harrington 1–2).

4.   Bibliography

   Harrington, Michael. <u>The Other America</u>. 1962. New York:
   Pelican Books, 1971.

5. Answers will vary.

POSSIBLE ANSWERS TO EDITING EXERCISES IN APPENDIX B

In addition to the answers given here, there may also be other ways to correct the errors.

When Babies Cry

1. interesting → interested
2. work → working *or* who work
3. are → have been
4. other infant → other infants
5. In reported experiment → In the reported experiment *or* In reported experiments
6. were making → made
7. crying; then → crying and then *or* crying; then they
8. have let → let
9. Amazing → Amazingly
10. most of infants → most of the infants
11. listen → listening
12. had shown → have shown *or* show
13. have conclude → have concluded
14. distinction → a distinction
15. babies, furthermore, that → babies, and furthermore that
16. who the baby's crying → whose crying
17. has been occurred → occurs

Women Executives and Daddies

1. success → successful
2. apparent → apparently
3. fascinate → fascinating
4. feature → features
5. a position gave → a position that gave *or* a position giving
6. this women → these women
7. youngs → young
8. were ignored → ignored
9. interest → interested
10. cook → cooking

11. what did society say → what society said
12. On the other hand → On the contrary *or* Quite the contrary
13. feminine → femininity
14. avoid → prevent *or* keep *or* stop
15. talk → talking
16. threat → threats
17. prouded very much → were very proud
18. competitive → competitive and
19. the strong → the strength
20. a few → few

The Successes of Debi Thomas

1. has begun → began
2. very → so
3. Although . . ., but she → Although . . ., she
4. determinated → determined
5. had only taken → took only
6. Disappointing → Disappointed
7. success → succeed
8. at least could → at least she could
9. to train → training
10. accepted → was accepted
11. one of the most difficult major → one of the most difficult majors
12. reward → rewarded
13. study → studies
14. specialize → specializing
15. confidence → confident

Musical Faces

1. Been → Being
2. researches seem → research seems
3. had been able → was able
4. to determinate → to determine
5. one or other side → one or the other side
6. amazing as may seem → amazing as it may seem
7. and look at → and looked at
8. this musicians → these musicians

9. controls → controlling
10. functions. Whereas → functions whereas
11. is appeared → appears
12. side of brain → side of the brain
13. this researchers' → this researcher's
14. you may had discovered → you may have discovered
15. for the music → for music

Going to School at Home

1. have decide → have decided
2. educating → to educate
3. the youngs → the children
4. daily, in other cases → daily. In other cases
5. uncomfort → uncomfortable
6. with send → with sending
7. however, home-schooling movement → however, the home-schooling movement
8. are accuse → are accused
9. independence thinking → independent thinking
10. and put → and of putting
11. has tried → tried
12. crush → crushes
13. that they accommodate → that accommodate
14. creating → create
15. laboratory rats paralyze → laboratory rats are paralyzed
16. Instead of teach → Instead of teaching
17. had turned → turn
18. Parents are happy → Parents happy
19. than would → than they would
20. are cover → cover
21. all case → all cases
22. While . . ., but for some → While . . ., for some

Acknowledgments

Page 126, Excerpt from "Developing Unity Among Women of Color: Crossing the Barriers of Internalized Racism and Cross-Racial Hostility" by Virginia R. Harris and Trinity A. Ordona from *Making Face, Making Soul: Haciendo Caras* (Aunt Lute Books). Reprinted by permission of Virginia R. Harris and Trinity A. Ordona.

Page 187, "The Dangers of Cramming," Keith Ablow from Newsweek, May 1985, © 1985, Newsweek, Inc. All rights reserved. Reprinted by permission.

Page 218, Kenneth Eskey, "School System a Key to Japan's Success," © Scripps Howard News Service. Reprinted by permission.

Page 234, "Grouping the Gifted: Pro," reprinted by permission of National Education Association.

Page 237, "Grouping the Gifted: Con," reprinted by permission of National Education Association.

Page 290, Revised text of "Their Manners are Decorous & Praiseworthy" from *Bury My Heart at Wounded Knee: An Indian History of the American West* by Dee Brown. © 1970 Dee Brown. Reprinted by permission of Sterling Lord Literistic, Inc. and Henry Holt and Company, Inc.

Page 295, "Discovering the Truth about Columbus" by Charles Sugnet and Joanna O'Connell. Reprinted by permission of Charles Sugnet and Joanna O'Connell.

Page 297, "Do Not Disturb" Copyright © 1986 Time Inc. Reprinted by permission.

Page 299, "Sacred Places" by Dan Baum. Reprinted by permission of Dan Baum.

Page 303, "Auto-cracy is being exported to the third world" by Mary Morse. Reprinted by permission of Mary Morse.

Page 312, "Taking the Bungee Plunge" by Ginia Bellafante. Reprinted by permission of Ginia Bellafante.

Page 315, "Darwin Revisited" by James Marti. Copyright © 1992 by James Marti. All rights reserved. Reprinted by permission.

Page 318, Excerpt from *Black Holes and Baby Universes and Other Essays* by Stephen W. Hawking. Copyright © 1993 by Stephen W. Hawking. Used by permission of Bantam Books, a division of Bantam Doubleday Dell Publishing Group, Inc. and Stephen Hawking c/o Writer's House, Inc. as agent for the proprietor.

Page 322, "The Quality of Mercy" by Rita Williams. Reprinted by permission of Rita Williams.

Page 327, Reprinted from *Eight Little Piggies: Reflections in Natural History* by Stephen Jay Gould, with the permission of W. W. Norton & Company, Inc. Copyright © 1993 by Stephen Jay Gould.

Page 331, From *Savage Inequalities* by Jonathan Kozol. Copyright © 1991 by Jonathan Kozol. Reprinted by permission of Crown Publishers, Inc.

Page 337, "History Proves It: Other Systems of Naming Work," excerpted with permission from the book *Naming Ourselves, Naming Our Children: Resolving the Last Name Dilemma,* by Sharon Lebell. Copyright © 1988 by Sharon Lebell.

Page 344, Deena R. Levine/Mara B. Adelman, *Beyond Language: Cross-Cultural Communication,* 2nd ed. © 1993, pp. 101–110. Reprinted by permission of Prentice Hall, Inc.

Page 349, "How to Spot a Liar" by Benedict Carey. Reprinted from *In Health* © 1990. Reprinted by permission.

Page 353, "Primate Studies and Sex Differences" by Sally Linton. Reprinted by permission of Sophi Smith Collection, Smith College.

Page 361, Excerpt from *Two Years in the Melting Pot* by Liu Zongren. Reprinted by permission of China Books & Periodicals, Inc., 2929 24th Street, San Francisco, CA 94110, Phone (415) 282–2994, Fax (415) 282–0994. Catalogue available.

Page 367, "Who Are Smarter—Boys or Girls?" Reprinted by permission of *Current Science* magazine. Published by Field Publications. Copyright © 1972.

Page 371, "Are men born with power," excerpt from *Anatomy of Love: The Natural History of Monogamy, Adultery, and Divorce* by Helen E. Fisher, Ph.D., by permission of W. W. Norton & Company, Inc. and Simon & Schuster. Copyright © 1992 by Helen E. Fisher.

Page 374, From *Savage Inequalities* by Jonathan Kozol. Copyright © 1991 by Jonathan Kozol. Reprinted by permission of Crown Publishers, Inc.

Page 378, "Is there a doctor in the classroom?" by Laurie Ouellette. Originally published in The *Utne Reader*. Reprinted by permission of Laurie Ouellette.

Page 382, "Voices from the College Front" by Natasha Tarpley. Copyright © 1993 by Essence Communications Inc. Reprinted by permission.

Page 389, "A View from Other Cultures: Must Men Fear 'Women's work'?" Reprinted from *Gender & Grace: Love, Work, and Parenting in a Changing World* by Mary Stewart Van Leeuwen. © 1990 by Mary Stewart Van Leeuwen. Used by permission of InterVarsity Press, P.O. Box 1400, Downers Grove, IL 60515.

Page 394, "On Kids and Slasher Movies" by Michael Ventura. Reprinted by permission of Michael Ventura.

Page 397, "Public Enemy Number One?" by Mike Males. Reprinted by permission of Mike Males.

Index

429

ABOUT THE AUTHOR

Ilona Leki (Ph.D., University of Illinois) is professor of English and director of ESL at the University of Tennessee. Coeditor of the *Journal of Second Language Writing* (with Tony Silva) and of *Reading in the Composition Classroom: Second Language Perspectives* (with Joan Carson), she is the author of *Understanding ESL Writers: A Guide for Teachers* (Boynton/Cook). She has taught ESL and trained teachers in the United States, France, Morocco, Colombia, Turkey, the former Yugoslavia, Brazil, and Egypt. Her publications and conference presentations focus on second language writing and reading. Her primary professional goals have been to understand what academic literacy in a second language entails and to use that understanding to help make academic writing in English a comfortable and rewarding experience for ESL students—and pleasant reading for their teachers.